Civil Liberties and the Vinson Court

I believe that the community is already in process of dissolution where each man begins to eye his neighbor as a possible enemy; where non-conformity with the accepted creed, political as well as religious, is a mark of disaffection; where denunciation, without specification or backing, takes the place of evidence; where orthodoxy chokes freedom of dissent; where faith in the eventual supremacy of reason has become so timid that we dare not enter our convictions in the open lists to win or lose.

JUDGE LEARNED HAND

Civil Liberties and the Vinson Court

C. HERMAN PRITCHETT

THE UNIVERSITY OF CHICAGO PRESS

CHICAGO & LONDON

STANDARD BOOK NUMBER: 226-68443-1
THE UNIVERSITY OF CHICAGO, CHICAGO 60637
THE UNIVERSITY OF CHICAGO, LTD., LONDON

Third Impression 1969. Printed in the
United States of America

IN MEMORY OF THE CHIEF

CHARLES E. MERRIAM

Preface to the Second Impression

Reissuance of this volume twelve years after its initial publication affords an opportunity to reconsider the place of the Vinson Court in American political history with the advantage of hindsight. After experiencing the excitement of the Warren Court and living with its massive involvement in the drive for political and social egalitarianism, the Vinson Court seems somewhat flat and undistinguished. Its center of gravity tended to lie with President Truman's four appointees—Fred Vinson, Harold Burton, Tom Clark, and Sherman Minton—plus the least sparkling of the Roosevelt holdovers, Stanley Reed. For writing and concepts which would rise above a competent legal journeyman's level, one had to go to the fringes of the Court where the brilliant Frankfurter, the lean, hard-hitting Black, the witty and unpredictable Jackson, and the mountain-climbing Douglas operated.

We can now see that the Vinson Court was in one of history's troughs. It sat between eras—one finished, another waiting to be born. Its predecessor, the Roosevelt Court, had met the challenge of its times by legitimating big government and the welfare state. By 1946, when Vinson was appointed, there was no longer any question about the power of the federal government or the states to tax or spend or regulate. The Court would never again interfere with the ameliorative efforts of the President or Congress. It had thoroughly absorbed the lesson of judicial liberalism as taught by Justice Holmes, whose dissenting opinions of the 1920's were the rule of the Court in the 1940's, that the judiciary must not get in the way of dominant legislative opinion. If, as Justice Frankfurter tended to believe, the Holmesian doctrine required judicial acquiescence as the proper response in all controverted situations, then the great days of the Court as a mover and shaker were over.

But judicial liberals were divided on this issue, and both wings of the Court could quote Holmes. The strong legislature–weak judiciary formula, said Justices Black and Douglas, was only appropriate when legislatures were doing things *for* people. When the legislature was doing things *to* people, then the judiciary's role was to act vigorously to guarantee to individuals their constitutionally protected rights against governmental coercion. When the government was engaged in criminal prosecutions; when it was deporting aliens; when legislative investigating committees were grilling witnesses; when Negroes were subjected to discrimination; when people were being taxed or coerced to support religious doctrines; when qualified citizens were being denied the right to vote—in these situations the liberal judicial activist saw intervention by the courts as the essential guarantee of the Constitution's libertarian text.

The Vinson Court tended to fall between these two stools, finding something persuasive in each position. Confronted with the scandal of McCarthyism, it was quiescent. Facing Smith Act prosecutions, the loyalty inquisition of federal employees, lists of subversive organizations, scrutiny of school teachers' associates, loyalty oaths, and deportation of ex-communists, the Court's response was generally to legitimate the government action. If this gambit of judicial restraint had been the Vinson Court's only tactic, then it would indeed have little to say to us now.

But in one field, significantly, there was another kind of response. When confronted with the issue of racial discrimination in whatever form, the Vinson Court marched under a different banner. Although moving cautiously, as was appropriate considering the enormity of the problem, this Court nevertheless proceeded effectively to bring the problem of Negro inequality out of the limbo of neglect and unconcern into the focus of national consciousness. In laying the foundation for the 1954 decision in *Brown* v. *Board of Education*, the Vinson Court met its obligation to history and lighted the fuse for the equal protection explosion that was to illuminate the world of its successor, the Warren Court, and the times in which we live.

Preface

"Writing a book," said Winston Churchill at the 1949 National Book Exhibition in London, "is an adventure; to begin with it is a toy, then an amusement, then it becomes a mistress, and then it becomes a master, and then it becomes a tyrant, and the last phase is that just as you are about to be reconciled to your servitude you kill the monster and strew him about to the public." This is the second time that toying with the fascinating problem of personal equations on the Supreme Court has involved the author in the current of events which Churchill describes so aptly. The first strewing about was done by *The Roosevelt Court: A Study in Judicial Politics and Values*, published in 1948. It dealt with a decade of Supreme Court experience, beginning with President Roosevelt's first appointment in 1937, and its primary purpose was to relate the extremely significant constitutional developments of that period to the ideological preferences of the Court's new members.

Trying to probe the influence of judicial personality on judicial decisions is no easy task. In *The Roosevelt Court* principal reliance was placed on data supplied by the Court's nonunanimous decisions. As was stated in the Preface to that volume:

> A unanimous judicial decision throws little light upon what Walton Hamilton calls "deliberation in process." It tells nothing of the conflicts around the judicial conference table, the alternative lines of argument developed, the accommodations and the compromises which went into the final result. A unanimous opinion is a composite and quasi-anonymous product, largely valueless for purposes of understanding the values and motivation of individual justices.
>
> A nonunanimous opinion admits the public to the Supreme Court's inner sanctum. In such a case the process of deliberation has failed to produce a conclusion satisfactory to all participants. Having carried the

argument as far as they usefully can, the justices find it necessary finally to take a vote, state and support the winning and losing positions, and place the arguments before the world for judgment. In informing the public of their divisions and their reasons, the justices also supply information about their attitudes and their values which is available in no other way. For the fact of disagreement demonstrates that the members of the Court are operating on different assumptions, that their inarticulate major premises are dissimilar, that their value systems are differently constructed and weighted, that their political, economic, and social views contrast in important respects. These differences and contrasts are not always evident on the surface of the conflicting opinions. It may be necessary to search out the true causes of dispute, and not all the searchers will come back with the same findings. But that the search is appropriate and essential to a fuller understanding of the judicial process, few will doubt.

The present volume is a successor to *The Roosevelt Court*, both in subject and in method. Slightly overlapping the period of the former study, it covers the seven years, 1946–53, during which Fred M. Vinson was Chief Justice of the United States. Unlike *The Roosevelt Court*, however, the present volume does not attempt to encompass all fields of constitutional development during the Vinson era. Rather it concentrates on what was far and away the most significant problem of the times—civil liberties.

Now that the Court has embarked upon a new period in its history under the Chief Justiceship of Earl Warren, it is hoped that this analysis will help to clarify the dilemmas with which the recent Court has been confronted and the lines of policy which it has been developing. This book is written not so much for the specialist as for the interested layman. The author is a political scientist, not a lawyer, and, as a lawyer has recently remarked, "political scientists have little effect upon the court of Constitutional law and history, as they seldom legislate, prepare briefs, or argue cases." However, they can, and do, write books.

The author desires to acknowledge how much he has profited over the past few years from association with his former colleague in constitutional law at the University of Chicago, Robert A. Horn, now at Stanford University. He is indebted to John P. Frank, of Yale Law School; David Fellman, of the University of Wisconsin; and his colleague Morton Grodzins, for their critical reading of the manuscript; to Carol Drath for typing much of the manuscript; and to Doreen Herlihy, secretary of the Department of Political Science at the University of Chicago, for invaluable help of many kinds.

Where this work is critical of the Vinson Court and its members, the criticism is that of a friend of the judicial process who wants only to see the Supreme Court live up to the greatness which destiny and the American constitutional system have thrust upon it. On Monday, October 5, 1953, as the Court met in its first session under Chief Justice Warren, the *New York Times* published an eloquent editorial which well expresses the author's sentiments. It concluded with these words:

> Liberty under the law is one of the noblest of human concepts. But how much liberty and how much law?
>
> If nine men, or five men out of nine, had to give the final answer, we could well despair, just as we might well despair if the perpetuation of this republic depended on the election or re-election every four years of a supreme genius as President. But the nine men, however detached, however scrupulously impartial, are part of the world in which they live and move. We do not vote for them or against them, and would not want to, but all honest thought has some influence upon them. They are, at their best, America thinking, just as the President, a general, a manufacturer, a labor leader, a professional man, may be America acting. We may well feel a sense of reverence as the Court walks in—not solely for nine men brought to this place in part by chance as well as by achievement and ability, but for the function they perform. They are a substitute for force—the best yet invented.
>
> The Court resumes. When its entrance is announced we can arise with alacrity, for here in this room, where orders are sometimes given that no other power can contravene, is a symbol of our civilization and our freedom.

Table of Contents

I. *The Vinson Court*

Fred M. Vinson was sworn in as Chief Justice of the United States on June 24, 1946, and held that post until his death on September 8, 1953. The Chief Justice is, of course, only one of nine members of the Supreme Court, but in his post there is both the expectation and to a considerable degree the potentiality of leadership. His actual authority over his colleagues is rather limited, to be sure, and stems primarily from his role as presiding officer at the judicial conferences where the Court's decisions are worked out and from his power to assign the writing of opinions.[1] The prestige and symbolic value of his office are great, but they may be insufficient to sway the Court. Thus Charles Evans Hughes, certainly one of the most gifted, forceful, and diplomatic of Chief Justices, was not able to maneuver the Court out of its head-on clash with the New Deal in 1935 and 1936. Nevertheless, he guided the Court with consummate skill, a fact which became even more evident after his retirement, by contrast with the record of his successor. Harlan F. Stone had been a brilliant Associate Justice, but his ineptness in the exacting role of Chief Justice was, to some extent at least, a contributing factor in the disintegration of the Court which occurred between 1941 and 1946.

Stone's death on April 22, 1946, gave President Truman an important decision to make. Justice Robert H. Jackson, who was at the time absent in Germany, where he was serving as Allied prosecutor at the war-guilt trials, was an avowed candidate for the post of Chief Justice. President Roosevelt had apparently given some thought to Jackson as Chief Justice in 1941; but when he asked Hughes for his judgment as to Jackson and Stone, Hughes had indicated his preference for the latter because of Stone's greater judicial experience. In 1946 Hughes was again asked for advice by President Truman and, according to his biographer, recommended Jackson.[2] However, the appointment went to Vinson, a close personal friend of Truman and a Democratic stalwart from Kentucky, who had had unique experience in all three branches of the federal government. Long a member of the House of Representatives and its pre-eminent expert in the drafting of tax legislation, he was appointed to the important court of appeals for the District of Columbia in 1938. After five years of service there, he was drafted by President Roosevelt for the wartime posts of director of Economic Stabilization and of War Mobilization and Reconversion. Soon after taking office in 1945, President Truman made him Secretary of the Treasury, and it was from the Treasury that Vinson moved to the Supreme Court.

THE PASSIVE PERIOD?

The Court over which Vinson was called to preside was badly split. During the term prior to his appointment, dissents had been filed in over half the opinions handed down by the Court. The 1944 term[3] had been marked by 30 five to four decisions, the ultimate in judicial disagreement. This record seemed to be attributable in part to strained personal relations on the Court. Jackson had reacted to his failure to obtain the Chief Justiceship by releasing a bitter attack on Justice Hugo Black for the pressure he had allegedly brought to block the appointment.[4] The differences were also doctrinal, though they were no longer the relatively clear liberal-conservative disagreements of the twenties and early thirties. Now the divisions were over issues considerably more subtle and refined but capable of generating just as much heat and controversy. The hope was widely expressed that Vinson's essential moderation and his gifts for conciliation and compromise would be effective in reducing the tension on the Court and in bridling its divergent tendencies.

This book proposes to examine the experience of the Supreme Court from 1946 to 1953 as, under Chief Justice Vinson's leadership, it went about its historic task of interpreting and applying the fundamental principles of the American constitutional system in the decision of controversies which came before it. Such a purpose requires some explanation; for seven years is not a very large slice of the history of the Court, and in such cramped quarters there is not much opportunity for the flowering of significant new constitutional doctrine. Moreover, it cannot even be contended that these years were very important in the life of the Court or in its relationship to the larger political scene. John Frank, who for the past several years has written extremely perceptive annual articles on the work of the Court, said of the 1948 term: "If Supreme Court justices ever wish they had a more interesting way to make a living, then the thought must have occurred to them frequently during the October, 1948 term; for as terms go, it was rather dull."[5] And in 1951 he summed up this era as the Court's "passive period," saying: "The affirmative influence of the Court and the Constitution on American life since 1946 has been very little. . . . Compared either with the other contemporaneous institutions of government or with some past courts, the influence on the actual conduct of affairs is small."[6]

There are a number of reasons for this state of affairs. One is that several of the issues historically most provocative to the Court had by 1946 been virtually liquidated as constitutional controversies. Thus the issue of congressional power under the commerce and taxing clauses of the Constitution had been a principal element in the Court's battle with the New Deal. But on the Court as reconstituted after 1937 (hereafter the Court for the period 1937–46 is referred to as the "Roosevelt Court") these federal grants of power were interpreted so broadly as substantially to eliminate them as sources of subsequent controversy.[7] On the level of state powers, the due process clause of the Fourteenth Amendment had been extensively employed since the 1890's to strike down regulatory and experimental legislation. But the Roosevelt Court killed substantive due process almost as dead as the proverbial doornail.[8]

A second reason for the Court's period of passivity can be found in the general characteristics of the period. The immediate postwar mood was one of relaxation after war's tensions and enforced purposiveness. It was a period of quest for normalcy, of drift and withdrawal, of the Eightieth Congress. Such times do not pose the challenge of new situations for the Court. Then, before any definite direction could develop out of this relief from war's preoccupations, a new, though colder, war had taken over the center of the stage in national policy. And the conduct of foreign relations is traditionally an executive and legislative matter which presents few issues for judicial determination.

There was one area, however, in which the Vinson Court found significant work to do—the general field of civil liberties. To a marked degree, civil liberty was the unfinished business of the Roosevelt Court, which had been responsible for elevating this problem to the apex of judicial concern. Never before had the Court encouraged suitors to come to it with such a variety and profusion of civil liberties problems. One unpopular religious group, Jehovah's Witnesses, carried no less than two dozen cases of alleged infringement of freedom to preach or print to the Supreme Court between 1937 and 1946.[9] Out of such a welter of new material, however, the Court had not, by 1946, succeeded in building a coherent constitutional theory, and its members were seriously at odds as to proper judicial policy. Thus the Vinson Court inherited a series of first-rate constitutional controversies, a fully opened Pandora's box.

FROM NONCONFORMITY TO SUBVERSION

The times, moreover, guaranteed the production of new civil liberties controversies for the Vinson Court, since the cold war was bound to harden ideological lines, create tensions, and encourage the adoption and application of various types of restrictive measures. Whereas the Roosevelt Court's typical First Amendment problem had been to balance the respective rights of Jehovah's Witnesses and a local community, the Vinson Court drew the much harder assignment of determining how far a free and democratic society is obliged to extend its freedom to individuals or organizations dedicated to the overthrow of democracy. Where the Roosevelt Court had to deal with nonconformity, the Vinson Court's problem was subversion.

Most of the legislation applied against Communists or the threat of Communist subversion since 1946 was a product of the period, and the Vinson Court was called upon to give the first authoritative judicial interpretation of these provisions. The Smith Act of 1940, making it unlawful to advocate the overthrow of the government of the United States by force or violence, or to organize a group for such a purpose, was first applied to the leadership of the American Communist party in a prosecution which the Supreme Court decided in 1951.[10] The provision of the 1947 Taft-Hartley Act requiring officials of labor unions to sign non-Communist affidavits passed its constitutional test in 1950.[11] The Internal Security (McCarran) Act of 1950, some of the provisions of which were re-enacted by the Immigration and Nationality (McCarran-Walter) Act of 1952, was very quickly involved in Supreme Court decisions on deportation of alleged alien Communists.[12] The McCarran Act also set up a Subversive Activities Control Board, with responsibility for determining whether organizations or individuals should be required to register as "Communist-front" or "Communist-action" organizations or members; but the first rulings of this board had not reached the Supreme Court by 1953.

Not all the Court's cold-war problems grew out of congressional legislation. The legislative investigative function as manipulated during recent years by Senators McCarthy and Jenner and Representatives Dies and Velde has seemed on many occasions to be aimed toward prosecution rather than information—a transformation not without constitutional significance. Executive rather than legislative action was at issue in the far-flung federal loyalty program inaugurated by President Truman's executive order of March 21, 1947. At the state and local level a wide variety of statutes or ordinances has sought to deal with the Communist problem by loyalty oaths, registration requirements, exclusion of the Communist party from the ballot, or declarations of the illegality of the Communist party.

Controversies generated by the cold war against communism have, of course, contributed only a portion of the civil liberties grist to the Vinson Court's mill; but they inevitably had an importance far beyond their numbers in influencing public attitudes toward the Court and the tone of the Court's own discussions. In so far as these cold-war cases led to significant new statements or reformulations of judicial theory on civil liberties, they are discussed under appropriate headings in the chapters which follow. But the decisions of greatest theoretical significance are not necessarily the ones which are most newsworthy or most effective in capturing public attention.

Consider the Vinson Court's involvement in the two most notorious prosecutions of the period—the case of Alger Hiss and that of the atom spies, Julius and Ethel Rosenberg. The Court's initial contact with the Hiss case was a most unusual one and saw Justices Frankfurter and Reed appearing at the trial as character witnesses for Hiss. The defendant's counsel had requested both justices to appear in that capacity. Justice Frankfurter felt that it was his duty to respond without the unnecessary formality of a subpoena, but Justice Reed refused to testify until subpoenaed. A bill was subsequently introduced in Congress by Representative Keating, of New York, prohibiting federal judges from appearing as character witnesses in court proceedings; but it was rejected by the House Rules Committee on the ground that it was "patently unconstitutional."[13] The Court escaped further problems in the Hiss case when on March 12, 1951, it denied certiorari for review of the court of appeals decision upholding Hiss's conviction in his second trial.[14]

In the Rosenberg case the Supreme Court likewise sought to avoid any involvement in review of the trial and conviction and would again have been successful had it not been for Justice Douglas. In view of the significant part played by the Court in the confused and hectic days prior to the Rosenberg executions on June 19, 1953, it may be worth while to give a chronology of the Court's action.

On March 29, 1951, the Rosenbergs had been found guilty under the Espionage Act of 1917 of passing atomic secrets to Russia in wartime and were sentenced to death by Judge Irving Kaufman on April 5. The conviction was affirmed by the court of appeals on February 25, 1952; and the Supreme Court refused to review the case by denying the petition for writ of certiorari on October 13.[15] Justice Black noted at the time that he thought the petition should be granted, but under the Court's rules it requires the votes of four justices to grant a petition for certiorari.[16]

On November 17, 1952, the Court denied a petition for rehearing, with Black again stating his disagreement.[17] On this occasion Justice Frankfurter also appended a statement, which could have been interpreted as hinting that he, too, thought the petition should have been granted. He pointed out that he had consistently refused ever to make known his disagreement with denial of a certiorari petition, but his opening sentence stated: "Petitioners are under death sentence, and it is not unreasonable to feel that before life is taken review should be open in the highest court of the society which has condemned them." However, he went on to note that Congress had not made such review by the Supreme Court available as of right, and he expressed his belief that the conduct of the trial had been carefully examined by the court of appeals.

There was then further maneuvering in the lower courts, and a petition for executive clemency was filed, which President Eisenhower denied on February 11, 1953. Another petition for certiorari was filed with the Supreme Court and denied on May 25.[18] This time Douglas joined Black in expressing the opinion that the writ should be granted, while Frankfurter noted that he adhered to his position as stated the preceding November. Judge Kaufman then fixed the week of June 15 for execution of sentence.

That week was one of unparalleled activity and confusion for the Supreme Court. On June 12 an application for stay of execution had been filed with the Court and was referred to Justice Jackson in his capacity as supervising justice for the Second Circuit, where the Rosenberg case was tried. Jackson recommended to the Court at its regular Saturday conference on June 13 that the stay application be set for oral hearing on Monday, June 15. When the Court met at noon on Monday, the last day of its term, it announced refusal to hear oral argument on the stay, denied the stay, and also denied a petition for rehearing of its May 25 decision.[19] The orders disclose that Black, Frankfurter, and Burton had supported Jackson's recommendation for oral argument on the stay. Only the vote of Douglas was necessary to make this the majority view. But he took the rather puzzling position that, since the Court was refusing to hear the case on the merits, which he favored, "there would be no end served by hearing oral argument on the motion for a stay. For the motion presents no new substantial question not presented by the petition for certiorari and by the petition for rehearing." In view of Douglas' later action, it is anomalous that his vote took from the Rosenbergs their first real opportunity to have any aspect of their case orally argued before the highest court. Having denied opportunity for oral argument, the Court then voted on the stay itself, which lost five to four. Burton voted to deny the stay, while Douglas favored it, along with Jackson, Frankfurter, and Black. Thus Burton and Douglas changed places on the second vote.

After completing the reading of a list of orders, including those disposing of the Rosenberg case, the Court concluded its Monday session by ordering a recess until October. But while the justices were still in their places on the bench, a Rosenberg attorney arose to inform the Court that he wished to file a petition for writ of habeas corpus. Chief Justice Vinson replied that the petition must be filed with the Court's clerk. This the lawyer did, and the Court reconvened in a special meeting that afternoon, announcing its denial of the writ at six o'clock that evening.[20] Black and Frankfurter dissented, the latter saying that he felt there should be a full hearing on the matter the next day. He added: "Oral argument frequently has a force beyond what the written word conveys."

The Rosenberg attorneys then pressed Justice Douglas to order a stay of execution. He pondered the matter all day Tuesday, and on Wednesday issued a stay order on the ground that the Espionage Act of 1917, under which the Rosenbergs had been sentenced to death, might have been superseded by the Atomic Energy Act of 1946, Section 10 of which provides for the death penalty in espionage cases only on recommendation of the jury. The Rosenberg jury had made no such recommendation. Strangely enough, this contention had never been pressed by the regular Rosenberg counsel but came from two volunteer lawyers who had injected themselves into the case. After consideration, Douglas concluded that this point was a substantial one which the Rosenbergs should have a chance to litigate; and so he granted a stay until the district court and the court of appeals could pass on it. After issuing his order, he left the capital, as several other justices had already done.

However, Attorney General Herbert Brownell, Jr., immediately asked the Supreme Court to convene a special term to review the Douglas order, and the Chief Justice complied.[21] The missing members returned to Washington, and the Court met at noon on Thursday to hear three hours of arguments. Decision was postponed until noon the next day, Friday; and the Rosenbergs, who were scheduled to die Thursday night, thus got an additional day of life. At noon on Friday, the Court announced the setting-aside of Justice Douglas' stay order.[22] For the Court, Chief Justice Vinson held that the Atomic Energy Act did not repeal or limit the provisions of the Espionage Act and that there was no substantial question needing further litigation. Douglas and Black dissented. Frankfurter neither dissented nor concurred but stated in a separate opinion that the questions raised were so complicated and novel that more time should be afforded for study and argument. That night, shortly after eight o'clock, Julius and Ethel Rosenberg died in the electric chair at Sing Sing, the first civilians in the history of the United States to be executed for espionage in peacetime. The week was hardly part of the Court's "passive period."

One postscript should be noted. The following Monday, June 22, Justice Frankfurter filed a fuller and definitely dissenting opinion, elaborating on the views he had stated the preceding Friday.[23] "I am clear," he said, "that the claim had substance and that the opportunity for adequate exercise of the judicial judgment was wanting." And then he added:

> To be writing an opinion in a case affecting two lives after the curtain has been rung down upon them has the appearance of pathetic futility. But history also has its claims. This case is an incident in the long and unending effort to develop and enforce justice according to law. The progress in that struggle surely depends on searching analysis

> of the past, though the past cannot be recalled, as illumination for the future. Only by sturdy self-examination and self-criticism can the necessary habits for detached and wise judgment be established and fortified so as to become effective when the judicial process is again subjected to stress and strain.

Another postscript was that Representative W. M. Wheeler of Georgia introduced a resolution in the House seeking to impeach Justice Douglas for his action in granting the stay, as well as for other "high crimes and misdemeanors." The Judiciary Committee gave Wheeler a hearing and a lecture on elementary constitutional law and then rejected his resolution. On July 16 Chief Justice Vinson filed a formal opinion, destined to be his last, elaborating on his brief holding of June 19, but also defending Douglas' action. He said:

> Mr. Justice Douglas, in issuing the stay, did not act to grant some form of amnesty or last minute reprieve to the defendants; he simply acted to protect jurisdiction over the case, to maintain the status quo until a conclusive answer could be given to the question which had been urged in the defendants' behalf.

FROM RELIGIOUS FREEDOM TO RELIGIOUS ESTABLISHMENT

The difference between nonconformity and subversion, then, is one measure of the increase in the difficulty and importance of the civil liberties controversies with which the Vinson Court has had to deal. Another indication of how much higher the stakes were for the Vinson Court than for its immediate predecessors is found in the recent decisions interpreting the establishment-of-religion clause in the First Amendment. The guarantee of "free exercise" of religion has been a subject of litigation for decades, the problems involved ranging all the way from conscientious objection to polygamy. Characteristically, however, these decisions have had a limited applicability and a limited interest for the general public. The establishment-of-religion provision, on the other hand, was a very nearly forgotten and untested clause of the First Amendment. Then suddenly on the Vinson Court its interpretation became important in the highly sensitive area of public aid to private schools, particularly Catholic parochial schools. Thus the Court was forced onto another hot spot, where any action it took was bound to be bitterly attacked.

There was one earlier case, in 1930, where the Court unanimously upheld a Louisiana law providing free textbooks to pupils in both public and private schools. The theory of the decision was that the aid was to the child and not to the school.[24] This reasoning was of some help to the Vinson Court when it came to deal with its first establishment case in 1947. *Everson* v. *Board of Education* (often called the "New Jersey bus case") tested a state arrangement under which parents could be reimbursed from public moneys for costs incurred in transportation of their children to parochial schools. By a five to four vote, with Black, Douglas, Murphy, Vinson, and Reed in the majority, the Court held that this was simply a social welfare measure and that the First Amendment did not require exclusion of persons of any faith from the benefits of "public welfare legislation." What the establishment-of-religion clause did mean, Black summed up as follows:

> Neither a state nor the Federal Government can set up a church. Neither can pass laws which aid one religion, aid all religions, or prefer one religion over another. Neither can force nor influence a person to go to or remain away from church against his will or force him to profess a belief or disbelief in any religion. No person can be punished for entertaining or professing religious beliefs or disbeliefs, for church attendance or nonattendance. No tax in any amount, large or small, can be levied to support any religious activities or institutions, whatever they may be called, or whatever form they may adopt to teach or practice religion.

Rutledge, Jackson, Frankfurter, and Burton, dissenting, took the general position that payment for transportation to church schools was a direct aid to religious education and hence unconstitutional.

In 1948 the Court had to decide, in *McCollum* v. *Board of Education*, whether a "released-time" program of religious education in the public schools of Champaign, Illinois, violated the establishment-of-religion clause. Under this program, public school children, with the consent of their parents, attended classes in Protestant, Catholic, or Jewish religious instruction during school hours and in the school building. The religious teachers were not paid by the schools but were under the supervision of the school superintendents, and attendance was compulsory for participants in the program. Justice Black, speaking for the Court majority, held that under this plan tax-supported school buildings were being used in disseminating religious doctrines and that the state's public school machinery was being employed to provide pupils for religious classes. Only Reed voted to hold the Champaign plan constitutional.

The McCollum decision created a furore in church circles, for similar released-time programs were in effect throughout the country. As Black himself later admitted: "Probably few opinions from this Court in recent years have attracted more attention or stirred wider debate."[25] The eminent constitutional scholar, Edward S. Corwin, charged that the Supreme Court was setting itself up as a "national school board."[26]

It was against this background that the Court was offered a second opportunity to consider the issue, in ruling on the New York program of released-time religious education in the 1952 case of *Zorach* v. *Clauson*. The New York plan called for religious instruction outside the schools, thus differing sufficiently from the Champaign arrangement to win the approval of six justices, including three who had voted to strike down the Champaign plan (Douglas, Vinson, Burton), two who had not been on the Court at the time of the earlier decision (Clark and Minton), and one (Reed) who had thought the Champaign plan valid. Justices Black, Jackson, and Frankfurter, all in the McCollum majority, dissented in this case.

Under the New York City program, students were released from classes during the school day, on written request of their parents, in order to attend religious exercises or classes in religious centers off the school grounds. Those not released stayed in the school classrooms. The churches made weekly reports to the schools, sending a list of children who had been released from school but had not reported for religious instruction. Because the program involved "neither religious instruction in public school classrooms nor the expenditure of public funds," Douglas ruled for the majority that the McCollum case was not controlling.

There were two elements in Douglas' argument, the first of

which was more persuasive than the second. He sought to show, first, that any rigid system of separation between church and state would be absurd and impossible. It would make church and state aliens to each other—

> hostile, suspicious, and even unfriendly. Churches could not be required to pay even property taxes. Municipalities would not be permitted to render police or fire protection to religious groups. Policemen who helped parishioners into their places of worship would violate the Constitution. Prayers in our legislative halls; the appeals to the Almighty in the messages of the Chief Executive; the proclamations making Thanksgiving Day a holiday; "so help me God" in our courtroom oaths—these and all other references to the Almighty that run through our laws, our public rituals, our ceremonies would be flouting the First Amendment.

And he concluded: "We cannot read into the Bill of Rights such a philosophy of hostility to religion."

All this, of course, makes sense, and it suggests that Black was somewhat too sweeping in his Everson decision when he said that the First Amendment prevented government from aiding all religions, for government has obviously aided all religions by such measures as tax exemption. Douglas' revised listing of what is forbidden the government by the First Amendment is as follows:

> Government may not finance religious groups nor undertake religious instruction nor blend secular and sectarian education nor use secular institutions to force one or some religion on any person. . . . It may not make a religious observance compulsory. It may not coerce anyone to attend church, to observe a religious holiday, or to take religious instruction.

But did not the New York plan here under attack actually coerce students to "take religious instruction"? Douglas thought not. If there were any evidence in the record that the system was administered in a coercive manner or that teachers sought to persuade or force students to take religious instruction, then a wholly different case would be presented, he said.[27] Without such evidence, the situation was merely that of schools' closing their doors or suspending their operations "as to those who want to repair to their religious sanctuary for worship or instruction. . . . The public schools do no more than accommodate their schedules to a program of outside religious instruction."

This latter statement cannot possibly be squared with the facts, as the dissenters promptly pointed out. The schools do not close their doors or suspend their operations. Students who do not participate in the religious program are compelled to attend other school activities. Thus the state is clearly making "religious sects beneficiaries of its power to compel children to attend secular schools." As Jackson put it, the school "serves as a temporary jail for a pupil who will not go to church." The system, he continued, was clearly within the condemnation of the McCollum decision. Douglas' attempt to distinguish between the two on the ground that the instruction was outside the school building in New York, he condemned as "trivial, almost to the point of cynicism, magnifying its nonessential details and disparaging compulsion which was the underlying reason for invalidity."

The weaknesses in the Douglas position suggest that the Court majority was disposed to use any available method to quiet the storm caused by the McCollum decision. This impression seems to be strengthened by the course the Court took in the New Jersey Bible-reading case, *Doremus* v. *Board of Education*, decided a month prior to *Zorach* v. *Clauson*. Here the Court avoided making any decision at all on the constitutionality of a state statute providing for the reading, without comment, of five verses of the Old Testament at the opening of each public school day. Its grounds were technical ones of lack of standing on the part of the plaintiffs to maintain the suit.[28] This theory of avoiding trouble, however, runs afoul of the fact that Douglas, Reed, and Burton, who composed half the Zorach majority, dissented in Doremus, contending that the Court should go ahead and pass on the Bible-reading question. In any case, there seems little doubt that additional controversies over the constitutional relation of church and state will continue to be pressed upon the Court and that this is another potentially explosive problem with which it will have to learn to live.[29]

PERSONALITY AND JUDICIAL REVIEW

The events of the week of June 15, 1953, and the establishment-of-religion cases just reviewed afford dramatic illustration of the burden of personal responsibility which falls on members of the Supreme Court and the range of discretion open to the justices in the decisions they are called upon to make. The Rosenberg case was difficult because of the great public tension present, though legally it was simply a matter of proper statutory interpretation. On large constitutional questions, such as the establishment-of-religion issues, the opportunities for division are even greater. The more basic principles of the Constitution are so broad and built so closely into the political system that legal learning is only one, and not necessarily the most important, of the guides for decision of constitutional issues. Judicial inquiry normally can supply not one but several answers to such questions, and the selection from among the available courses of decision is inevitably affected by the social philosophy and policy preferences of the judges passing on the issue.

At no level in our judicial system is the judge an automaton, and least of all on the highest court. Who the judges are makes a difference in the decisions. It made a difference that John Marshall, an ardent nationalist, was Chief Justice of the United States from 1801 to 1835 and thus able to make his private policy preferences part of the fundamental public law of the new nation. It made a difference that Messrs. McReynolds, Butler, Sutherland, and Van Devanter were justices of the Supreme Court in 1935 and 1936 when the first New Deal measures had to face constitutional inquiry. It made a difference when civil rights issues came before the Court in the 1940's that Justices Black, Douglas, Murphy, and Rutledge were among those present and voting.[30]

That a relationship between judicial personality and judicial decisions exists is obvious. But it is not an obvious or simple matter to develop means for appraising the influence of individual justices upon the course or direction of the Court's decision-making. Justice Frankfurter is fond of quoting an old English saying that "the devil himself knoweth not the mind of men."[31] The mind of a man who happens to be a judge is the center of many contending forces when he is making it up, and an external reconstruction of the process is quite impossible. However, the rules of the game require that judges supply clues to their thought-processes in the form of written opinions. In every major case decided by the Supreme Court, one or more of its justices provide a written justification for the decision announced.

The individualistic tradition of Anglo-Saxon jurisprudence, moreover, permits judges who do not agree with the views of their brethren to say so and to give their reasons for dissenting. Thus the Supreme Court on decison day takes on the aspect of a small legislature in which votes are cast pro and con on significant issues of public policy, with accompanying explanations much more coherent and systematic and better-reasoned than are customarily available in explanation of votes cast, say, in the United States Senate.

Capitalizing on the availability of such excellent material, there are two principal ways one might proceed to study the relationship between individual justices and the judicial institution of the Supreme Court. The first is the biographical method. This approach would take an individual justice and attempt to discover all the facts about his life that might have a bearing on the way he decided cases on the bench. It would examine the circumstances of his boyhood, the nature of his education, the kind of clients he represented at the bar if he was a practicing lawyer, the way he voted if he was a member of a legislature—everything short of psychoanalytic data (which presumably would not be available to the investigator) would be related to the subject's judicial behavior. Of course, numerous biographies have been written of Supreme Court justices, one of the most notable and recent being Pusey's life of Charles Evans Hughes. Such a biography may not actually "explain" a judge's decisions, but it certainly illuminates the broad outlines of a pattern of thought and development which gave direction to a judicial philosophy.

The second approach gives major emphasis to the judicial institution and looks at the individual justices primarily as participants in the manufacture of an institutional product. This is the method which the great historians of the Court—Charles Warren, Andrew C. McLaughlin, Charles Grove Haines, Gustavus Myers —have followed. But covering as they do broad sweeps of the Court's history, they have inevitably been limited in the attention they could give to, or the techniques they could employ for discovering, the personal background of judicial decisions.

A more intensive inquiry into such problems would require two things: (1) limitation of the study to a relatively brief period an actuality. Clark, a Texan, had been an official in the Department of Justice since 1937 and was appointed Attorney General by President Truman in 1945. Subsequent congressional investigations raised questions as to Clark's judgment in selecting some of his subordinates in the Department of Justice and also caused criticism of his actions in connection with the Kansas City vote fraud investigations in 1946.[38] Minton, like Burton, had been a Senate colleague of President Truman. During his term, from 1935 to 1941, he had served as Democratic whip and had enjoyed a reputation as a fire-eating New Dealer. President Roosevelt appointed him as one of his administrative assistants in January, 1941, and later that year named him to the court of appeals for the seventh circuit.

These men, then, were the justices through whom the Vinson Court spoke and who were responsible for balancing the conflicting claims of freedom and order, liberty and authority, in the civil liberties cases which that Court decided.

DISSENTING RECORD

If there was a hope that the reconstituted Court would achieve a greater degree of harmony than the Roosevelt Court, it was largely doomed to disappointment. In fact, the Court over which Vinson presided, if tested by the proportion of nonunanimous decisions handed down, was more divided than any in Supreme Court history. Prior to 1935, the Court had seldom decided less than 85 per cent of its cases unanimously. But since that time a marked change has occurred in the Court's habits, a change fully documented by the data collected in Table 1.[39]

Only a few comments need be made to emphasize the facts of disagreement. During the 1936 term, 19 per cent of the Court's decisions failed to win the approval of the entire Court. Ten years later, in the first year of the Vinson Court, 64 per cent of the decisions were nonunanimous. During the same term, 26 of the 92 nonunanimous decisions involved a five to four division among the justices. The indexes of division continued to show an increase during the next two terms, reaching a high of 74 per cent nonunanimous decisions and 35 five to four decisions in the 1948 term. The departure of Murphy and Rutledge from the

of the Court's history and (2) the development of new methods of analyzing individual participation in judicial decisions. In a previous volume the author attempted to achieve these goals by limiting the period of study to the ten years from 1937 to 1947 and by adding to the familiar methods of judicial study certain techniques for analyzing the voting alignments and behavior of the justices in their decisions during that period. The result seemed sufficiently rewarding to justify applying the same methods to the Vinson Court, with special reference to its civil liberties decisions.

PERSONNEL OF THE VINSON COURT

The Court as it stood at the end of the term in June, 1953, was composed of nine justices, four of whom had been appointed by President Truman. The remaining five had been named by President Roosevelt, who by his nine appointments between 1937 and 1943 had had an opportunity completely to reorient the predominantly conservative Court which he had inherited from his predecessors.[32]

The first of the Roosevelt appointees still serving on the Vinson Court was Hugo L. Black. Beginning his service in 1937 on what was alleged to be a "spite" appointment to embarrass the Senate, under the cloud of former Ku Klux Klan membership, and with the supposed handicap of no previous judicial experience save for a brief term on a police court, Black had rapidly established himself as an extremely keen and able jurist and the leader of the Court's more liberal wing. He wrote opinions in a lean, hard-hitting style, which often burned with the fire of an active social conscience.[33]

Justice Stanley Reed, Roosevelt's second appointee, was a Kentucky lawyer who had represented tobacco and railroad interests before coming to Washington under President Hoover as counsel for the Federal Farm Board. Under Roosevelt he was first made general counsel for the RFC and then promoted to the solicitor general's post, where he defended the constitutionality of the initial New Deal measures. He lacked Black's activist, legislative type of mind, and, while supporting labor's gains and the enlargement of governmental powers sponsored by the New

Deal, he found himself a middle-of-the-roader and "swing man" on the Roosevelt Court.

Justice Felix Frankfurter, appointed from Harvard Law School in 1939, was destined to become one of the great puzzles of the Roosevelt Court. Known before his appointment for his liberal reputation and his fecundity in providing ideas and personnel for the New Deal, his record on the Court quickly departed from the expected liberal pattern, particularly on civil liberties questions. One explanation offered was that he was more concerned with developing a consistent philosophy of limited judicial power than in the social results of particular decisions. Whatever the reason, Frankfurter and Black quickly became the intellectual leaders or focal points of two conflicting tendencies on the Roosevelt Court.[34]

Justice William O. Douglas, with his background of Yale Law School and the Securities and Exchange Commission, approached more nearly the Black pattern. In fact, Black and Douglas had almost identical voting records during their first terms; and, while they differed increasingly, the longer they stayed on the bench, the differences seemed to be more over details than over basic principals. Perhaps more than any other member of the Roosevelt Court, Douglas seemed to chafe under the limitations which the Court imposed, and he sought escape by spending his summers in far-flung and sometimes perilous travels.[35] He received serious consideration for the Democratic vice-presidential nomination in 1944 and had some supporters for the presidential nomination in 1948 and 1952.

Justice Robert H. Jackson, who came to the Court by way of the solicitor general's and attorney general's posts, proved to be relatively close to Frankfurter in voting performance; but the rather erratic nature of his opinions made it difficult to catalogue him. He demonstrated in his opinions an acute mind and a brilliant style, which produced many felicitous phrases but which also on occasions descended to personalities and wisecracks.

These five justices constituted, of course, a majority of the Vinson Court and guaranteed that the principal orientations of the Roosevelt Court would be reproduced on its successor. But, since these five justices were themselves split up, with Black

paired with Douglas, Frankfurter with Jackson, and Reed somewhere in between, the Roosevelt holdovers were unlikely to vote often as a unit on controversial issues. Consequently, control of the Court would depend upon how the new appointees fitted themselves into the existing alignments or whether they developed new focal points of their own.

The first opportunity for a Truman appointment came with Justice Owen Roberts' resignation in 1945. Roberts was the only pre-Roosevelt appointee to last through Roosevelt's twelve years in office, and by 1945 he had earned a place on the far right of the Court as its most conservative member. To replace him, President Truman apointed one of his former Senate colleagues, Harold H. Burton, a Republican—in fact, the first Republican to join the Court since the Hoover administration.[36] Burton had been mayor of Cleveland and had been elected to the Senate in 1940. His views on internal affairs had proved to be those of a moderate conservative, while on foreign problems he had gradually moved over to the internationalist wing of the Republican party. His appointment was apparently attributable to President Truman's feeling that some gesture should be made toward bipartisan representation on the Court and to the respect which he had developed for Burton when they were serving together on the Special Committee To Investigate National Defense, better known as the Truman Committee.

After Vinson's appointment in 1946, the Court's membership was stable for the next three terms. Then in the summer of 1949 occurred the deaths of Justices Murphy and Rutledge. They had both been closely associated with Black and Douglas on many issues, particularly in the civil liberties field. This cohesive bloc had within itself the four votes needed to grant certiorari petitions and needed to find only one additional recruit in order to control the Court's decisions.[37] It was this four-judge group which, more than any other factor, gave the Roosevelt Court its distinctive character; and the loss of Rutledge and Murphy opened the possibility that the Court's direction might be fundamentally altered.

Announcement of the two new appointees, Tom C. Clark and Sherman Minton, made it clear that this possibility would become

Court resulted in a drastic decline in five to four decisions, but the ratio of nonunanimous decisions dropped much less noticeably. By the 1951 term it was up again to 71 per cent, and in 1952 an all-time high of 81 per cent was registered.[40]

It is scarcely necessary at this late date to defend the dissenting opinion as an institution. Without the right to file dissents, members of the Supreme Court would do their work behind faceless

TABLE 1

DISAGREEMENT ON THE SUPREME COURT, 1940–52 TERMS

Term	Total Decisions by Full Opinion	Nonunanimous Decisions		Dissenting Votes		5 to 4 Votes
		Number	Per Cent	Number	Per Decision	
1940....	169	47	28	117	0.69	3*
1941....	162	59	36	160	0.99	16
1942....	171	75	44	176	1.03	10*
1943....	137	80	58	194	1.42	16
1944....	163	94	58	245	1.50	30
1945....	137	77	56	156	1.14	†
1946....	144	92	64	246	1.71	26
1947....	118	82	69	224	1.90	26
1948....	123	91	74	273	2.22	35
1949....	98	65	66	125	1.27	2*
1950....	98	62	63	168	1.71	15
1951....	94	67	71	167	1.78	11
1952....	108	87	81	204	1.90	9

* Less than a full Court sitting during a considerable portion of the term.
† Only eight justices sitting during the entire term.

masks of anonymity. The sense of personal participation in and responsibility for the Court's decisions would be lost. Moreover, the public would be deprived of the debates on fundamental issues and the statements of alternative constitutional theories which are now supplied by majority and minority opinions. Chief Justice Hughes was almost mystical on this subject when he said: "A dissent in a court of last resort is an appeal to the brooding spirit of the law, to the intelligence of a future day, when a later decision may possibly correct the error into which the dissenting judge believes the court to have been betrayed."[41] And Justice Frankfurter, before his appointment to the Court, wrote: "Divisions on the Court and the greater clarity of view and candor of expression to which they give rise, are especially productive of insight."[42]

On the other hand, it is possible to have too much even of a good thing. Certainly the fact that a unanimous opinion is beginning to seem like a rarity on the Supreme Court indicates that some important change has occurred in judicial attitudes. There are those who see the record of nonunanimous decisions as the fever line of the Court, as an index to the politicization of judicial opinion. Thomas Reed Powell says of the present situation:

> One gets the impression of a company of independent essay writers rather than of members of an official body wielding governmental power. A court is an institution and it would seem to be intrinsically desirable that its members should be dominated by an institutional ethos in so far as that is feasible without putting them in a seriously false position by silence.[43]

It is precisely because the Court's institutional ethos has become so weak that we must examine the thinking of the individual justices if we are to understand the civil liberties decisions of the Vinson Court or to appraise their significance for American life and politics. Before turning to that task, however, some background on pre-1946 judicial doctrines must be supplied.

II. *Free Speech before Vinson*

"Congress shall make no law . . . abridging the freedom of speech, or of the press. . . ." This great principle of an open society was incorporated in the Constitution of the United States when the First Amendment was ratified on December 15, 1791; but it was over one hundred years before the Supreme Court had to undertake any significant exploration of the scope and meaning of this prohibition. For one thing, the amendment was directed only at Congress, not at the state legislatures, and Congress during the nineteenth century was little concerned with domestic legislation of a police character.

There was, to be sure, the Sedition Act of 1798,[1] which later commentators have regarded as definitely unconstitutional; but no test of that law got to the Supreme Court before it expired in 1801. However, the popular verdict against the Federalist party, which sponsored that legislation, was more effective than any judicial pronouncement; and it was not until the first World War that Congress again consciously resorted to antilibertarian controls over speech, under the prodding of popular hysteria. This time the Supreme Court was quickly drawn into the argument, and, ever since, the American judiciary has been a principal contributor to freedom of speech doctrine. The following discussion is a brief and necessarily inadequate summary of the Court's thinking from 1919 to 1946, organized around three general standards which its members have developed and applied.

CLEAR AND PRESENT DANGER

Justice Oliver Wendell Holmes was the Court's spokesman in its first encounters with the free speech problem. The Espionage Act of 1917, which prohibited the making of false statements intended to interfere with the successful prosecution of the war, as well as acts obstructing recruiting or causing insubordination in the armed forces, was at issue in the 1919 case of *Schenck* v. *United States.* The defendants had mailed circulars to men eligible for the draft, declaring conscription to be unconstitutional despotism and urging them in impassioned language to assert their rights. Holmes spoke for a unanimous Court in finding such actions to be clearly illegal under the statute: "The question in every case is whether the words are used in such circumstances and are of such a nature as to create a clear and present danger that they will bring about the substantive evils that Congress has a right to prevent. It is a question of proximity and degree." And he added, with particular reference to the problems of the Schenck case: "When a nation is at war many things that might be said in time of peace are such a hindrance to its effort that their utterance will not be endured so long as men fight and that no Court could regard them as protected by any constitutional right."

In the same month, March, 1919, Holmes wrote two more unanimous decisions for the Court, upholding convictions in Espionage Act cases. In *Frohwerk* v. *United States* the culprit had inserted several articles in a Missouri German-language newspaper on the constitutionality and merits of the draft and the purposes of the war. Holmes was obviously in some doubt as to whether the clear-and-present-danger test had been met here, but, because of the inadequacy of the record, he concluded: ". . . it is impossible to say that it might not have been found that the circulation of the paper was in quarters where a little breath would be enough to kindle a flame and that the fact was known and relied on by those who sent that paper out."

The third case was the conviction of Eugene V. Debs, one of whose speeches at a Socialist convention was charged with being an attempt to cause insubordination in the army and obstruct recruiting. The speech was not designed for soldiers, nor did Debs urge his hearers to resist the draft. Nonetheless, Holmes felt unable to go behind the jury's verdict and accepted it as proof that actual interference with the war was intended and was the proximate effect of the words used.[2]

Thus in its first three applications the clear-and-present-danger test proved a rather illusory protection to freedom of speech in wartime. It was, in effect, a rationalization for sending men to jail because of their speech, though it did have the virtue of insisting that the relationship between speech and illegal acts must be proximate, not remote and indirect. Professor Zechariah Chafee, Jr., praised the Schenck ruling as supplying "for the first time an authoritative judicial interpretation in accord with the purpose of the framers of the Constitution."[3]

In the fall of 1919 Holmes, along with his colleague, Louis D. Brandeis, sought to show that the test did have protective value, but the two justices were unable to carry the Court majority with them. The crime in *Abrams* v. *United States* was printing and circulating pamphlets attacking the government's action in sending American troops to Vladivostok and Murmansk in the summer of 1918 and calling for a general strike of munition workers. Holmes's dissent is probably his most famous piece of rhetoric; but here we need note only the effort he made to sharpen up and strengthen the clear-and-present-danger test by these words:

> . . . we should be eternally vigilant against attempts to check the expression of opinions that we loathe and believe to be fraught with death, unless they so imminently threaten immediate interference with the lawful and pressing purposes of the law that an immediate check is required to save the country. . . . Only the emergency that makes it immediately dangerous to leave the correction of evil counsels to time warrants making any exception to the sweeping command, "Congress shall make no law abridging the freedom of speech."

In two additional cases during the same term, the same two justices, with Brandeis writing the dissents, protested the Court's failure to apply the "rule of reason" which the clear-and-present-danger test supplied.[4]

Two later foundation stones of the theory remain to be inspected. The first is *Gitlow* v. *New York*, a 1925 decision upholding a conviction under the New York criminal anarchy statute for publication of a radical manifesto. The Court majority this time did not even pay lip service to clear and present danger. Justice Sanford argued that the test had been relevant in Espionage Act cases, for that act made certain actions unlawful and the purpose of the test was to determine at what point words became the equivalent of unlawful acts. But in the New York statute, the legislature had itself determined that certain words of incitement were dangerous. In reviewing such a legislative finding, the sole responsibility of the Supreme Court was to decide whether there was a reasonable basis for such a legislative conclusion. Justice Sanford, embracing the "remote-possibility" or "bad-tendency" test, felt that there was: "A single revolutionary spark may kindle a fire that, smoldering for a time, may burst into sweeping and destructive conflagration. It cannot be said that the state is acting arbitrarily or unreasonably when . . . it seeks to extinguish the spark without waiting until it has enkindled the flame or blazed into the the conflagration."

Holmes came up again with some fine prose to the effect that "every idea is an incitement"; but the enduring positive contribution of Gitlow was the majority's casual, almost incidental, admission that the free speech protections of the First Amendment, applicable by their terms only against congressional action, are also effective in the states by reason of the "liberty" provision of the Fourteenth Amendment.

This was a startling constitutional development. Ever since 1884 the Supreme Court had denied that the Fourteenth Amendment imported into the states all the criminal prosecution provisions of the Fourth through the Eighth Amendments,[5] and as late as 1922 the Court had opined that "the Constitution of the United States imposes on the States no obligation to confer upon those within their jurisdiction . . . the right of free speech."[6] But in 1923 the Court had ruled that "liberty" to teach a foreign language in private schools was protected by the Fourteenth Amendment from state infringement.[7] And one week before the Gitlow decision the Court invalidated an Oregon law interfering with the "liberty" of parents to send their children to private schools.[8] Although in each case there was a deprivation of property element for schools and teachers, the decisions did clear the way for a holding that liberty of thought, without any property nexus, was protected under the Fourteenth Amendment. And so we find Sanford saying in Gitlow: ". . . we may and do assume that freedom of speech and of the press . . . are among the fundamental personal rights and 'liberties' protected . . . from impairment by the states."[9]

Finally, we must note Brandeis' concurring opinion in *Whitney* v. *California*, a 1927 case where, speaking for Holmes as well, he wrung out of the clear-and-present-danger test the maximum protection of which it seems capable. A legislative declaration that a danger exists which justifies restrictions on speech and assembly creates, he said, merely a "rebuttable presumption." If the conditions alleged by the legislature do not, in fact, exist, then the courts, guided by the clear-and-present-danger test, must refuse to enforce the statute. Brandeis admitted that the standards for the test had not yet been clearly fixed, and he undertook once more the task of formulation:

> To courageous, self-reliant men, with confidence in the power of free and fearless reasoning applied through the processes of popular government, no danger flowing from speech can be deemed clear and present, unless the incidence of the evil apprehended is so imminent that it may befall before there is opportunity for full discussion. If there be time to expose through discussion the falsehood and fallacies, to avert the evil by the processes of education, the remedy to be applied is more speech, not enforced silence. Only an emergency can justify repression. . . . Moreover, even imminent danger cannot justify resort to prohibition of these functions essential to effective democracy, unless the evil apprehended is relatively serious. Prohibition of free speech and assembly is a measure so stringent that it would be inappropriate as the means for averting a relatively trivial harm to society. . . . The fact that speech is likely to result in some violence or in destruction of property is not enough to justify its suppression. . . . Among free men, the deterrents ordinarily to be applied to prevent crime are education and punishment for violations of the law, not abridgment of the rights of free speech and assembly.

Though Holmes assented to this statement, it clearly goes beyond his own previous efforts to clarify the clear-and-present-danger test; and Alexander Meiklejohn, in fact, contends that it amounts to an abandonment of that test in favor of the principle of absolute freedom of public discussion.[10]

LEGISLATIVE REASONABLENESS

Looking back, we see that the clear-and-present-danger test was, at first, not a test for the validity of legislation—the Espionage Act was admittedly constitutional—but rather a test for determining how closely words had to be related to illegal acts in order to be infected with their illegality. Even in Gitlow, Holmes did not appear to challenge the New York statute. He merely doubted whether Gitlow's "redundant discourse" was included in the statutory prohibition. It was not until Whitney that clear and present danger was definitely set forth as a basis on which courts and, indeed, all Americans could "challenge a law abridging free speech and assembly by showing that there was no emergency justifying it."

This development brought the clear-and-present-danger test into direct conflict with an earlier standard of judicial review, namely, that legislative conclusions embodied in statutes must be upheld by courts if there is any basis on which a "reasonable man" could have reached the same conclusion as the legislature. The reasonable-man theory was embraced by the majority in Gitlow and Whitney. Those decisions held that the function of the Court, when confronted with a statute alleged to infringe basic civil liberties, was limited to judging whether a reasonable man could have reached the legislature's conclusion as to the existence of a danger demanding that protective action be taken. As Sanford said in Gitlow: "Every presumption is to be indulged in favor of the validity of the statute." Legislatures should be rebuked only if they act "arbitrarily or unreasonably."

Now there is sound authority for the reasonable-man theory of judicial review. Holmes himself was ordinarily one of the most ardent exponents of this test. As he said in his famous dissent to *Lochner* v. *New York*, he would not invalidate any statute "unless it can be said that a rational and fair man necessarily would admit that the statute proposed would infringe fundamental principles as they have been understood by the traditions of our people and our law." Of course, Lochner was not a civil liberties case; the issue was whether New York could limit the hours of employment in bakeries. But in 1923 Holmes did apply the reasonable-man test in what came very close to being a civil liberty case, *Meyer* v. *Nebraska.* The Court majority here, as previously noted, held invalid a state law which was aimed to prevent the teaching of the German language in the primary schools. Holmes refused to go along with his colleagues, because he believed that whether children in their early years should hear and speak only English at school was "a question upon which men reasonably might differ and therefore I am unable to say that the Constitution of the United States prevents the experiment being tried."

This quotation epitomizes the doctrine upon which Holmes's reputation for liberalism was based. The reasonable-man theory was a method of letting the legislatures have their own way. A conservative Supreme Court, from 1880 on, had insisted on the right to substitute its judgment for that of Congress or the state legislatures as to the constitutionality of laws which changed the rules respecting rights and uses of property. Holmes thought that the Court had no such license from the Constitution to override the views of popularly elected legislatures, except to veto statutes for which no case could possibly be made that would satisfy a reasonable man. This was the core of his liberalism.

Why, then, did Holmes abandon the reasonable-man test in the civil liberties field? And how could it be liberalism to advocate a doctrine of narrow judicial review in dealing with economic regulation and broad judicial review over regulations limiting freedom of speech and press?

This apparent paradox was explained in two different ways on the Roosevelt Court, and the divergence was the basis for some of its classic arguments, as in the two flag-salute decisions.[11] One explanation was that Holmes had not really meant to challenge the reasonable-man theory or to develop an alternative to it as a test for the validity of legislation. Justice Frankfurter, who claims the role of Holmes's principal disciple and interpreter, developed this main theme with variations in a number of decisions. For present purposes, his position can be illustrated by two freedom of speech cases in which individuals had been convicted of contempt of court for their out-of-court comments on pending judicial controversies.

The first case was *Bridges* v. *California*, a 1941 decision involving contempt citations of a powerful newspaper and a powerful labor leader. The California court here had acted on the basis of its general common-law powers; no state statute existed granting or defining the conditions under which courts could summarily punish publications dealing with pending litigation. Consequently, the Supreme Court, in Justice Black's eyes, was free to decide as an original question whether summary punishment was justified; and his test was the Schenck test, as interpreted by Gitlow, that the publications must have created "such likelihood of bringing about the substantive evils" as to deprive them of constitutional protection. "Likelihood" was to be determined on the basis of clear and present danger. Reviewing the various Holmes and Brandeis formulations on the subject, Black came up with his own "working principle," namely,

> that the substantive evil must be extremely serious and the degree of imminence extremely high before utterances can be punished. Those cases do not purport to mark the furthermost constitutional boundaries of protected expression, nor do we here. They do no more than recognize a minimum compulsion of the Bill of Rights. For the First Amendment does not speak equivocally. . . . It must be taken as a command of the broadest scope that explicit language, read in the context of a liberty-loving society, will allow.

Justice Frankfurter, dissenting with three colleagues, could not accept this statement. State action "to assure the impartial accomplishment of justice is not an abridgement of freedom of speech or freedom of the press, as these phases of liberty have heretofore been conceived even by the stoutest libertarians." The "age-old . . . prohibition against interference with dispassionate adjudication" should not be displaced by "a phrase which first gained currency on March 3, 1919." The Court's duty, Frankfurter thought, was not discharged by the unthinking "recitation of phrases that are the shorthand of a complicated historic process"; and he denied that the difference between the "reasonable tendency" test used by the California court and the clear-and-present-danger test was one of "constitutional dimension."

Frankfurter was only getting warmed up in Bridges, however. In 1946 another contempt of court case growing out of newspaper comment on judicial conduct came up, *Pennekamp v. Florida;* and again the Bridges rule was applied by the Court, this time speaking through Justice Reed, who said: "We conclude that the danger under this record to fair judicial administration has not the clearness and immediacy necessary to close the door of permissible public comment. When that door is closed, it closes all doors behind it." Justice Frankfurter, though concurring with the Court's judgment on technical grounds, attacked the use of this test as unjustified:

> "Clear and present danger" was never used by Mr. Justice Holmes to express a technical legal doctrine or to convey a formula for adjudicating cases. It was a literary phrase not to be distorted by being taken from its context. . . . "The clear and present danger" with which its two great judicial exponents were concerned was a clear and present danger that utterance would "bring about the . . . evils" which Congress sought and "has a right to prevent." Among "the substantive evils" with which legislation may deal is the hampering of a court in a pending controversy, because the fair administration of justice is one of the chief tests of a true democracy. And since men equally devoted to the vital importance of freedom of speech may fairly differ in an estimate of this danger in a particular case, the field in which a State "may exercise its judgment is necessarily a wide one." Therefore, every time a situation like the present one comes here the precise problem before us is to determine whether the State court went beyond the allowable limits of judgment in holding that conduct which has been punished as a contempt was reasonably calculated to endanger a State's duty to administer impartial justice in a pending controversy.

These cases are perhaps sufficient to give a fairly clear picture of Frankfurter's position.[12] His argument may be summarized as follows: (1) that the test was being used for a *purpose* other than Holmes intended—namely, to determine the constitutionality of legislation; (2) that it was being applied in much different *areas* than Holmes contemplated, including contempt of court proceedings and violation of petty police regulations; and (3) that the *spirit* of its use was much different than Holmes would have approved.

But what, then, is the field of usefulness for clear and present danger? Does it have any validity at all? It is difficult to say what Frankfurter's position up to 1946 was in this respect. He did not himself write any opinions for the Roosevelt Court relying upon the clear-and-present-danger test; his views were expressed only in attacks on other justices for their use of it. But he did, particularly in the earlier years of the Roosevelt Court, participate without objection in some decisions in which the test was employed. One was the famous picketing decision, *Thornhill* v. *Alabama,* where the Court extended the protection of the free speech clause to labor picketing. Writing the Court's opinion, Justice Murphy, citing Holmes's views in Schenck and Abrams, said:

> Abridgement of the liberty of . . . discussion can be justified only where the clear danger of substantive evils arises under circumstances affording no opportunity to test the merits of ideas by competition for acceptance in the market of public opinion. . . . No clear and present danger of destruction of life or property, or invasion of the right of privacy, or breach of the peace can be thought to be inherent in the activities of every person who approaches the premises of an employer and publicizes the facts of a labor dispute involving the latter.

Frankfurter registered no disagreement, nor did he one month later when Justice Roberts, for a unanimous Court, referred to clear and present danger as the test of a state's power to prevent or punish "riot, disorder, interference with traffic upon the public streets, or other immediate threat to public safety, peace, or order."[13] But in subsequent cases he did not permit such arguments to pass without protest.

THE PREFERRED-POSITION ARGUMENT

We now turn to the other explanation of the Holmes paradox, one adopted on numerous occasions by the Roosevelt Court and associated with the judicial quartet of Black, Douglas, Murphy, and Rutledge. This view holds that Holmes definitely intended to supplant the reasonable-man test by clear and present danger in areas where legislative action trenched upon civil liberties. The reasonable-man test was appropriate in all other fields; but where the basic freedoms of the First Amendment were at issue, then the judiciary had to hold itself and the legislature to higher standards. The higher standards were required because of the "preferred position" which the Constitution gives to the basic First Amendment freedoms.

This is an explanation which Holmes himself never used, of course. Its effect is to exalt the clear-and-present-danger test, instead of minimizing it, as Frankfurter does. It supplies a foundation, a justification, which the test otherwise lacks. It induces in a judge a mental set favorable to civil liberties claims.

The essence of the preferred-position argument was stated in an extreme form by Frankfurter to be that "any law touching communication is infected with presumptive invalidity."[14] A more moderate statement is that, because First Amendment values are so essential to a free society, legislative action infringing those values must be shown to be not only "reasonably" adapted to the attaining of valid social goals but justified by overwhelmingly conclusive considerations.

The development of the preferred-position view must be indicated rather summarily. The origin might be found in Justice Cardozo's statement in a 1937 decision that First Amendment liberties were on "a different plane of social and moral values." Freedom of thought and speech, he said, is "the matrix, the indispensable condition, of nearly every other form of freedom. . . . Neither liberty nor justice would exist if they were sacrificed."[15] A somewhat similar position was taken a little earlier in the same year, in the case of *Herndon* v. *Lowry*. But the credit for the invention is usually given to Justice Stone, in a footnote which he appended to a 1938 decision.[16]

The case in question concerned application of a congressional act prohibiting transportation of certain types of compounded milk products in interstate commerce, and Stone was rehearsing the familiar arguments for the "reasonable-man" theory of judicial review:

> . . . the existence of facts supporting the legislative judgment is to be presumed, for regulatory legislation affecting ordinary commercial transactions is not to be pronounced unconstitutional unless in the light of the facts made known or generally assumed it is of such a character as to preclude the assumption that it rests upon some rational basis within the knowledge and experience of the legislators.

At this point occurred the footnote:

There may be narrower scope for operation of the presumption of constitutionality when legislation appears on its face to be within a specific prohibition of the Constitution, such as those of the first ten Amendments, which are deemed equally specific when held to be embraced within the Fourteenth. . . . It is unnecessary to consider now whether legislation which restricts those political processes which can ordinarily be expected to bring about repeal of undesirable legislation, is to be subjected to more exacting judicial scrutiny under the general prohibitions of the Fourteenth Amendment than are most other types of legislation. . . . Nor need we enquire . . . whether prejudice against discrete and insular minorities may be a special condition, which tends seriously to curtail the operation of those political processes ordinarily to be relied upon to protect minorities, and which may call for a correspondingly more searching judicial inquiry.

This is admittedly a tentative and qualified pronouncement; Frankfurter, who vigorously challenges the whole preferred-position argument as "mischievous," is justified in concluding that "it did not purport to announce any new doctrine" and that, if it had, a footnote would hardly have been an "appropriate way" of doing so.[17] But within a year and a half the idea which Stone had at least suggested leaped from the footnotes to become the doctrine of an almost unanimous Court, Justice Frankfurter included, in the 1939 handbill cases.[18] Speaking through none other than Justice Roberts, the Court said:

In every case, therefore, where legislative abridgement of the rights [to freedom of speech and press] is asserted, the courts should be astute to examine the effect of the challenged legislation. Mere legislative preferences or beliefs respecting matters of public convenience may well support regulation directed at other personal activities, but be insufficient to justify such as diminishes the exercise of rights so vital to the maintenance of democratic institutions. And so, as cases arise, the delicate and difficult task falls upon the courts to weigh the circumstances and to appraise the substantiality of the reasons advanced in support of the regulation of the free enjoyment of the rights.

McReynolds was the only dissenter.

The "preferred-position" phrase was apparently not actually employed until Stone, by then Chief Justice, used it in 1942 in his dissent to *Jones* v. *Opelika*, where the Court majority upheld municipal license taxes on booksellers as applied to Jehovah's Witnesses and cited the fact that these were general tax ordinances, not levies aimed at this particular group. In reply Stone observed:

> The First Amendment is not confined to safeguarding freedom of speech and freedom of religion against discriminatory attempts to wipe them out. On the contrary the Constitution, by virtue of the First and the Fourteenth Amendments, has put those freedoms in a preferred position. Their commands are not restricted to cases where the protected privilege is sought out for attack. They extend at least to every form of taxation which, because it is a condition of the exercise of the privilege, is capable of being used to control or suppress it.

One year later Justice Douglas restated this thought, but now for the Court majority, in *Murdock* v. *Pennsylvania*, which overruled *Jones v. Opelika:* "Freedom of press, freedom of speech, freedom of religion are in a preferred position." The phrase reappears in several subsequent decisions.[19] Even Justice Jackson, whose more recent thoughts have been most antagonistic to the preferred-position argument, lent it support in his 1943 holding in the second flag-salute case.[20] The point he made there was that a reviewing court must be very careful in invalidating legislation on ordinary due process grounds because that standard is so indefinite, but the definiteness of the First Amendment permits the replacement of the reasonable-man test by considerably stricter standards. He explained:

> . . . It is important to distinguish between the due process clause of the Fourteenth Amendment as an instrument for transmitting the principles of the First Amendment and those cases in which it is applied for its own sake. The test of legislation which collides with the Fourteenth Amendment, because it also collides with the principles of the First, is much more definite than the test when only the Fourteenth is involved. Much of the vagueness of the due process clause disappears when the specific prohibitions of the First become its standard. The right of a State to regulate, for example, a public utility may well include, so far as the due process test is concerned, power to impose all of the restrictions which a legislature may have a "rational basis" for adopting. But freedoms of speech and of press, of assembly, and of worship may not be infringed on such slender grounds. They are susceptible of restriction only to prevent grave and immediate danger to interests which the state may lawfully protect.

What Frankfurter regards as "perhaps the strongest language dealing with the constitutional aspect of legislation touching utterance" was Justice Rutledge's statement in the 1945 case of *Thomas* v. *Collins:*

> . . . Any attempt to restrict those liberties must be justified by clear public interest, threatened not doubtfully or remotely, but by clear and present danger. The rational connection between the remedy provided and the evil to be curbed, which in other contexts might support legislation against attack on due process grounds, will not suffice. These rights rest on firmer foundation. Accordingly, whatever occasion would restrain orderly discussion and persuasion, at appropriate time and place, must have clear support in public danger, actual or impending. Only the gravest abuses, endangering paramount interests, give occasion for permissible limitation.

It must be added that this was the view of only four justices, since Jackson, who supplied the fifth vote in the case, concurred on other grounds.

This, then, was the preferred-position argument as developed by the Roosevelt Court. The reasonable-man test placed the burden of proof of unconstitutionality on any person attacking a legislative conclusion. The clear-and-present-danger test shifted the burden of proof to the defenders of any legislation which limited First Amendment freedoms. The preferred-position argument reinforced the clear-and-present-danger test and supplied its reason for being. These three formulations give us a shorthand version of the civil liberties heritage of the Vinson Court.

III. *Free Speech: Previous Restraint*

With the foregoing understanding of the Vinson Court's ideological inheritance on civil rights, we may turn to an examination of its own contributions and performance, examining first the basic problem of freedom of speech. The decisions to be considered in this area have been grouped into two general categories, according as the limitations at issue were imposed in advance of speaking or publication or were in the nature of punishment for speech or publication which had been found to violate statutory standards. More simply, it is the distinction between censorship of speech and punishment for having spoken. It is the difference between officials banning a meeting or silencing a newspaper and prosecuting individuals after the event for allegedly unlawful speech or publication. The present chapter will concern itself with the censorship cases, leaving the punishment cases for the succeeding chapter.

THE CENSORSHIP ISSUE

The Anglo-Saxon tradition has been strongly against censorship for several centuries and has regarded it much more seriously than the threat of subsequent punishment. "The liberty of the press," wrote Blackstone, "consists in laying no *previous* restraints upon publications."[1] He went on to argue that liberty of the press meant nothing more than this; and here he was clearly wrong. But in declaring the invalidity of official censorship he was stating a principle which had become established in England by 1695, and in the colonies by 1725.[2] The issue had thus been closed for decades by the time the First Amendment was adopted; and, whatever other doubts there might be about its intent, there could be no doubt that it intended to restate the ban on previous restraints of speech and press.

The case against censorship was, in fact, so thoroughly established that, apart from some temporary wartime situations, attempts at previous restraint have been so few or so localized throughout our history as to provide little material for judicial review. When censorship was attempted through official instrumentalities, it was more often concerned with morals than with politics. Thus there was the 1915 case in which the Supreme Court upheld state censorship of motion pictures.[3] The motion picture, which was then purely an entertaining novelty and rather completely devoid of any ideational content, was regarded by the Court as merely a "spectacle" like the circus and the theater and not part of the press of the country or an organ of public opinion.

The Supreme Court's first great anticensorship decision was the 1931 case of *Near* v. *Minnesota*, in which a Minnesota statute providing for the abating, as a public nuisance, of "malicious, scandalous and defamatory" newspapers or periodicals and the enjoining of anyone maintaining such a nuisance was declared unconstitutional by a five to four vote. It is noteworthy that Chief Justice Hughes's opinion found no necessity for using either the reasonable-man or the clear-and-present-danger test. There was no need to ask whether a legislature could reasonably have regarded this device as adapted to meeting an evil, because the Constitution and American practice under it had simply forbidden legislatures to use censorship as a method of meeting social problems. The clear-and-present-danger test was irrelevant, because it is a way of measuring differences in degree—differences which, if established, may turn an illegal interference with speech into a justifiable restriction. But prior restraint, the Court seemed to say, is always illegal; so circumstances cannot make it legal.[4]

The minority of Butler, Van Devanter, McReynolds, and Sutherland did not accept this analysis. In their view, censorship was not unconstitutional per se. They would leave resort to this device within the area of legislative choice, and in this case they felt that the legislature could reasonably have decided that it met their needs. Butler noted: "It is of the greatest importance that the states shall be untrammeled and free to employ all just and appropriate measures to prevent abuses of the liberty of the press."

Near v. *Minnesota* thus forecast the line which all subsequent censorship decisions have taken. For some justices it is necessary to establish only that a statute accomplishes prior restraint; it is *ipso facto* condemned. Other justices feel that there is room even here for legislative balancing of interests and that restraints may be justified by desirable social consequences.

The first censorship cases to come to the Roosevelt Court found it practically unanimous in acting on the absolutist view and condemning various city ordinances which required the permission of city officials for the distribution of handbill literature.[5] In 1940 a Connecticut statute which made it a crime to engage in house-to-house canvassing for religious or philanthropic causes without the prior approval of a county welfare official was unanimously declared to constitute "a censorship of religion."[6]

However, subsequent cases involving prior restraints of a perhaps milder nature brought out divisions between the absolutists and the believers in a "rule of reason" on the Court. In 1943 the Court held invalid a city ordinance making it unlawful to ring doorbells or knock on doors for the purpose of summoning the occupants to the door to give them handbills or circulars; but Justices Reed, Jackson, and Roberts could not see in this "trivial town police regulation," intended to protect the daytime sleep of swing-shift workers, any violation of the First Amendment.[7] Two 1946 decisions upheld the right to distribute literature on the premises of a federal housing authority project in Texas and a "company town" in Alabama, without becoming liable to the penalty provided by state law for remaining on the premises of another after being warned not to do so.[8] Again three members of the Court—this time Stone, Reed, and Burton—were in dissent.

The division was even closer in declaring invalid municipal license fees on transient merchants or book agents, as applied to the Jehovah's Witnesses engaged in door-to-door peddling of religious tracts. When this issue first came before the Court in 1943, it split five to four in upholding the taxes.[9] But after Rutledge replaced Byrnes, the matter was reconsidered, and the decision went five to four the other way.[10]

On the other hand, there was a 1941 case, *Cox* v. *New Hampshire*, in which the Roosevelt Court unanimously upheld a regulation challenged as prior restraint. A group of Jehovah's Witnesses had been convicted for marching single file along the downtown sidewalks of Manchester, New Hampshire, carrying placards to advertise a meeting, without securing the special license required by state statute for "parades or processions" on a public street. The act was upheld by Chief Justice Hughes as a reasonable police regulation, administered under proper safeguards. He made clear that the Court was treating the license as merely a traffic regulation and that the conviction was not for conveying information or holding a meeting. Thus any breach which the Cox holding made in the principle of no prior restraints was quite narrow.

For the Vinson Court's attitude on prior restraint, we may begin with the two 1952 movie censorship decisions, which unanimously overruled the Mutual Film pro-censorship decision of 1915.[11] The Mutual Film doctrine antedated the period of the Court's concern with civil liberties problems, and several justices had given intimations from time to time that moving pictures were entitled to the protection of the First and Fourteenth Amendments. Thus in *United States* v. *Paramount Pictures*, a 1948 antitrust case, the Court said: "We have no doubt that moving pictures, like newspapers and radio, are included in the press whose freedom is guaranteed by the First Amendment." On the other hand, the practice of movie censorship was widely established.

Burstyn v. *Wilson* concerned Rosselini's film *The Miracle*, which had been licensed for exhibition in New York and shown for about two months. Then, after a Catholic campaign against the film, appropriate administrative review was undertaken, and the license was withdrawn on the ground that the picture was "sacrilegious." A state statute authorized denial of a license to a movie found to be "obscene, indecent, immoral, inhuman, sacrilegious, or . . . of such a character that its exhibition would tend to corrupt morals or incite to crime."

Justice Clark wrote the Court's opinion holding that states cannot constitutionally censor motion pictures on the ground that they are sacrilegious. First, Clark definitely brought movies within the protection of the First Amendment, by way of the Fourteenth. Contrary to the view in the Mutual Film case that movies were merely spectacles, Clark said: "It cannot be doubted that motion pictures are a significant medium for the communication of ideas." The fact that the production, distribution, and exhibition of movies is a large-scale business conducted for profit is irrelevant to the issue, for, of course, newspapers and magazines have the same status.

The rest of Clark's opinion is a little puzzling. In part he seems to base his rejection of censorship on the rather narrow ground that "sacrilege," the standard applied here, is too loose and meaningless and sets the censor "adrift upon a boundless sea amid a myriad of conflicting currents of religious views, with no charts but those provided by the most vocal and powerful orthodoxies." Justice Frankfurter in his concurring opinion further emphasizes the vagueness issue and says that sacrilege as a standard "inevitably creates a situation whereby the censor bans only that against which there is a substantial outcry from a religious group."

If the Court's objection is simply to the breadth of the standard, then the *Miracle* decision may be of little value in determining the constitutionality of movie censorship on other grounds. Clark himself warns that the Court is expressing no opinion on "whether a state may censor motion pictures under a clearly-drawn statute designed and applied to prevent the showing of obscene films." But his opinion does contain one rather strong sentence related less to the vagueness issue and more to the general invalidity of prior restraints: "From the standpoint of freedom of speech and the press, it is enough to point out that the state has no legitimate interest in protecting any or all religions from views distasteful to them which is sufficient to justify prior restraints upon the expression of those views."

The fact that there was actually a division on the Court on the censorship issue, in spite of the unanimous opinion in the Burstyn case, became evident one week later, when the Court reviewed censorship of the movie *Pinky* by a Texas city.[12] This picture, dealing with a racial theme, had been refused a license under a city ordinance authorizing denial when the board of censors believed the movie "of such character as to be prejudicial to the best interests of the people of said city." The Court ruled the ordinance unconstitutional in a per curiam opinion which merely cited the Burstyn case and *Winters* v. *New York*, a 1948 decision in which a New York criminal statute had been invalidated on the ground of vagueness. But in a concurring opinion Douglas ignored the vagueness issue, concluding rather that the ordinance was invalid because it was a "flagrant form" of prior restraint. "If a board of censors can tell the American people what it is in their best interests to see or to read or to hear . . . then thought is regimented, authority substituted for liberty, and the great purpose of the First Amendment to keep uncontrolled the freedom of expression defeated." Thus it appears that part of the Court, probably a majority, found movie censorship unconstitutional only where the standards were too vague, while others on the Court objected to it as a matter of principle.

Next we may look at another pair of cases, both decided on the same day in 1951, involving the use of licensing systems to control speech. The Court condemned both licensing efforts, but unanimously in one case and by a five to four vote in the second. The easier of the two cases was *Niemotko* v. *Maryland*, involving a group of Jehovah's Witnesses who wished to give a series of Sunday Bible talks in the public park of Havre de Grace. There was no ordinance prohibiting or regulating the use of the park, but, by custom, organizations desiring to hold meetings there obtained a permit from the park commissioner, with an appeal lying to the city council from an adverse decision. In this case the applicants came to the council, which, after questioning them as to their alleged refusal to salute the flag and their views on the Bible, denied the request. The witnesses then proceeded to hold their meeting without a permit, but their speaker was arrested as soon as he began his discourse and was subsequently convicted of disorderly conduct.

The Supreme Court, through Chief Justice Vinson, unanimously reversed the conviction. The evidence showed that the conduct of the speaker had been quite orderly and that the only basis for the charge was the failure to have a permit. The Court pointed to its long line of decisions condemning license requirements as a prior restraint on speech or press or religion, which can be justified only if "narrowly drawn, reasonable and definite standards" are provided for the licensing officials to follow. This was an unusually clear case of "unwarranted discrimination" in a refusal to issue a license, and a denial of equal protection.[13]

The second license case, *Kunz* v. *New York*, was more troublesome. It concerned a New York City ordinance making it unlawful to hold public worship meetings on the street without first obtaining a permit from the city police commissioner. Kunz, whose custom it was to engage in outdoor preaching, in 1946 applied for and received a permit good for the calendar year. In November, 1946, the permit was revoked after a hearing, on evidence that Kunz had ridiculed and denounced other religious beliefs in his meetings. His applications for permits in 1947 and 1948 were disapproved, no reason being given. When he spoke without a permit in Columbus Circle, he was arrested and fined $10.00.

For the Chief Justice and the Court majority, this was another clear case of prior restraint, the ordinance giving to "an administrative official discretionary power to control in advance the right of citizens to speak on religious matters on the streets of New York," with "no appropriate standards to guide his action." To the argument that Kunz's religious meetings had in the past caused some disorder, the Court replied that "there are appropriate public remedies to protect the peace and order of the community if appellant's speeches should result in disorder or violence."

Justice Jackson, dissenting, felt it was "quixotic" to give "hateful and hate-stirring attacks on races and faiths" the classic protections of free speech. New York City is a "frightening aggregation" of people all legally free to live, labor, and travel where they please.

> Is it not reasonable that the City protect the dignity of these persons against fanatics who take possession of its streets to hurl into its crowds

defamatory epithets that hurt like rocks? . . . If any two subjects are intrinsically incendiary and divisive, they are race and religion. . . . These are the explosives which the Court says Kunz may play with in the public streets, and the community must not only tolerate but aid him. I find no such doctrine in the Constitution.

Third come the two well-known sound-truck cases, decided while Murphy and Rutledge were still on the Court. Here Chief Justice Vinson's shift between cases gave conflicting results in the two decisions. *Saia* v. *New York*, decided in 1948, involved a Jehovah's Witnesses minister in Lockport, New York, who gave lectures at a fixed place in a public park on designated Sundays, using sound equipment mounted on top of his car to reach a wider audience. Lockport had an ordinance which forbade the use of sound-amplification devices except with the permission of the chief of police. Saia had such a permit; but when it expired, renewal was refused on the ground that there had been "complaints." The minister proceeded to use his equipment without a permit, and he was tried and convicted for the violation.

Justice Douglas, in a short opinion classically illustrating the absolutist position, held the ordinance unconstitutional on its face as a previous restraint on the right of free speech, with no standards prescribed for the exercise of discretion by the chief of police in using his licensing powers. There might be abuses in the use of loudspeakers, but, if so, they would have to be controlled by "narrowly drawn statutes" aimed at those abuses, not by giving a police officer power to deny the use of loudspeakers entirely. People might allege that they were annoyed by noise when they were really annoyed by the ideas noisily expressed. "The power of censorship inherent in this type of ordinance reveals its vice."

Both Frankfurter and Jackson wrote dissenting opinions, in the former of which Reed and Burton concurred. Frankfurter pointed out that the park in question was a small one; the loudspeaker was powerful enough to cover a large part of the park and might seriously interfere with the recreational uses to which people wished to put the park. Uncontrolled noise is an "intrusion into cherished privacy." It disturbs "the refreshment of mere silence, or meditation, or quiet conversation." The Founders were drawn into the debate by Frankfurter's noting that the members of the Constitutional Convention in 1787 had shown their appreciation of the virtues of quiet by having "the street outside Independence Hall covered with earth so that their deliberations might not be disturbed by passing traffic."

Jackson's dissent, characteristically, was somewhat more vigorous. He was astonished to think that the Constitution prevents municipalities from regulating or prohibiting "the irresponsible introduction of contrivances of this sort into public places." This was not, to Jackson, a free speech case. It was a case testing whether society can exercise control over "apparatus which, when put to unregulated proselyting, propaganda and commercial uses, can render life unbearable." Obviously, more cases would be required to spell out the law on this subject.

Kovacs v. *Cooper*, decided the following year, seemed to offer this opportunity. The proceeding arose out of the operation of a sound truck in Trenton, New Jersey, for the purpose of commenting on a local labor dispute. A Trenton ordinance made it unlawful for sound trucks or similar amplifying devices emitting "loud and raucous" noises to be operated on the public streets. On its face this ordinance was more stringent than the one in Lockport, for it appeared to be a complete prohibition of sound apparatus. This was, in fact, the interpretation placed upon the ordinance by the state courts.

In a rather cloudy opinion for the Supreme Court, however, Justice Reed appeared to interpret the ordinance as prohibiting only "loud and raucous" sound trucks. He stated specifically that "absolute prohibition within municipal limits of all sound amplification, even though reasonably regulated in place, time and volume, is undesirable and probably unconstitutional as an unreasonable interference with normal activities." But, on the other hand, "unrestrained use throughout a municipality of all sound amplifying devices would be intolerable," and the "loud and raucous" test he accepted as a satisfactory one. Though he saved the ordinance in this fashion, he never did make it clear whether a sound truck could be operated in other than a loud and raucous manner. If not, the decision overruled the Saia case, though

Reed held they were clearly distinguishable; the Saia ordinance, he said, established a previous restraint on free speech, whereas the Trenton ordinance was aimed at preventing disturbing noises.

This was a distinction without a difference to Justice Jackson, though he was one of the five justices making up the majority. Neither was he impressed by Reed's "loud and raucous" test; to him the ordinance unconditionally banned all sound trucks from Trenton streets, and it was on this basis that he supported the ordinance. The four dissenting justices, speaking through Black and Rutledge, took the same view of the ordinance's intention, which in their minds made it unconstitutional under the Saia doctrine. Thus Justice Reed achieved the dubious distinction in the Kovacs case of writing an opinion for the Court to which five justices objected, and of upholding a conviction on a different interpretation of local law from that of the state courts. Jackson summed up the situation by saying that the two sound-truck decisions would "pretty hopelessly confuse municipal authorities as to what they may or may not do."[14]

The streetcar "captive audience" case from the District of Columbia, though it is not in form a censorship case, is related in some ways to the sound-truck cases, since both deal with the rights of privacy in public places. The privately owned transit system of the District of Columbia arranged for musical programs to be received in its streetcars, with interspersed commercial announcements covering about three minutes in every hour. The public utilities commission of the District, after investigation and hearing, held that the programs were not inconsistent with public interest, comfort, and safety.

The Supreme Court concluded that no constitutional violation had resulted. If a legislature wishes to prohibit raucous sounds in public places, it can do so, as the Kovacs case held. But if, on the other hand, a public body, after due process, concludes that the broadcasting of radio programs in a public place such as a streetcar does not interefere with public convenience or comfort, the courts should not interfere on constitutional grounds. An individual does not have the same right to privacy on a public vehicle as he has in his home.

Justice Black agreed, provided that "news, public speeches,

views, or propaganda of any kind" were not included in the broadcasts. Justice Frankfurter took no part in the case because his feelings were "so strongly engaged as a victim of the practice in controversy." Justice Douglas dissented on the ground that "government should never be allowed to force people to listen to any radio program. . . . The right to be let alone is indeed the beginning of all freedom."[15]

Finally, we have three cases in which the Vinson Court definitely approved prior-restraint legislation.[16] The first was *United Public Workers* v. *Mitchell*, a 1947 decision rejecting by a four to three vote a claim of unconstitutionality brought against the Hatch Act, which limits the political activity of government employees and requires the removal from their jobs of those who take an "active part in political management or in political campaigns." Justice Reed, speaking for Frankfurter, Vinson, and Burton as well, held the statute not to be an unconstitutional invasion of the employees' rights of free speech. Congress had concluded that it was in the best interests of an efficient public service for classified employees to be prohibited from active participation in politics: "To declare that the present supposed evils of political activity are beyond the power of Congress to redress would leave the nation impotent to deal with what many sincere men believe is a material threat to the democratic system."

Justices Black, Douglas, and Rutledge (Murphy not participating) would have held the statute unconstitutional. Douglas contended that if political influences needed to be limited, the legislation should be more narrowly drawn, to get at the specific conduct constituting a clear and present danger. Black's argument was in more general terms and more vigorous language. He bitterly condemned a policy which muzzles several million citizens and deprives the body politic of their political participation and interest. He believed that the statute endowed the Civil Service Commission "with the awesome power to censor the thoughts, expressions, and activities of law-abiding citizens in the field of free expression from which no person should be barred by a government which boasts that it is a government of, for, and by the people—all the people."

The second case was the 1951 decision of *Breard* v. *City of*

Alexandria, in which the Court permitted a municipal ordinance against door-to-door solicitation to be applied against itinerant salesmen of magazine subscriptions, over the contention that such a prohibition was an unconstitutional restraint on freedom of the press. Such ordinances, commonly referred to as the "Green River type," have been adopted in a number of cities, allegedly as a protection to the privacy of the home but undoubtedly sponsored in most cases by local merchants interested in cutting off bothersome competition. The original Green River ordinance had been upheld against the challenge of a Fuller brush man by the Supreme Court in 1937, but, of course, no First Amendment question was presented in that case.[17]

Again in Breard, as in Kovacs, it fell to Justice Reed to reconcile an antilibertarian decision with the libertarian precedents. A large part of his unusually jocular opinion deals with the due process and commerce clause objections to the ordinance, with which we are not here concerned. As a free press problem, the case turned on "a balancing of the conveniences between some householders' desire for privacy and the publisher's right to distribute publications in the precise way that those soliciting for him think bring the best results." Reed's conclusion was that communities which had found house-to-house canvassing "obnoxious" had a right to control it by ordinance. Magazines could be sold some other way.

The Chief Justice dissented on commerce clause grounds without reaching the First Amendment problem. Douglas agreed with him, but he also went along with Black's dissent, which was a short but sharp defense of the principles of the Court's earlier decisions protecting door-to-door canvassing from taxation and other restrictions. These precedents, he believed, had been in effect overruled by Reed, and he concluded: "Today's decision marks a revitalization of the judicial view which prevailed before this Court embraced the philosophy that the First Amendment gives a preferred status to the liberties it protects. I adhere to that preferred position philosophy."

Finally, in the 1953 case of *Poulos* v. *New Hampshire* the Court held constitutional a city ordinance providing for licensing of meetings in public streets or parks, where the state supreme court had required that the licensing system must be "uniform, nondiscriminatory and consistent." Justice Reed for the Court concluded that, under the system, licensing officials had "no discretion as to granting permits, no power to discriminate, no control over speech.".

The ordinance was identical with the language of the state statute unanimously upheld by the Supreme Court as applied in the 1940 Cox case. In Poulos, however, Douglas and Black dissented vigorously, distinguishing between the clear speech issue raised here and the street-procession–traffic-control problem involved in Cox. Douglas' dissent denied that the licensing system could be administered in a ministerial fashion; discretion would inevitably be exercised. No standards or procedural safeguards could save a licensing system, for "even a reasonable regulation of the right to free speech is not compatible with the First Amendment." The preferred position of civil rights forbids *any* regulation: "The command of the First Amendment . . . is that there shall be *no* law which abridges those civil rights. The matter is beyond the power of the legislature to regulate, control, or condition."

Douglas did not undertake to reconcile this absolutist position with his statement in the Saia case that a statute narrowly drawn to get at possible abuses by sound trucks would be constitutional. Perhaps he would say that the unamplified human voice cannot be guilty of abuses which would justify regulation of amplified speech. Or perhaps Douglas and Black, disturbed by the trends on the Vinson Court and the declining influence of the preferred-position argument, felt it necessary to take an increasingly dogmatic position in the opposite direction.

In summary, it would seem that seven years of the Vinson Court left prior restraint still suspect, but no longer unconstitutional on its face. In 1940 Justice Roberts and a unanimous Court in the Cantwell case referred to previous restraint as simply "inadmissible." The 1953 rule is the rule of reasonableness as stated by Justice Reed in the Poulos case: "Regulation and suppression are not the same, either in purpose or result, and courts of justice can tell the difference."[18]

RESTRAINT OF PICKETING

A special but perennial and important problem in restraint of expression grows out of the use of injunctions to limit or forbid picketing in labor disputes. Here again, as in the censorship cases just reviewed, the Vinson Court executed a gradual retreat from the absolutist position, originally stated by Justice Murphy in the 1940 case of *Thornhill* v. *Alabama*. In that decision the Supreme Court for the first time equated picketing with speech and put peaceful picketing under the protection of the First Amendment. Interpreting a state law which made peaceful picketing a misdemeanor, the Court, with only the unreconstructed McReynolds dissenting, held that "the dissemination of information concerning the facts of a labor dispute must be regarded as within that area of free discussion that is guaranteed by the Constitution." A statute completely blocking such dissemination must be adjudged unconstitutional on its face, and, as in *Near* v. *Minnesota*, justifications for the restraint were irrelevant.

It soon appeared, however, that the Court was far from clear or unanimous on the implications of its new doctrine. Within the next few years varying interpretations turned up in contemporaneous decisions. In 1941 the Thornhill doctrine was applied and even extended to protect peaceful "stranger picketing" (i.e., by pickets not employed by the picketed concern) in *A.F.L.* v. *Swing*. But on the same day Justice Frankfurter, author of Swing, also wrote the Meadowmoor opinion holding that the Illinois courts could enjoin *all* picketing in a labor dispute which had been so marred by past violence that it was believed impossible for future picketing to be maintained on a peaceful basis.[19]

Again on the same day in 1942 the Court unanimously struck down a New York court injunction against picketing in the Wohl case,[20] while upholding a Texas injunction in *Carpenters and Joiners Union* v. *Ritter's Cafe*. Ritter was having a house built by nonunion labor, but the pickets were operating around his cafe, a mile away. By a five to four vote the Court ruled that Texas had the right to restrict picketing "to the area . . .

within which a labor dispute exists." Then in 1943 the Court swung back to a broad view of picketing rights in the Angelos case by unanimously upholding the peaceful picketing of a cafeteria by a union whose grievance was that the cafeteria was operated by its owners and so hired no employees for the union to organize.[21]

This backing and filling was a clear indication that the Thornhill doctrine was not an entirely satisfactory guide for the Court's answers to picketing problems. It merely held that a state could not flatly prohibit all picketing, because of the communication element therein. This would seem to leave open the possibility of regulation in two general types of situations—where the communications process results in, or even seeks, damage to other social values protected by law or the Constitution, or where the communication element in picketing is of only minor importance compared with other functions which the picketing is being made to serve.

The Meadowmoor case is an illustration of the former situation. Clearly, the prevention of violence is a goal which may justify restraints on picketing where experience has shown that real danger of violence exists. This factor, of course, accounts for the emphasis on "peaceful picketing." But, as our second category suggests, picketing may be peaceful and still subject to restraint, if it can be shown that the communications purpose, which is the only justification for constitutional protection, is less important than other purposes which are unprotected.

Actually, it is quite clear that on many picket lines the purpose is not so much publicity as it is economic coercion. The International Brotherhood of Teamsters can shut off the flow of supplies into an establishment by posting a single picket at each of its truck entrances. Of course, this kind of "signal picketing" is a far cry from the circulation of ideas which the First Amendment is intended to protect. Archibald Cox has suggested that, unless the Court is to abandon the Thornhill rule entirely and withdraw constitutional protection from all picketing, it must undertake to distinguish between "publicity picketing" and "signal picketing," so that each can be appropriately treated.

But he admits that this distinction is a very difficult one to draw, for the "same picket line usually appeals both to public opinion and to group discipline backed by economic sanctions."[22]

The Vinson Court did not proceed quite so logically as Cox suggests. It continued to treat picketing as communication, at least in theory; but in a series of important cases it found a conflict between rights of communication and other lawful social interests, which justified the issuance of injunctions against picketing.[23] In each case two elements were essential to the Court's conclusion: (1) that these competing values represented public policy as laid down by competent authorities acting within their legal and constitutional powers and (2) that these interests were, in fact, of greater social value than the rights of communication which were being restrained. It is instructive to see how these findings were reached in the specific cases.

In the first case, *Giboney* v. *Empire Storage & Ice Co.*, decided in 1949, the conflict was with Missouri's law on restraint of trade. A union of retail ice peddlers in Kansas City sought agreements with wholesale ice distributors not to sell to nonunion peddlers. Under state law such agreements were punishable by $5,000 fines and five-year prison terms, plus liability to suit for treble damages by the injured parties. Empire, which refused to sign the agreement or discontinue such sales, was picketed and secured an injunction against the picketing. The union's justification was that a labor dispute existed with the company and that the picketers were publicizing only truthful information in exercise of their rights to free speech.

Speaking through Justice Black, the Court unanimously ruled against the union. As for the first test mentioned above, the constitutionality of antitrust legislation was, of course, well established. On the second point, Black agreed that a state could not abridge fundamental freedoms "to obviate slight inconveniences or annoyances," but he said that Missouri's interest in enforcement of its policy against restraints of trade could not be so classified. The union was attempting to enforce its own policy in violation of that officially declared by the state; the speech restrained was "an essential and inseparable part of a grave offense against an important public law." Consequently, the

First Amendment did not immunize that unlawful conduct from state control.

In two other cases where the conflict was likewise with a policy laid down by state legislation, the Giboney rule was applied. In *Building Service Employees Union* v. *Gazzam* the picketing was for the purpose of compelling an employer to sign a contract with a labor union which would force his employees to join the union, in contravention of a Washington state law forbidding employer coercion of employees in selection of collective bargaining representatives. In *Local Union No. 10* v. *Graham* a Virginia court injunction was upheld on the ground that the picketing, while peaceful and carried on by only one or two pickets with signs reading "This Is Not a Union Job" in front of a school construction project, had the purpose of forcing the contractor to fire nonunion workers, in violation of the state Right to Work statute.[24] The union's defense was that they were not trying to get nonunion men fired but to get union men to stay away from the project.[25]

In these three cases where the picketing was for a purpose declared unlawful by statute, the Court's task was comparatively easy. But in *Hughes* v. *Superior Court of California*, decided the same day as Gazzam, the determination of illegal purpose rested on judge-made rather than on statute law. Here a grocery store, about half of whose customers were Negroes, was picketed by a citizens' group with the demand that the store's employees be in proportion to the racial origin of the customers. An injunction against the picketing was upheld by the California supreme court on the ground that the picketing, though peaceful, was for an unlawful purpose—"to demand discriminatory hiring on a racial basis." The court assumed, without deciding the question, that if discrimination in employment did exist, "picketing to protest it would not be for an unlawful objective"; but here the picketers were demanding that employment be based on race and color rather than on individual qualifications, and this was contrary to California's public policy.

Justice Frankfurter, approving this position for a unanimous Court, said it was immaterial that the state policy on this point was expressed by the judicial organ rather than by the legislature. California was free to strike at the evils inherent in a "quota system" of employment by means of a limited injunction rather than by statute law. Justices Black, Minton, and Reed concurred on the basis of the Giboney case rather than on the basis of Frankfurter's reasoning.

This indication of differing views grew into full-fledged dissent in the next and most difficult picketing case which the Vinson Court had to decide, *International Brotherhood of Teamsters* v. *Hanke*. The facts were that two used-car businesses in Seattle, operated by their owners without employees, were picketed to enforce a demand that they become union shops. The union was seeking to set up a schedule whereby used-car dealers would be closed evenings and on week ends, and these two self-employers contended they could not afford to operate on this basis. The state courts, in enjoining the picketing, were apparently impressed by the fact that all but 10 of the 115 used-car dealers in Seattle were self-employers, and concluded:

> The union's interest in the welfare of a mere handful of members . . . is far outweighed by the interests of individual proprietors and the people of the community as a whole, to the end that little businessmen and property owners shall be free from dictation as to business policy by an outside group having but a relatively small and indirect interest in such policy.

What distinguishes this case from the preceding ones is that the union in its picketing was not making an unlawful demand. If Hanke had entered into the contract which the union was demanding, it would presumably have been enforced by the state courts. Thus the injunction was based simply on court disapproval of the union's objectives. Nevertheless, Justice Frankfurter, with the support of Vinson, Jackson, and Burton,[26] upheld the injunction on the ground that Washington was free to strike a balance between competing economic interests and that the balance here achieved was not "so inconsistent with rooted traditions of a free people that it must be found an unconstitutional choice."

Frankfurter's principal feat was in making the famous 1937 case of *Senn* v. *Tile Layers' Protective Union*, which had been favorable to picketing, support a conclusion here which restricted picketing. In the former case Senn, a self-employed tile-layer, who occasionally hired other tile-layers to assist him, was picketed when he refused to yield to the union demand that he himself no longer work at his trade. The injunction he sought was refused in accordance with the terms of a Wisconsin statute authorizing the giving of publicity to labor disputes and making peaceful picketing lawful and nonenjoinable. Senn contended that the restriction on his freedom was a denial of his liberty under the Fourteenth Amendment; but Justice Brandeis for the Supreme Court ruled that it lay in the domain of policy for Wisconsin to permit such picketing and to put it as a "means of publicity on a par with advertisements in the press." The meaning of this precedent for the present case, said Frankfurter, was that "if Wisconsin could permit such picketing as a matter of policy it must have been equally free as a matter of policy to choose not to permit it and therefore not to 'put this means of publicity on a par with advertisements in the press.' "

But Frankfurter was careful not to quote another sentence from the Senn opinion, the sentence which was the keystone of the Thornhill decision, in which Brandeis said: "Members of a union might, without special statutory authorization by a State, make known the facts of a labor dispute, for freedom of speech is guaranteed by the Federal Constitution." Frankfurter also sought to minimize the protective quality of the Swing, Wohl, and Angelos decisions by contending that in those cases the Court had "held only that a State could not proscribe picketing merely by setting artificial bounds, unreal in the light of modern circumstances to what constitutes an industrial relationship or a labor dispute."

Black, Minton, and Reed dissented from Frankfurter's opinion, and Douglas did not participate. Black did not seek to particularize the reasons for his disagreement beyond calling attention to his Ritter's Cafe dissent, but Minton wrote a substantial dissent, in which Reed joined, challenging Frankfurter's interpretation of the Senn holding:

. . . Because Wisconsin could permit picketing, and not thereby encroach upon freedom of speech, it does not follow that it could forbid like picketing; for that might involve conflict with the Fourteenth Amend-

> ment. It seems to me that Justice Brandeis, foreseeing the problem of the converse, made the statement above quoted in order to indicate that picketing could be protected by the free speech guaranty of the Federal Constitution. Whether or not that is what Justice Brandeis meant, I think this Court has accepted that view, from Thornhill to Angelos. It seems to me too late now to deny that those cases were rooted in the free speech doctrine. I think we should not decide the instant cases in a manner so alien to the basis of prior decisions.

No subsequent cases offered an opportunity to continue the debate begun in the Hanke case.[27] That decision would seem to justify a conclusion that the Thornhill principle has been confined to its narrowest limits, namely, invalidation only of flat restraints against all picketing, leaving legislatures and judges free in all other respects to define public purposes which would override picketing rights. Considering the willingness of the Vinson Court to grant the validity of some prior restraint even on bona fide speech, as noted in the earlier part of this chapter, it is hardly surprising that picketing—a dubious form of speech at best—was quickly stripped of the constitutional protection tentatively accorded it by the Roosevelt Court.

IV. *Free Speech: Subsequent Punishment*

The theoretical objection to prior restraint, as seen in the preceding chapter, is that speech must not be throttled in advance. Abuses of speech are not to be anticipated. But the libertarian theory does not deny that freedom of speech may be abused. It admits that possibility and agrees that such abuses can be punished, after proof in proper judicial proceedings. However, unless closely controlled, punishment for what one has said can be just as effective in discouraging free discussion as censorship.

For individual injuries resulting from speech which is malicious and false, the libel and slander laws are available. But are there public values which may be threatened by speech or press, for which the speaker or publisher may be punished in the name of the public without infringing the First Amendment? We recall Justice Holmes's comment that no one has the right falsely to cry fire in a crowded theater. Such an extreme example is good for making a point, but it does not help much in dealing with cases where the public evil resulting from speech is less drastic and demonstrable. Starting a panic in a theater is practically murder. But how much less than murder is society obligated to put up with in order to protect the rights of free speech?

SPEECH AS BREACH OF THE PEACE

First, we may consider situations in which free exercise of speech appears to threaten the maintenance of public order. Obviously, preservation of the peace is a prime responsibility of a community's officials. How far may speech be permitted to go in creating a disturbance of the public peace before the authorities are justified in hauling the speaker off to jail? The Roosevelt Court had to answer a question of this sort in the 1942 Chaplinsky case, in which a member of Jehovah's Witnesses had created a public disturbance in Rochester, New Hampshire, by his open denunciations of all religion as a "racket." When he called a city marshal "a God damned racketeer" and "a damned Fascist," he was arrested and convicted of violating a state statute against calling anyone "offensive or derisive" names in public. Justice Murphy, perhaps more sensitive to claims of personal freedom than any other justice in the history of the Court, spoke for a unanimous bench in upholding the conviction on the ground that insults and "fighting" words "are no essential part of any exposition of ideas and are of such slight social value as a step to truth that any benefit that may be derived from them is clearly outweighed by the social interest in order and morality."[1]

The Vinson Court's questions in this field were somewhat harder to answer. The first was presented by *Terminiello* v. *Chicago* in 1949. The case arose out of a Fascist-type speech made under riotous conditions by an associate of Gerald L. K. Smith in a Chicago auditorium in 1946. An unfrocked Catholic priest, Terminiello specialized in attacks upon the Jews and the Roosevelt administration. On this occasion eight hundred sympathizers were present in a packed hall, while outside a larger crowd picketed the building in protest, threw rocks through the windows, and sought to force the doors. Police had all they could do to keep the doors shut, and only by their aid was the speaker's party able to enter and leave the building. Following the affair Terminiello was found guilty of disorderly conduct under an ordinance covering "all persons who shall make, aid, countenance, or assist in making any improper noise, riot, disturbance, breach of the peace, or diversion tending to a breach of the peace." The conviction was upheld by two higher Illinois courts.

These facts seemed to give the Supreme Court an opportunity and an obligation to consider further the important question as to whether speech which is composed of "derisive, fighting words" calculated to cause violent reaction is entitled to constitutional protection. However, a strange coalition of Reed plus Black, Douglas, Murphy, and Rutledge, speaking through

Douglas, decided the case on a basis which never permitted the Court to reach this issue.

It appeared from an examination of the record that the trial judge had charged the jury that "breach of the peace" consists of any "misbehavior which violates the public peace and decorum" and that the "misbehavior may constitute a breach of the peace if it stirs the public to anger, invites dispute, brings about a condition of unrest, or creates a disturbance, or if it molests the inhabitants in the enjoyment of peace and quiet by arousing alarm." The defendant's counsel took no exception to this instruction to the jury; it was not objected to in the two appellate courts; nor was it mentioned in the petitions for certiorari or the briefs in the Supreme Court. "In short," as Vinson said in dissent, "the offending sentence in the charge was no part of the case until this Court's independent research ferreted it out of a lengthy and somewhat confused record."

Nevertheless, the majority held that this construction of the ordinance was as relevant and as binding on the Court as though the "precise words had been written into the ordinance." Consequently, the issue was whether an ordinance which penalized speech that might "invite dispute" or "bring about a condition of unrest" was constitutional. Douglas' brief opinion, almost without argument and completely without reference to the facts of the riotous meeting, concluded that speech could not be censored or punished on such grounds but only where it was "shown likely to produce a clear and present danger of a serious substantive evil that rises far above public inconvenience, annoyance, or unrest." The ordinance as construed by the Court was probably not invalid in its entirety, Douglas reasoned, but, since the verdict was a general one, the Court could not be sure that it did not "rest on the invalid clauses," and so the conviction was reversed.

This decision was effectively rebutted by the four-judge minority. Actually, Vinson would have agreed with the majority on the merits if objection to the constitutional validity of the trial court's instructions had been properly made by Terminiello's counsel. But the action of the Court in itself "ferreting" such a defect out of the record led him to join in the dissent.[2]

If the Court was going to make such exceptions to its rules, Frankfurter added, he was amazed that it chose to do so for people indulging in "such stuff" as had been heard in the Chicago hall and in a proceeding where life or liberty was not at stake, only a paltry $100 fine.

Jackson's dissent, concurred in by Frankfurter and Burton, was a vigorous examination of the merits of the case in his best style. He supplied a detailed summary of the factual situation on which the prosecution was based and which was in the trial judge's mind as he charged the jury.[3] He conveyed some sense of the inflammatory situation at the meeting by quoting at length from the stenographic record of Terminiello's speech and his testimony at the trial. For Jackson, who had been to Nuremberg, this exhibition of political, racial, and ideological conflict was not an isolated or unintended collision of forces: "It was a local manifestation of a world-wide and standing conflict between two organized groups of revolutionary fanatics, each of which has imported to this country the strong-arm technique developed in the struggle by which their kind has devastated Europe." American cities have to cope with this problem, he said. They should not be paralyzed by sweeping decisions which would encourage hostile ideological forces to use city streets as battlegrounds, with resulting destruction of public order.

The Constitution and the Court's precedents did not require or support such a sterilization of state powers, Jackson continued. Surely if, as the Chaplinsky case had held unanimously, an individual can be punished for the use of "fighting words" like "damned racketeer," how can it be unconstitutional "to punish civilly one who precipitated a public riot involving hundreds of fanatic fighters in a most violent melee." Freedom of speech exists only under law and not independent of it. Terminiello could not have spoken at all had it not been for the police protection provided his meeting. "Can society be expected to keep these men at Terminiello's service if it has nothing to say of his behavior which may force them into dangerous action?" The authorities are entitled to place some checks upon those whose behavior or speech calls mobs into being; and the courts should support these checks, so long as the claim of "danger to public order is not invoked in bad faith, as a cover for censorship or suppression. The preamble declares domestic tranquility as well as liberty to be an object in founding a Federal Government." And, finally: "The choice is not between order and liberty. It is between liberty with order and anarchy without either. There is danger that, if the Court does not temper its doctrinaire logic with a little practical wisdom, it will convert the constitutional Bill of Rights into a suicide pact."

Jackson's rhetoric was persuasive, but, in fact, he was battling a man of straw. Douglas might have made the contest a real one by arguing the case for the right of a speaker to address willing listeners in a private hall and by examining the nature of the community's obligation to defend that right against violent interruptions from outsiders. He ignored this opportunity to make a constructive contribution to civil liberties theory, confining himself instead to an academic lecture about the importance of "unrest" or even "anger" in preventing the "standardization of ideas." While such language may seem almost ridiculously irrelevant to the problem of controlling riots, actually the decision established no barrier to untrammeled consideration of the relationship between free speech and the expectation of violence, should the issue be successfully raised in future cases.

In fact, it was only a year and a half until the Court was again confronted with this problem, though in a considerably less acute form than in the Terminiello riot—in the 1951 case of *Feiner* v. *New York*. Feiner, a university student, made a soapbox speech on a Syracuse street corner to publicize a meeting of the Young Progressives of America, his voice being carried over loudspeakers mounted on a car. The seventy-five or so people who gathered, mixed white and Negro, blocked the sidewalk, so that pedestrians had to go out into the street to get around. Feiner spoke in a "loud, high-pitched voice," and in the course of his remarks reportedly said that the mayor of Syracuse, President Truman, and Mayor O'Dwyer of New York were all "bums"; that the "American Legion is a Nazi Gestapo"; and that "the Negroes don't have equal rights; they should rise up in arms and fight for their rights."[4] Two police officers, originally attracted by the traffic problem caused by the crowd, mixed in the gathering and became aware of "angry mutterings," "shoving and milling around," and "restlessness." One man in the audience told the officers that if they didn't take that "son of a bitch" off the box, he would.[5] The officers then approached Feiner, and one of them "asked" him to get off the box. When Feiner continued his speech, the officer "told" him to get down. When this failed, the officer "demanded" that he get down, telling him he was under arrest. Feiner asked why he was arrested, and the officer said the charge was "unlawful assembly." The ground was later changed to disorderly conduct.

Speaking for a six-judge majority, Vinson upheld the conviction. The evidence as to whether "a clear danger of disorder" threatened as a result of the speaker's remarks had been weighed by the trial court, and its conclusion had been affirmed by two higher state courts. Feiner had a right to speak, but he had no right to "incite to riot." He was "neither arrested nor convicted for the making or the content of his speech. Rather, it was the reaction which it actually engendered." Besides, he was guilty of "deliberate defiance" of the police officers.

Justice Frankfurter's concurring opinion stressed deference to the state court's knowledge of local conditions and the danger of "abstract or doctrinaire" interpretations of the Fourteenth Amendment. He had a high opinion of the sensitivity of the New York Court of Appeals to civil liberties problems, and, since it had ruled unanimously against Feiner, he would not question its judgment.

As would be expected, Black and Douglas dissented vigorously, but Minton unexpectedly joined them, which may serve as an index to the weakness of the Vinson opinion. For Black this decision made it "a dark day for civil liberties in our Nation." Douglas felt that the record showed no likelihood of riot.

> It shows an unsympathetic audience and the threat of one man to haul the speaker from the stage. It is against that kind of threat that speakers need police protection. If they do not receive it and instead the police throw their weight on the side of those who would break up the meetings, the police become the new censors of speech.

The Feiner case does, indeed, approve a formula which can make police suppression of speech ridiculously simple. Any group which wishes to silence a speaker can create a disturbance in the audience, and that will justify police in requesting the speaker to stop. If the speaker refuses, he is guilty of disorderly conduct. Both Vinson and Frankfurter suggested that there were limits to the use of this formula and that the Supreme Court would not let it be abused. But if the Court could be convinced from the facts in this case that the speaker was "inciting to riot," then the judicial protection to be expected is slim indeed. Frankfurter was reassured because he trusted New York's highest court to be on guard against civil liberties violations. But what would he suggest as a safeguard in states where the highest court cannot be similarly trusted?

Justice Jackson agreed with the Feiner decision, but in his dissent to the Kunz case, decided the same day, he charged that the Court-approved Feiner type of police control was actually much more dangerous than the permit system which the Court disapproved in Kunz:

> City officials stopped the meetings of both Feiner and Kunz. The process by which Feiner was stopped was the order of patrolmen, put into immediate effect without hearing. Feiner may have belived there would be no interference, but Kunz was duly warned by refusal of a permit. He was advised of charges, given a hearing, confronted by witnesses, and afforded a chance to deny the charges or to confess them and offer to amend his ways. The decision of revocation was made by a detached and responsible administrative official and Kunz could have had the decision reviewed in court. . . . It seems to me that this procedure better protects freedom of speech than to let everyone speak without leave, but subject to surveillance and to being ordered to stop in the discretion of the police.

One final test remained for the Vinson Court, the "group libel" case, *Beauharnais* v. *Illinois*, decided in 1952. An Illinois statute makes it unlawful for persons or corporations to publish or exhibit any writing, picture, drama, or moving picture which "portrays depravity, criminality, unchastity, or lack of virtue of a class of citizens, of any race, color, creed or religion . . . [or] exposes the citizens of any race, color, creed or religion to contempt, derision, or obloquy or which is productive of breach of the peace or riots."

Joseph Beauharnais, head of an organization called the White

Circle League, circulated on Chicago street corners anti-Negro leaflets which were in the form of petitions to the mayor and city council. They asked the use of the police power "to halt the further encroachment, harassment and invasion of white people, their property, neighborhoods and persons, by the Negro." They referred to the need "to prevent the white race from becoming mongrelized by the negro . . ." and to the "rapes, robberies, knives, guns and marijuana of the negro." The leaflets also appealed for persons to join the White Circle League and asked for financial contributions. Beauharnais was convicted of violating the statute and was fined $200. He challenged the statute as violating liberty of speech and press and too vague to support conviction for crime.

The Supreme Court upheld the conviction and statute by a five to four vote, Justice Frankfurter writing the opinion. The statute he treated as a "group libel law." Every state provides for the punishment of libels directed at individuals. Clearly, it is libelous falsely to charge a person "with being a rapist, robber, carrier of knives and guns, user of marijuana." The question, then, is whether the Fourteenth Amendment prevents states from punishing libels "directed at designated collectivities and flagrantly disseminated."

Frankfurter's answer is that the Illinois legislature might reasonably have decided to seek ways "to curb false or malicious defamation of racial and religious groups made in public places and by means calculated to have a powerful emotional impact on those to whom it was presented." He pointed to the long history of race tension in Illinois, "from the murder of the abolitionist Lovejoy in 1837 to the Cicero riots of 1951." He noted the recent emphasis of social scientists on the importance of groups, supporting the view that "a man's job and his educational opportunities and the dignity accorded him may depend as much on the reputation of the racial and religious group to which he willy-nilly belongs, as it does on his own merits." Thus, where the individual is "inextricably involved" in the group, speech which could be libelous if directed to the individual may also be treated as libelous when directed at the group. Truman's four appointees joined with Frankfurter to make this the majority view.

Black, Douglas, Reed, and Jackson dissented, though Jackson's position differed from that of the other three. To Black, this decision manifested the shocking results of the reasonable-man test in the civil liberties field. By treating the Illinois statute as a libel law, Frankfurter had taken the case out of the context of all the Court's free speech decisions on "the bland assumption that the First Amendment is wholly irrelevant. It is not even accorded the respect of a passing mention." The result is the upholding of a statute which "imposes state censorship over the theater, moving pictures, radio, television, leaflets, magazines, books and newspapers."[6] It is held to be punishable "to give publicity to any picture, moving picture, play, drama or sketch, or any printed matter which a judge may find unduly offensive to any race, color, creed or religion." Such a law, Black was sure, would present "a constant overhanging threat to freedom of speech, press and religion."

Frankfurter's reply was twofold. First, we must trust the legislatures; we must allow them room for a "choice of policy"; we must accept "the trial-and-error inherent in legislative efforts to deal with obstinate social issues." Black rejoined: "My own belief is that no legislature is charged with the duty or vested with the power to decide what public issues Americans can discuss. . . . State experimentation in curbing freedom of expression is startling and frightening doctrine in a country dedicated to self-government by its people."

Second, Frankfurter contended that "while this Court sits," it could "nullify action which encroaches on freedom of utterance under the guise of punishing libel." But what was to be the Court's standard of review? Frankfurter rejected clear and present danger as completely inapplicable. Libel is, like obscenity, bad in and of itself. Conviction depends only on establishing the facts, not on appraising the probable consequences of the action.

But Justice Jackson, usually as critical as Frankfurter of the clear-and-present-danger test, found this to be one of the situations where its application would be most helpful. He agreed as to the power of states to adopt group libel laws and would not apply clear and present danger as a test of their constitutionality. However, he did think that, in order to convict under them, the prosecution should be required to show "actual or probable consequences" of the libel:

> Punishment of printed words, based on their *tendency* either to cause breach of the peace or injury to persons or groups, in my opinion, is justifiable only if the prosecution survives the "clear and present danger" test. It is the most just and workable standard yet evolved for determining criminality of words whose injurious or inciting tendencies are not demonstrated by the event but are ascribed to them on the basis of probabilities. . . .
>
> In this case, neither the court nor jury found or were required to find any injury to any person, or group, or to the public peace, nor to find any probability, let alone any clear and present danger, of injury to any of these . . . in this case no actual violence and no specific injury was charged or proved. The leaflet was simply held punishable as criminal libel *per se* irrespective of its actual or probable consequences.

This, Jackson concluded, was error. There should have been some account taken of the particular form, time, place, and manner of this communication. Is a leaflet inherently less dangerous than the spoken word, because less "emotionally exciting"? Is the publication "so foul and extreme" as to defeat its own ends? Perhaps its appeal for money, "which has a cooling effect on many persons," would negative its inflammatory effect. Perhaps it would impress the passer-by "as the work of an irresponsible who needed mental examination." By failing to insist on such an inquiry into the circumstances, Jackson charged that the majority had failed to achieve a constitutional balance between state power and individual rights.[7]

ANTI-COMMUNIST LEGISLATION

Now we come to the two cases in which the Vinson Court made perhaps its most important statements on civil liberties theory. In contrast with the preceding cases, which involved state or local action, these two cases arose out of congressional legislation aimed at communism. The first was the non-Communist affidavit provision of the Labor Management Relations Act of 1947, better known as the Taft-Hartley Act. The second was the more general Smith Act of 1940. In both cases the opinion for the Court was written by the Chief Justice.

American Communications Assn. v. *Douds*, decided in 1950, upheld the constitutionality of the Taft-Hartley oath requirement. Section 9(h) of that act denied the protections of the act to any labor organization unless each of its officers filed an affidavit with the NLRB "that he is not a member of the Communist party or affiliated with such party, and that he does not believe in, and is not a member of or support any organization that believes in or teaches, the overthrow of the United States Government by force or by any illegal or unconstitutional methods." It should be noted at once that the language covers not only members of the Communist party but also a second and much less easily defined group. Section 9(h) was widely resented in labor circles, and some labor leaders who had been most active in fighting communism within their unions were the most bitter in their attacks on the section.

Vinson's opinion began by pointing out that the purpose of Congress in setting up the oath requirement was to remove the "political strike" as an obstruction to interstate commerce. By extensive hearings Congress had assembled a great mass of evidence

> which tended to show that Communists and others proscribed by the statute had infiltrated union organizations not to support and further trade union objectives, including the advocacy of change by democratic methods, but to make them a device by which commerce and industry might be disrupted when the dictates of political policy required such action.

Congress has power to take such protective action under the commerce clause unless results are achieved which are forbidden by other provisions of the Constitution. The labor unions argued that the necessary effect of section 9(h) was to make it impossible for persons who could not sign the oath to be officers of unions, and consequently that the statute violated fundamental rights guaranteed by the First Amendment—"the right of union officers to hold what political views they choose and to associate with what political groups they will, and the right of unions to choose their officers without interference from government." On the other hand, the government denied there was any First Amendment problem, because the sole sanction provided by the statute was "the withdrawal from noncomplying unions of the 'privilege' " of using the act's facilities.

Neither of these views, Vinson concluded, accurately stated the practical effects of the oath. The statute did not merely withdraw "a privilege gratuitously granted" by the government; a noncomplying union would, in fact, have imposed upon it "a number of restrictions which would not exist if the Board had not been established." On the other hand, the Court could not accept the union view that this was "a licensing statute prohibiting those persons who do not sign the affidavit from holding union office."

The Court's position was that the effect of the statute was to exert "pressures upon labor unions to deny positions of leadership to certain persons who are identified by particular beliefs and political affiliations." Normally, beliefs and affiliations are "irrelevant to permissible subjects of government action," but that does not mean that they are "never relevant."[8] Here the Court conceived that beliefs and affiliations bore a reasonable relationship to the apprehended evil. But the problem lay in the fact that, while lessening the threat to interstate commerce, Congress at the same time was undeniably discouraging "the lawful exercise of political rights protected by the First Amendment."

For light on whether this restriction was constitutional, Vinson turned to the clear-and-present-danger test. Examining the statements of Holmes and Brandeis, Vinson found the gist of their position to be that "ideas and doctrines thought harmful or dangerous are best fought with words," and only "when force is very likely to follow an utterance before there is a chance for counter-argument to have effect may that utterance be punished or prevented." This formulation he believed inapplicable to the present situation:

> Government's interest here is not in preventing the dissemination of Communist doctrine or the holding of particular beliefs because it is feared that unlawful action will result therefrom if free speech is practiced. Its interest is in protecting the free flow of commerce from what

> Congress considers to be substantial evils of conduct that are not the products of speech at all. Section 9(h), in other words, does not interfere with speech because Congress fears the consequences of speech; it regulates harmful conduct which Congress has determined is carried on by persons who may be identified by their political affiliations and beliefs.

The persons identified by the statute do not cause their damage by speech, and it is not their speech that the statute seeks to restrain, but their use of force through the political strike. "Speech may be fought with speech. . . . But force may and must be met with force. Section 9(h) is designed to protect the public not against what Communists and others identified therein advocate or believe, but against what Congress has concluded they have done and are likely to do again."

How clear and present must these dangers be to justify congressional action? By way of reply, Vinson cites a wide variety of statutes, ranging from compulsory vaccination to the Hatch Act limitation on the political activities of civil servants, by which legislators have sought to protect the public from evils of conduct, even though First Amendment rights are thereby in some degree infringed. Decisions as to the necessity for controlling conduct to prevent evils are for the legislature to make, and courts must not interfere except in clear cases of undue infringement on personal freedom.

In the present situation the Court found numerous justifications for the congressional decision. The oath is a part of the "very complex machinery" set up by Congress to encourage the peaceful settlement of labor disputes. This machinery has increased union power, and "public interest in the good faith exercise of that power is very great." Moreover, the statute is not aimed at the suppression of ideas. It does not prevent or punish by criminal sanctions the making of a speech. There is no prohibition, no censorship, no stifling of beliefs. Congress has not restrained the activities of the Communist party as a political organization. Only a "relative handful of persons" are affected by the act, and they are "free to maintain their affiliations and beliefs subject only to possible loss of positions which Congress has concluded are being abused to the injury of the public."

Vinson's opinion spoke for Reed and Burton. Douglas, Clark, and Minton did not participate. Frankfurter and Jackson concurred with Vinson in all respects save one. They both denied the constitutionality of the act's coverage of persons who "believe in" the overthrow of the government by force or unconstitutional methods. Vinson admitted that if this language was read "very literally," it would create constitutional problems; but the Court was obliged to construe the act so as to avoid the danger of unconstitutionality if at all possible. That could be done here by interpreting the language

> to apply to persons and organizations who believe in violent overthrow of the Government as it presently exists under the Constitution as an objective, not merely a prophecy. Congress might well find that such persons . . . would carry that objective into their conduct of union affairs by calling political strikes designed to weaken and divide the American people.

Frankfurter, on the other hand, felt that asking men to take oath that they did not favor illegal or unconstitutional methods of changing the government was to "open the door too wide to mere speculation or uncertainty," considering that "constitutionality or legality is frequently determined by this Court by the chance of a single vote." Apart from the uncertainty angle, this "probing into men's thoughts trenches on those aspects of individual freedom which we rightly regard as the most cherished aspects of Western civilization." Finally, holding that the proscribed type of beliefs indicated no necessary relationship to the Communist party and the dangers which the statute was seeking to avert, he said:

> I cannot deem it within the rightful authority of Congress to probe into opinions that involve only an argumentative demonstration of some coincidental parallelism of belief with some of the beliefs of those who direct the policy of the Communist Party, though without any allegiance to it. To require oaths as to matters that open up such possibilities invades the inner life of men whose compassionate thought or doctrinaire hopes may be as far removed from any dangerous kinship with the Communist creed as were those of the founders of the present orthodox political parties in this country.

Jackson's widely quoted dissent is noteworthy for its hard-hitting analysis of the Communist party's differences from other political parties in the United States, which he felt justified the singling-out of the party in this statute. But he was equally vigorous in declaring that Congress has no power "to proscribe any opinion or belief which has not manifested itself in any overt act." He concluded: "I think that under our system, it is time enough for the law to lay hold of the citizen when he acts illegally, or in some rare circumstances where his thoughts are given illegal utterance. I think we must let his mind alone."

Justice Black's dissent, unlike that of Frankfurter and Jackson, was based on a complete rejection of section 9(h). He could not believe that "the Commerce Clause restricts the right to think." He stood on

> the basic constitutional precept that penalties should be imposed only for a person's own conduct, not for his beliefs or for the conduct of others with whom he may associate. Guilt should not be imputed solely from association or affiliation with political parties or any other organization, however much we may abhor the ideas which they advocate.

The test oath was in itself a suspect weapon, Black felt, for "history attests the efficacy of that instrument for inflicting penalties and disabilities on obnoxious minorities."[9] He could not see what were the limits on the Court's holding, for its reasoning would apply just as readily to support "statutes barring Communists and their suspected sympathizers from election to public office, mere membership in unions, and in fact from getting or holding any jobs whereby they could earn a living." His final word was: "Never before has this Court held that the Government could for any reason attaint persons for their political beliefs or affiliations. It does so today."[10]

The issue in the 1951 case of *Dennis* v. *United States* was the validity of the Smith Act as applied in the conviction of eleven leaders of the American Communist party. The indictment made two charges against them: (1) wilfully and knowingly conspiring to organize as the United States Communist party a society, group, and assembly of persons who teach and advocate the overthrow and destruction of the government of the United States by force and violence and (2) knowingly and wilfully advocating and teaching the duty and necessity of overthrowing and destroying the government by force and violence. It is important to note at the outset that no overt revolutionary acts other than teaching and advocating were alleged. There is a statute against "seditious conspiracy,"[11] but the Communist leaders were not charged with a conspiracy to overthrow the government. Rather they were charged with conspiracy *to form a party* to teach and advocate the overthrow of the government.

The trial on these charges before Judge Medina in the federal district court in New York City lasted for nine months and was filled with sensations. The conviction was upheld by the court of appeals, Chief Judge Learned Hand writing the opinion.[12] The Supreme Court granted certiorari limited to questions of the constitutionality of the Smith Act, "inherently or as construed and applied in the instant case," and then, by a vote of six to two, with Vinson writing the opinion and Clark not participating, confirmed the convictions.[13]

The major issue confronting the Court was how to reconcile with the free speech guaranty of the Constitution convictions which treated speaking and teaching as criminal offenses. For, admittedly, the eleven had taken no action with the immediate intention of initiating a revolution. The trial judge spanned the gap between speech and action by the bridge of intent; he charged the jury that the Communists could be found guilty, provided that they had the intent "to overthrow the government by force and violence as speedily as circumstances permit." The jury could not convict, Medina continued, if they found that the defendants did "no more than pursue peaceful studies and discussions or teaching and advocacy in the realm of ideas." Thus a college course explaining the philosophical theories of communism would not be banned by the Smith Act.

For Douglas, dissenting, this was dangerous doctrine. He admitted that intent "often makes the difference in the law" where ordinary acts are concerned, but speech has a special constitutional status. Under the Medina test, Communist books are not outlawed but can be taught lawfully only if the teacher does not believe in them. "The crime then depends not on what is taught but on who the teacher is. That is to make freedom of speech turn not on *what is said,* but on the *intent* with which it is said. Once we start down that road we enter territory dangerous to the liberties of every citizen."

The Court majority, however, upheld the district judge's interpretation and ruled that the Smith Act was "directed at advocacy, not discussion." But that did not solve the problem completely. For advocacy has two aspects. It is action against which, when aimed toward unlawful ends, the government has the undoubted power to protect itself. But it also "contains an element of speech," as Vinson said; and consequently his opinion for the Court majority had inevitably to return again to the clear-and-present-danger test.

There is no doubt that Vinson's argument amounts to a substantial reinterpretation of the Holmes-Brandeis doctrine, which he purports to follow. His principal affirmative contribution is his definite rejection of the Court's restrictive holding in the Gitlow case that any statute punishing advocacy of overthrow of the government is valid and that the courts are limited to determining whether in a particular case the evidence supported the conviction. Holmes and Brandeis had dissented from this holding, and Vinson accepted their protest. However, he did not go so far as Holmes and Brandeis had proposed in that case; he did not accept their view that courts should affirm such statutes only if the likelihood of success for the subversive activity is immediate and pressing.

Vinson took a middle ground, preserving the right of judicial review but permitting the statute to be upheld wherever the facts as determined by the Court indicate some appreciable probability at some point in time of successful overthrow of the government. The actual formula he adopted was that used by Learned Hand in the court of appeals: "Whether the gravity of the 'evil,' discounted by its improbability, justifies such invasion of free speech as is necessary to avoid the danger." Obviously, said Vinson, the clear-and-present-danger test "cannot mean that before the Government may act, it must wait until the *putsch* is about to be executed, the plans have been laid and the signal is awaited. . . . We must therefore reject the contention that success or probability of success is the criterion."

Jackson and Frankfurter each added his own interpretation of clear and present danger. For Jackson, the problem was easy. Holmes and Brandeis had developed this test in cases which presented only "technical or trivial violations . . . arising before the era of World War II revealed the subtlety and efficacy of modernized revolutionary techniques used by totalitarian parties." Jackson would save the test, "unmodified, for application as a 'rule of reason' in the kind of case for which it was devised," namely, hotheaded speeches on street corners or circulation of a few incendiary pamphlets. But when the issue is the probable success of a world-wide revolutionary conspiracy, it is futile for the courts to attempt prophecy in the guise of a legal decision. "The judicial process simply is not adequate to a trial of such far-flung issues."

Frankfurter took the occasion to state again his rejection of the clear-and-present-danger test, which had, he contended, by reason of the Court's recent decisions become nothing but a formula, an inflexible dogma supporting "uncritical libertarian generalities." What was called for was not the application of a formula but a "candid and informed weighing of the competing interests." Moreover, this weighing is, in the first instance, for legislatures to undertake, "and the balance they strike is a judgment not to be displaced by ours, but to be respected unless outside the pale of fair judgment." Neatly reversing the original emphasis of the doctrine, he contended that clear and present danger was meant by its originators to emphasize that exercise of freedom of speech must be compatible with the preservation of other freedoms essential to a democracy:

> It were far better that the phrase be abandoned than that it be sounded once more to hide from the believers in an absolute right of free speech the plain fact that the interest in speech, profoundly important as it is, is no more conclusive in judicial review than other attributes of democracy or than a determination of the people's representatives that a measure is necessary to assure the safety of government itself.

One of those "believers in an absolute right of free speech" was Justice Black, who charged that the Court's decision repudiated "directly or indirectly" the clear-and-present-danger rule: "I cannot agree that the First Amendment permits us to sustain laws suppressing freedom of speech and press on the basis of Congress' or our own notions of mere 'reasonableness.' Such a doctrine waters down the First Amendment so that it amounts to little more than an admonition to Congress." He would hold Section 3 of the Smith Act "a virulent form of prior censorship of speech and press," and "unconstitutional on its face."

Douglas took up a subsidiary clear-and-present-danger issue, namely, whether the trial judge had been correct in limiting the jury to determining the fact of guilt under the statute, while reserving to himself as a matter of law the finding as to whether a danger existed sufficient to justify the application of the statute. Vinson held that this question was properly one for the judge to decide; but Douglas regarded it as "so critical an issue in the case" that it should have gone to the jury. However, he could not see how either judge or jury could have decided the question of danger on the basis of a record which contained no evidence on the "strength and tactical position" of the Communist party in the United States. In the absence of such evidence, he himself could see no danger from these "miserable merchants of unwanted ideas." "Free speech—the glory of our system of government—should not be sacrified on anything less than plain and objective proof of danger that the evil advocated is imminent."

Obviously, the Dennis decision is a serious defeat for the traditional libertarian position, and Black and Douglas were not without grounds for the concern they expressed. But there are at least three aspects of the decision which, in greater or lesser degree, tend to minimize its impact on freedom of speech. First, the Vinson decision refused to adopt Jackson's startling application of the "conspiracy" concept to this type of case. Here is the background for his case: "The basic rationale of the law of conspiracy is that a conspiracy may be an evil in itself, independently of any other evil it seeks to accomplish. . . . Congress may make it a crime to conspire with others to do what an individual may lawfully do on his own." The reason for this distinction is, of course, the increased effectiveness which men can achieve by combination:

> . . . a combination of persons to commit a wrong, either as an end or as a means to an end, is so much more dangerous, because of its increased power to do wrong, because it is more difficult to guard against and prevent the evil designs of a group of persons than of a single person, and because of the terror which fear of such a combination tends to create in the minds of people.

Jackson readily admitted that criminal conspiracy was "a dragnet device capable of perversion into an instrument of injustice in the hands of a partisan or complacent judiciary"; but he said that it had "an established place in our system of law" and should be available where the conspiracy charged was one to "undermine our whole Government":

> I do not suggest that Congress could punish conspiracy to advocate something, the doing of which it may not punish. . . . But it is not forbidden to put down force or violence, it is not forbidden to punish its teaching or advocacy, and the end being punishable, there is no doubt of the power to punish conspiracy for that purpose.

The meaning of Jackson's doctrine is this: Individual speech for purposes which Congress has forbidden is protected by the necessity of showing some clear and present danger to result from the speech. But advocacy of an unlawful end in which two or more persons have joined (and there are certainly very few cases where an individual speaking or publishing does not have some consultation or assistance) is punishable as criminal conspiracy, and no showing of danger need be made. Thus Jackson, who earlier in his argument had contended that the clear-and-present-danger test was to be applied only in dealing with "trivialities," now narrows its application further to trivialities which involve only one individual. Alongside the Jackson position, Vinson's begins to look much more reasonable. Douglas' reaction may be noted: "The doctrine of conspiracy has served divers and oppressive purposes and in its broad reach can be made to do great evil. But never until today has anyone seriously thought that the ancient law of conspiracy could constitutionally be used to turn speech into seditious conduct."[14]

Second, it may not be irrelevant to note that Frankfurter and Jackson, whose votes were necessary to the majority position, both took pains to state their view that the Smith Act, while legal, was unwise and a poor way to fight communism. Frankfurter's peroration went as follows:

> In finding that Congress has acted within its power, a judge does not remotely imply that he favors the implications that lie beneath the legal issues. . . . When legislation touches freedom of thought and freedom of speech, such a tendency is a formidable enemy of the free spirit. . . . A persistent, positive translation of the liberating faith into the feelings and thoughts and actions of men and women is the real protection against attempts to strait-jacket the human mind. . . . Without open minds there can be no open society. And if society be not open the spirit of man is mutilated and becomes enslaved.[15]

Jackson was less eloquent but more pointed:

> While I think there was power in Congress to enact this statute and that, as applied in this case it cannot be held unconstitutional, I add that I have little faith in the long-range effectiveness of this conviction to stop the rise of the Communist movement. Communism will not go to jail with these Communists. No decision by this Court can forestall revolution whenever the existing government fails to command the respect and loyalty of the people and sufficient distress and discontent is allowed to grow up among the masses. Many failures by fallen governments attest that no government can long prevent revolution by outlawry.

Finally, it should be noted that the effect of the decision is not, strictly speaking, to adopt the rule of guilt by association and to brand every member of the Communist party as one who of necessity has engaged in unlawful activity. It is true that the government's success against the party's leaders in the Dennis case was immediately followed by similar Smith Act prosecutions of second- and third-string Communists throughout the country. In April, 1952, six regional leaders were convicted in Baltimore. That summer, fourteen were convicted in Los Angeles. In January, 1953, a second New York prosecution found thirteen guilty, and in June the trial of seven Communists in Honolulu came to a similar conclusion. In all, between 1947 and the beginning of 1953, eighty-seven Communists were indicted under the Smith Act.

In spite of the government's unvarying success in these prosecutions, it should be clear that the Supreme Court has not yet held the Communist party to be an illegal organization. No federal statute directly brands membership in the Communist party as criminal. There are such laws in at least three states—Georgia, Pennsylvania, and Massachusetts—but none has yet had a full court review. In all the Smith Act prosecutions it has been necessary for the government to prove that what the defendants actually said or did was conspiracy of the sort prohibited by the act. In the second New York prosecution (which incidentally was a much more dignified affair than the first trial under Judge Medina), Judge Edward J. Dimock directed the acquittal of two defendants because of the "slim evidence" as to their participation in the alleged conspiracy.

Presumably the next big government attack on the Communist party to come before the Supreme Court for review will involve the Internal Security Act of 1950. Under this statute the Subversive Activities Control Board in April, 1953, ordered the Communist party of the United States to register with the Department of Justice as a "Communist-action" organization and to make its records available to the government. Also, various state legislative attacks on the party will no doubt continue to reach the Court. One such statute is the Michigan Communist Control Law, requiring registration of the state party and forbidding the name of any Communist to appear on the ballot in that state. In March, 1953, the Supreme Court refused to pass on the constitutionality of this law, because it had not yet been construed in the state courts.[16]

The present cloudy half-legal, half-illegal status of the Communist party is almost matched by the confusion attending the present status of the clear-and-present-danger test. Recent doctrinal developments and personnel changes on the Court have effectively stripped it of the ideological support supplied it during the 1940's by the preferred-position argument. The Breard and Poulos decisions leave only Black and Douglas as adherents of the preference theory. Frankfurter would abandon clear and present danger entirely, on the ground that it has been turned into a slogan which supports absolutist conceptions of freedom and gets in the way of "judgmatical" appraisals. Jackson finds it still useful for weighing the pros and cons in relatively small controversies, where no long-range predictions are required of the Court. Chief Justice Vinson (and the majority for which he spoke) professed acceptance of the Holmes-Brandeis doctrine but actually were impervious to the later modifications which these two justices tried to build into the test. The Holmes whom Vinson was following was the Holmes of the Schenck case, and his clear-and-present-danger test was a rationalization for putting men in jail despite the provisions of the First Amendment.

V. *Legislatures and Loyalty*

In the preceding chapter the two outstanding cases were discussed in which congressional legislation directed against Communists was measured against the classic freedom of speech standards developed by the Court in previous civil liberties proceedings. However, the cold war was fought on numerous other fronts by both federal and state legislatures. In this chapter attention is centered on judicial reaction to two favorite legislative devices. The first is the legislative investigating committee, which undertakes to engage directly in sleuthing activities aimed at bringing to light Communist activities of all sorts and in all fields. The second is the loyalty oath for public employees.

LEGISLATIVE INVESTIGATIONS OF UN-AMERICANISM

In its excellent report published in 1947, the President's Committee on Civil Rights deplored the use of methods of outlawry and repression in dealing with the internal Communist threat and favored, instead, the devices of investigation and exposure.[1] While the FBI has no doubt performed the most effective services in this field, the House of Representatives Committee on Un-American Activities has achieved the most publicity.[2]

This committee had been a storm center ever since its organization in 1938 under Representative Martin Dies; and challenges to the constitutionality of its operations and methods began to reach the federal courts during the latter part of the 1940's. The first occasion which the Supreme Court had to pass on the handiwork of the Dies Committee did not involve any direct test of the committee's status or powers. Representative Dies, in a House speech in 1943, had named thirty-nine federal employees as Communists or fellow-travelers and "crackpot bureaucrats." Subsequent proceedings before a special House committee brought this total down to three, who were specifically forbidden in a deficiency appropriation act to receive any salary from funds carried by that measure. President Roosevelt, unable to veto this provision without killing the whole act, signed it with a sharp warning that the provision was an unconstitutional usurpation of executive and judicial functions.

By a five to two vote in the case of *United States* v. *Lovett*, the Supreme Court agreed, holding the provision to be a "bill of attainder." This medieval English legislative weapon is prohibited by Article I, Section 9, of the Constitution. In two post–Civil War cases, growing out of Missouri's imposition of a test oath of loyalty as a qualification for holding office or engaging in the professions of law, teaching, or the ministry, a bill of attainder was authoritatively defined by the Supreme Court as "a legislative act which inflicts punishment without a judicial trial."[3] Justice Black concluded for the Court in the Lovett case that "permanent proscription from any opportunity to serve the Government is punishment, and of a most severe type."

Direct challenges to the constitutionality of the operations and methods of the Un-American Activities Committee began to reach the lower federal courts about 1947. Review of five courts of appeals decisions dealing with the committee was sought from the Vinson Court, but it denied review in every case except one.[4] In that instance the flight of the appellant from the country prevented the Court from rendering a decision on the merits of the controversy.[5] The four decisions which the Court left in effect by refusing to grant certiorari all denied the various challenges made against the committee and its functioning, though two of the decisions were by two to one votes.[6] The following summary, then, while not based upon the Supreme Court's own holdings, does represent views which it saw no compelling reason to question.

The primary matter for consideration in all these proceedings was whether there could be any doubt as to the general authority of Congress to set up an investigating committee in this area. Congress has no specifically delegated power to investigate any subject. Its investigative powers are derived from its powers to legislate, to judge the qualifications of its members, and other constitutional functions the performance of which requires that Congress secure information on which to act. Because of the breadth of these constitutional powers, it may seem that it would be practically impossible for Congress to select a subject for investigation which would not be related to some proper area of congressional concern. Actually, however, there has been one notable occasion when the Court failed to find such relevance. This was the 1880 case of *Kilbourn* v. *Thompson*, testing the legitimacy of a House investigation into the bankrupt firm of Jay Cooke and Company and its interest in a District of Columbia real estate pool. The Supreme Court ruled that this was not a subject on which Congress could validly legislate.[7] But subsequent decisions have been more friendly to congressional authority, particularly the 1927 case of *McGrain* v. *Daugherty*, upholding the Senate's inquiry into the conduct of the Department of Justice under President Harding.

So far as the case for the Un-American Activities Committee is concerned, obviously no matter is of greater importance to Congress than the security of the nation and the protection of its independence and integrity against conspiratorial or subversive attacks. For these clearly proper congressional concerns it is scarcely necessary to cite such expressly stated congressional powers as to "provide for the common defense," "to raise and support armies," and the like. The Un-American Activities Committee might seem to have dissipated somewhat this strong constitutional support by being so largely uninterested in making legislative recommendations to Congress.[8] However, the mere fact that the House had stated in setting up the committee that it was for a legislative purpose was generally regarded as binding on the courts. Judge Charles E. Clark, dissenting in the Josephson case, said that upholding the committee on this basis made the congressional investigative power limitless, for "the dram of good must always sanctify the dubious remainder."

There seems little reason to doubt that Clark's conclusion is actually the correct one to draw from these appellate court decisions, for all the grounds on which limits might have been based were rejected in these cases. For one thing, attempts were made in several ways to show that the results achieved by the committee involved conflict with the provisions of the First Amendment. A kind of syllogistic argument was presented: (A) The power to investigate is limited by the power to legislate. (B) Congress has no power to legislate on matters of speech and thought. (C) Consequently, a committee of Congress cannot constitutionally seek to achieve through investigation goals that it could not achieve directly by legislation.

Judge Clark, in spelling out this position, said that if Congress had adopted a law in the same terms as the authorization of power to the committee, the law would clearly be held unconstitutional.[9] The Josephson majority, however, disposed of this contention by reminding that Congress can curtail freedom if justified by the clear-and-present-danger rule; the courts cannot assume in advance that Congress will make an unconstitutional use of its investigatory powers in an admittedly valid field.

But what if we discard syllogisms and advance judgments and concentrate rather on the charge that the committee had actually and deliberately sought to get, by publicity and exposure, results which could not constitutionally be secured by legislation? Clark believed this charge had been proved and that "the intended and actual consequences of the investigation are to limit freedom of speech." Again, it was contended that the committee's persistent questioning of witnesses as to whether they were members of the Communist party violated a right to privacy and to freedom from inquiry about political beliefs established by the First Amendment.

On both claims the committee has received a clean bill of health from the appellate courts. These inquiries have been regarded as incidental to the committee's main function of securing information. The questioning of witnesses as to their political and propaganda activities must, of necessity, be broad where the purpose is to determine whether such activities do, in fact, constitute a clear and present danger. If political affiliations or activities affect the public welfare, then the normal right to privacy is overridden by congressional interest in their nature and extent. In the Lawson case, involving ten Hollywood writers, the court held that questions as to Communist affiliation were obviously pertinent when addressed to men "who, by their authorship of the scripts, vitally influence the ultimate production of motion pictures seen by millions."

From the First Amendment the argument moved on to Fifth Amendment grounds. One principal contention here has been that the area of investigative powers given the committee is so broad and vague that any attempt to use the criminal statutes against persons refusing to co-operate with the committee necessarily runs afoul of the established rule that crimes must be defined with sufficient specificity that persons may know what conduct is legal and what is not. The Supreme Court's prior decisions, such as *Kilbourn* v. *Thompson* and *McGrain* v. *Daugherty*, clearly contemplate that witnesses may contest the legitimacy of a congressional inquiry by refusing to answer specific questions which they regard as outside the legitimate subject matter of inquiry, though, of course, a witness takes such action at the peril of being prosecuted for his refusal.

But when, as in the case of this committee, its charter authorizes it to examine into "the extent, character, and objects of un-American propaganda activities in the United States," a witness would be hard put to it to know what such a vague term as "un-American" embraces, and consequently how far his obligation to answer questions extends. The courts have tended to give more attention to this objection than to the First Amendment problems, but in the end they have again upheld the committee. Josephson had refused to be sworn or to answer any questions at all, and so he was held to be precluded from raising this defense. In the Lawson case Judge Bennett Clark ruled that a question as to membership in the Communist party was quite pertinent to an inquiry into "un-American" activity.

Some other minor constitutional arguments have been offered against the committee and its work. One is that it had inflicted punishment against witnesses before it, thus violating the constitutional prohibition against bills of attainder.[10] Another has struck at the alleged discrimination of the committee in investigating certain types of un-American propaganda and ignoring others. Scraping the bottom of the barrel, it has even been contended that the exclusion of Negroes from voting in certain southern states voids the election of representatives from those states and so invalidates all congressional acts in which they have participated, including committee activities.

So far as the Un-American Activities Committee inquiries into communism or the comparable efforts of Senators McCarthy and Jenner are concerned, then, the Vinson Court found no transgressions of constitutional limits of legislative power. The only committee to be subjected to restraint by the Court was one which operated at the other end of the political spectrum. *United States* v. *Rumely*, decided in 1953, grew out of the efforts of the House Select Committee on Lobbying Activities to get information from the secretary of the self-styled Committee for Constitutional Government. The Regulation of Lobbying Act required disclosure of contributions of $500 or more received or expended by organizations to influence legislation. This committee adopted a technique of accepting contributions of over $490 only if the donor specified that the funds be used for distribution of its books or pamphlets, thus enabling the organization to represent the contribution as a "sale" of books which did not have to be reported. The lobbying committee, seeing in this device a violation of the act, asked the organization for the names of the purchasers of its literature. Rumely declined and was convicted of contempt.

The Supreme Court unanimously reversed the conviction, but differing reasons were given. For the Court, Frankfurter ruled that Congress had meant to authorize the committee only to investigate lobbying "in its commonly accepted sense," that is, representations made directly to Congress or its members, not the influencing of opinion by the circulation of books or pamphlets. Thus he avoided any ruling on what he obviously regarded as a serious constitutional challenge to the committee action. Douglas and Black, concurring, felt that Congress had definitely authorized the committee to act as it had, and so they could not avoid the constitutional issue. Their conclusion was that the kind of inquiry attempted here "might be as serious as censorship" and added: "Once the government can demand of a publisher the names of the purchasers of his publications, the free press as we know it disappears."

The Rumely case does demonstrate, then, that one may still, at the risk of a contempt citation, force a test of the jurisdiction of a congressional investigating committee.[11] Another tactic of defense is refusal to testify on grounds of possible self-incrimination. The privilege of not giving evidence against one's self, guaranteed by the Fifth Amendment, was widely publicized during the televised hearings of the Kefauver committee, when more than one underworld character parroted the talismanic phrases as justification for his refusal to testify.

Up to 1950, witnesses before the Un-American Activities Committee who wished to remain silent generally justified their action on First Amendment grounds. When witnesses did claim their privilege against self-incrimination, however, it was the original policy of the committee not to attempt to compel answers. Beginning in 1950, the committee reversed its policy and ordered the prosecution of witnesses who employed this plea. While no case raising this issue has reached the Supreme Court from the Un-American Activities Committee, decisions in other cases have made it clear that the Fifth Amendment, when understandingly employed, can be an effective bar to legislative committee questioning, whatever damage it may do the witness in the public mind.[12]

The principal decision is *Blau* v. *United States,* in which the Supreme Court in 1950 unanimously ruled that a witness before a federal grand jury could legitimately refuse to answer questions about the Communist party of Colorado. Because of the Smith Act, Justice Black said, prosecution of anyone who admitted knowledge about the party or employment by it was more than an "imaginary possibility." Under these circumstances, compulsion to testify violated the Fifth Amendment. The principle of this case seems perfectly adequate to cover testimony before a congressional committee also.

A similar holding was arrived at in the second Blau case in 1951.[13] But very shortly thereafter the Court, in *Rogers* v. *United States,* substantially impaired this protection and made the process of claiming the right to remain silent before an investigating body more risky. Jane Rogers, subpoenaed by a federal grand jury in Denver, testified that she had been treasurer of the Communist party in Denver. In that capacity she had had possession of membership lists and dues records but, by the time of the inquiry, had turned them over to another person. She refused to identify the person to whom she had given the party's books, saying that she did not want to subject anyone else to the same thing she was going through. It was not until two days later that she justified her refusal by the privilege against self-incrimination, which she had apparently just learned about through an oral argument in the courtroom while she was waiting for her turn before the judge. Her claim was denied, and she was sentenced to four months for contempt.

The Supreme Court, through Chief Justice Vinson, held that Mrs. Rogers had waived the privilege of silence by her initial testimony and that the further questions which she refused to answer did not involve a "reasonable danger of further crimination." Justices Black, Frankfurter, and Douglas dissented. They felt that the Court was undermining the broad scope of constitutional privilege as interpreted in the Blau cases by an equally broad construction of the "waiver" doctrine. The result of the holding was to create a dilemma for witnesses who wanted to claim immunity:

> On the one hand, they risk imprisonment for contempt by asserting the privilege prematurely; on the other, they might lose the privilege if they answer a single question. The Court's view makes the protection depend on timing so refined that lawyers, let alone laymen, will have difficulty in knowing when to claim it.

The perils in relying upon the self-incrimination claim were also demonstrated in the case of Julius Emspak, who in February, 1951, was found guilty in a District of Columbia court of contempt of Congress for refusing to answer questions of the Un-American Activities Committee. He had claimed the right to remain silent under "constitutional guaranties"; but the trial judge ruled that he had to specify that he was doing so because of possible self-incrimination.[14] However, the next month Frederick V. Field was upheld in his refusal on self-incrimination grounds to answer questions of a Senate subcommittee investigating communism in government. Judge Goldsborough said that "if the defendant had answered . . . these . . . questions in the affirmative . . .

it would have taken very little more evidence to put him in the penitentiary."[15] Subsequent decisions, arising mostly out of the Kefauver hearings, have generally followed this same line.

The constitutional aspects of legislative inquiries have been examined from one other point of view by the Vinson Court, though the case in question concerned the California Senate Un-American Activities Committee rather than the United States House committee.[16] An individual named Brandhove, who had publicly attacked the California committee, was called before it. When he refused to testify, he was cited for contempt. This proceeding failed, and Brandhove then instituted a suit of his own against the members of the committee, alleging that he had been summoned before the committee not for a legislative purpose but to intimidate him and to prevent him from using his constitutional rights of free speech. He contended that the committee by this action had deprived him of rights guaranteed by the federal Constitution, in violation of the Civil Rights Act of 1871, and he sought damages in a civil suit.

For the Court, Justice Frankfurter ruled that the general principle of legislative immunity protected the committee from this kind of liability. He reviewed briefly the development in the English parliament of the privilege of legislators to be free from arrest or civil process for what they did or said in legislative proceedings and its transfer to this country in both federal and state constitutions. It seemed clear to him that Congress had not mean to limit this fundamental immunity by the general language of the 1871 statute here invoked. Nor did the claim of "unworthy purpose" on the part of the committee destroy the immunity of its members. In any case, this particular inquiry was "in a field where legislators traditionally have power to act," and the Court would not be justified in finding that a committee had exceeded the bounds of legislative power unless it was "obvious that there was a usurpation of functions exclusively vested in the Judiciary or the Executive."

Frankfurter also stressed that the case for the legislature was stronger here, where legislative privilege was directly attacked in the courts, than it would be in cases where the legislature was seeking the affirmative aid of the courts in asserting its powers.

Black picked up this point in his concurring opinion, to draw out the principle that "the validity of legislative action is [not] co-extensive with the personal immunity of the legislators." In other words, the fact that the committee members here could not be sued did not mean necessarily that "their alleged prosecution of Brandhove is legal conduct." If the committee sought to fine or imprison Brandhove on perjury, contempt, or other charges, he could, Black assumed, defend himself on the ground that the committee had been given powers broader than it could constitutionally exercise.[17]

For Douglas, Frankfurter's opinion carried judicial self-restraint too far. Frankfurter would leave erring legislators to "self-discipline and the voters." Douglas saw no reason why the courts could not also step in, if a legislative committee "departs so far from its domain" as to deprive a citizen of a right protected by the Constitution. "It is one thing to give great leeway to the legislative right of speech, debate, and investigation. But when a committee perverts its power, brings down on an individual the whole weight of government for an illegal or corrupt purpose, the reason for the immunity ends."

Quite apart from constitutional limits on legislative authority to investigate are issues arising out of the *procedures* followed by the principal congressional agencies. Much of the criticism that has been directed at investigating committees during the past decade has concerned their failure to give witnesses the benefit of procedures which are regarded as elementary due process of law in the courts. Secret hearings, refusal to permit the presence of counsel, acceptance and publication of character-damaging hearsay evidence, refusal to permit witnesses to make statements, abusive and harassing questioning—these and similar practices have substantially damaged the reputation of the investigative process. Reaction against these abuses has led the committees themselves to some rectification of their procedures, and various proposals have been placed before Congress for procedural codes which committees must observe or for judicial redress in case of character damage by investigating committee action.[18]

The Vinson Court contributed almost nothing to this movement, in spite of the fact that it handed down three decisions touching on procedural issues. In the first, *Christoffel* v. *United States*, decided in 1949 while Murphy and Rutledge were still on the Court, a five to four decision invalidated a conviction for perjury before a House committee, on the ground of failure to show that a quorum of the committee was in the room at the actual time the perjured testimony was given, even though a quorum had admittedly been present at the beginning of the session in question. Jackson for the minority said it was universal parliamentary practice that, after the presence of a quorum had been ascertained and recorded at the beginning of a session, the record stood unless and until the point of no quorum was raised. The majority's technical interpretation would, he added, make it impossible for a member of a legislative committee even to "visit a washroom" without running the risk of nullifying a whole committee proceeding.

Actually, the majority's somewhat absurd doctrine was soon limited, and the Court, after the 1949 personnel changes, quickly swung over to the other extreme. In *United States* v. *Bryan*, a 1950 case growing out of refusal to produce records subpoenaed by the Un-American Activities Committee, the Court not only held the quorum issue irrelevant but also permitted testimony given before the committee to be used in the prosecution, contrary to the apparent intent of the statute. Black and Frankfurter dissented, as they also did in *United States* v. *Fleischman*, decided the same day. Here a board member of the same organization whose records had been subpoenaed in the Bryan case was convicted for failing to help produce the records, even though they were not in her possession or under her control. These decisions help to point up a record of judicial timidity and confusion in dealing with the difficult problems posed by wholly new assertions of legislative investigatory powers.

GOVERNMENT EMPLOYEE LOYALTY

One of the special concerns of the cold-war period has been the loyalty of government employees, apprehension on this score being heightened by the Hiss case and a few others. A common legislative reaction, at all levels of government, was to require public employees to take an oath attesting to their loyalty and freedom from Communist sympathies. Several of these oath requirements came to the Supreme Court on claims of unconstitutionality.

In so far as the oaths related to actual membership of government employees in the Communist party, they caused the Court no more trouble than the non-Communist oath for labor-union officials which was upheld in the Douds case. A Los Angeles city ordinance requiring the filing of an affidavit by city employees that they were not and never had been members of the party was upheld in the 1951 case of *Garner* v. *Board of Public Works*, Justice Frankfurter saying: "In the context of our time, such membership is sufficiently relevant to effective and dependable government, and to the confidence of the electorate in its government."

But where the oaths dealt with less definite indicia of disloyalty, the Court felt it necessary to exert some restraining influence on legislative enthusiasm. Particularly did it insist that the principle of guilt by association be handled with care. This issue was raised in three important cases, the first two of which the Court was able to decide favorably to the oath requirement.

Gerende v. *Board of Supervisors of Elections* grew out of a Maryland statute requiring candidates for public offices in the state to file with their nomination certificates affidavits that they were not subversive persons. Standing alone, this would have been an absurdly vague standard, but Maryland's highest court had given it a more definite meaning by defining "subversive person" as one who was engaged "in one way or another in the attempt to overthrow the government by force and violence" or who was "knowingly a member of an organization engaged in such an attempt." On the basis of this interpretation the Court was able to uphold the oath requirement unanimously.

The Garner case, already mentioned, involved not only a non-Communist affidavit but also a requirement that city employees take an oath that they had not advocated or taught the overthrow of the government by force and violence or belonged to or been affiliated with an organization which so advocated or taught and that they would not do so during their period of employment by the city. The Supreme Court upheld this requirement by a scant five to four margin.

Black, Douglas, and Burton were convinced that the oath was a bill of attainder under the principles announced in the Lovett case and the post–Civil War decisions. Justice Frankfurter, who had shown a distaste for the bill of attainder argument in the Lovett decision, likewise avoided it here by basing his objection on the due process clause. The oath, according to his interpretation, was faulty because it did not ask the employee to swear that he "knowingly" or "to the best of his knowledge" had no proscribed affiliation. "Certainty is implied in the disavowal exacted." To ask a city employee for such certainty about every organization to which he may have belonged was an "irrational demand," going beyond the Gerende requirement, and would certainly operate as a deterrent to public employees joining in even "innocent associations." "Such a demand is at war with individual integrity; it can no more be justified than the inquiry into belief which Mr. Justice Black, Mr. Justice Jackson, and I deemed invalid in American Communications Association v. Douds."

Justice Jackson, however, did not see the parallel, and his vote gave the decision to supporters of the oath. Clark's opinion for the majority met Frankfurter's contention by assuming that the "knowing" requirement was "implicit in each clause of the oath," while the bill of attainder contention was explained away by holding that the statute was mere "legislative definition of standards of qualification for public or professional employment." In other words, there was no difference in principle between this oath requirement and a statute "forbidding the practice of medicine by any person who had been convicted of a felony"!

In the 1952 case of *Wieman* v. *Updegraff*, however, the Garner majority and minority both joined in unanimously invalidating an Oklahoma oath for state employees which, as interpreted by the state supreme court, did adopt the guilt-by-association test. Persons who were or had been members of proscribed organizations were to be excluded from the state service, regardless of their knowledge concerning the organizations to which they had belonged. Justice Clark said:

. . . Under the Oklahoma Act, the fact of association alone determines disloyalty and disqualification; it matters not whether association existed innocently or knowingly. To thus inhibit individual freedom of movement is to stifle the flow of democratic expression and controversy at one of its chief sources. . . . Indiscriminate classification of innocent with knowing activity must fall as an assertion of arbitrary power. The oath offends due process.

The loyalty oath has not been deemed sufficient protection against disloyal government employees, however. In numerous jurisdictions a more active program of checking official loyalty has been instituted. The program of the federal government has, of course, received major attention.[19] For present purposes we need go back no further than the Hatch Act of 1939, which required the removal of any federal employees belonging to an organization which advocated the overthrow of the constitutional form of government in the United States.[20] In 1940 the Civil Service Commission announced that, as a matter of policy, it would not certify for employment "the name of any person when it has been established that he is a member of the Communist Party, the German Bund, or any other Communist or Nazi organization." This policy was incorporated in the War Service Regulations of March 16, 1942, denying appointment where there existed "a reasonable doubt as to loyalty to the Government of the United States."[21]

On March 21, 1947, President Truman established a broad new federal loyalty program by Executive Order 9835.[22] This order required checking of the loyalty of all incumbent employees and of all applicants for employment. The former task was assigned to the heads of departments and agencies, assisted in each case by one or more agency loyalty boards. The latter was assigned to the Civil Service Commission, assisted by fourteen regional loyalty boards. An over-all Loyalty Review Board of 24 members, appointed by the Civil Service Commission, was set up to hear appeals from both employees and applicants.

The procedure of the loyalty probe as it operated from 1947 to May 1953, can be indicated briefly. A routine check was made on each incumbent or applicant. If derogatory information appeared, a full field investigation by the FBI was instituted.

The FBI had a purely investigative role; it laid its information before the agency or regional board without making any findings, recommendations, or evaluations. If there was doubt in the minds of the board members after receiving the FBI report, a statement of charges or an interrogatory would be sent to the individual, to which he could reply in writing. If this did not clear up the case, a hearing was given by the appropriate board, at which the employee or applicant could appear with an attorney or friend and produce witnesses or testimony. The hearing was private, and the procedure was not that of a court. The FBI was not required to reveal the names of its confidential agents and informants. The charges were required to be stated as specifically and completely as security considerations permitted. If the charges were sustained by the board, an appeal would lie to the Loyalty Review Board. For employees there was an intermediate appeal to the head of the agency.

The standard of judgment on which all loyalty boards operated, as revised in 1951, was that "on all the evidence, there is a reasonable doubt as to the loyalty of the person involved to the Government of the United States."[23] To assist the boards in their findings, the Attorney General was authorized by the executive order to designate organizations which he found to be "totalitarian, fascist, communist or subversive, or as having adopted a policy of advocating or approving the commission of acts of force or violence to deny others their rights under the Constitution of the United States, or as seeking to alter the form of government of the United States by unconstitutional means."

The violently conflicting views as to the constitutionality of this program came up to the Supreme Court for consideration in April, 1951, but the Court's resolution of them was not particularly satisfactory or effective. *Bailey* v. *Richardson* was a challenge to the validity of the entire program on due process and First Amendment grounds. The government had been upheld by a two to one vote in the court of appeals,[24] and the Supreme Court, finding itself split four to four, with Clark not participating, of necessity affirmed the lower court's decision without opinion. Actually, however, six of these eight justices took advantage of the decision in *Joint Anti-Fascist Refugee Committee* v. *McGrath,* decided the same day, to explain their positions in the Bailey case; and so it is to the McGrath case that we turn.

The Joint Anti-Fascist Refugee Committee, which claimed to be a charitable organization administering relief to Spanish Republicans, and two other organizations had been designated on the Attorney General's list and specifically classified as "Communist." The organizations sought declaratory judgments and injunctions for removal of their names from the list. Their complaints contended that they were not subversive organizations and that their inclusion on the list was an arbitrary act. The government's motion to dismiss the complaints was granted by the trial court, and judgment was affirmed by a two to one vote in the court of appeals.[25]

Five Supreme Court justices upheld the complaining organizations, but for such a variety of reasons that there was no "opinion for the Court." Justice Burton, who "announced the judgment," took the narrowest view, one which only Justice Douglas supported, and even he only partially. Burton, feeling that the case "bristled with constitutional issues" which the Court should avoid if at all possible, found a way of disposing of it on procedural grounds. The legal effect of the government's motion to dismiss the complaints was to admit the allegations of the complaints, allegations which constituted the entire record in the case and which presented the Attorney General's action as "patently arbitrary." The executive order provided that the Attorney General's findings were to be made "after appropriate investigation and determination"; and such a determination, said Burton, "must be the result of a process of reasoning. It cannot be an arbitrary fiat contrary to the known facts." Since the government had presented no facts in support of the Attorney General's procedure or conclusions, his action had to be condemned.

Justice Frankfurter, unlike Burton, could not avoid the broader constitutional issue of due process, which he eulogized as "perhaps the most majestic concept in our whole constitutional system." Due process requires notice and a fair hearing. "No better instrument has been devised for arriving at truth than to give a person in jeopardy of serious loss notice of the case against him and opportunity to meet it." Measured by this standard, the Attorney General's listing fell woefully short, for it was "made without notice, without disclosure of any reasons justifying it, without opportunity to meet the undisclosed evidence or suspicion on which designation may have been based, and without opportunity to establish affirmatively that the aims and acts of the organization are innocent."

Black, Douglas, and Jackson also wrote concurring opinions. Black argued that such lists amounted to bills of attainder and that the executive had no authority to issue them, no matter what kind of procedural protection was provided. Douglas agreed but reserved most of his decision for comments on the Bailey case. Jackson castigated the "extravagance" and "intemperance" of some of his colleagues (presumably Black and Douglas) and was doubtful whether the organizations had suffered any legal harm or had standing to seek relief; but he nonetheless concurred in the judgment on the ground that they could vindicate an unconstitutional deprivation of the rights of their members.

The dissent was written by Reed, with Vinson and Minton joining. Their position was that the designation was without legal effect or consequences: "These petitioners are not ordered to do anything and are not punished for anything." Listing them does not prohibit their business or deprive them of liberty or property. It is a "mere abstract declaration" and constitutes simply one piece of evidence in subsequent disloyalty proceedings. Not until steps are taken "to punish or enjoin their activities" will the organizations be entitled to judicial redress.

Because of the diverse holdings of the majority justices, the effectiveness of the judgment was difficult to determine. All it did was to remand the proceedings to the trial court and reinstate the three organizations' complaints. Senator Pat McCarran believed that the Attorney General could disprove the allegations by evidence at the trial and that no change in existing procedure would be required.[26] On the other hand, Seth Richardson, former chairman of the Loyalty Review Board, felt that the opinion made it necessary that "suitable hearings should be granted" to organizations before inclusion on the list.[27] Actually, it appears that the list continued to be used during the Truman administration and that no procedural reforms were instituted.[28]

It is obvious from the views expressed in the Joint Anti-Fascist case that the lineup in *Bailey* v. *Richardson* was Vinson, Minton, Reed, and Burton against Frankfurter, Jackson, Black, and Douglas. Burton's switch and the Court's consequent tie vote resulted in the paradox, to quote Jackson, of the Court's granting "judicial review and relief to the group while refusing it to the individual. So far as I can recall, this is the first time this Court has held rights of individuals subordinate and inferior to those of organized groups. I think this is an inverted view of the law—it is justice turned bottom-side up."

Dorothy Bailey, a training officer in the Federal Security Agency, had been charged with being a Communist and with activity in a Communist-front organization. Names of the informants who gave evidence against her to the FBI were not disclosed at the hearings. Their statements were not made under oath, and the Loyalty Review Board had not "the slightest knowledge" about them. As Judge Edgerton said, dissenting in the court of appeals, to support a finding of disloyalty "there were only the unsworn reports in the secret files to the effect that unsworn statements of a general sort, purporting to connect appellant with Communism, had been made by unnamed persons."[29] To Douglas, this was unacceptable procedure. To be sure, the employee was not faced with a criminal charge. "But she was on trial for her reputation, her job, her professional standing. A disloyalty trial is the most crucial event in the life of a civil servant. If condemned, he is branded for life as a person unworthy of trust or confidence. To make that condemnation without meticulous regard for the decencies of a fair trial is abhorrent to fundamental justice."

Jackson sought to come to grips more directly with the argument primarily relied on by the court of appeals, namely, that all employees hold office at the pleasure of the appointing authority and that courts will not review the action of executive officials in dismissing employees, except to insure compliance with statutory requirements. His rebuttal went as follows:

> Ordinary dismissals from government service which violate no fixed tenure concern only the Executive branch, and courts will not review such discretionary action. However, these are not discretionary discharges pursuant to an order having force of law. Administrative machinery is publicly set up to comb the whole government service to discharge persons or to declare them ineligible for employment upon an incontestable finding, made without hearing, that some organization is subversive. To be deprived not only of present government employment but of future opportunity for it certainly is no small injury when government employment so dominates the field of opportunity.
>
> The fact that one may not have a legal right to get or keep a government post does not mean that he can be adjudged ineligible illegally.

On the other side, the Reed dissent in the Joint Anti-Fascist case denied that employees removed on disloyalty charges were entitled to any different procedural protection than employees removed on other grounds. "Employees under investigation have never had the right to confrontation, cross-examination and quasi-judicial hearing." All they were entitled to was "notice and charges." The loyalty procedure gave them that.[30]

The uncertainties of the Bailey case were largely dissolved a year later when six justices upheld the New York Feinberg law providing for removal of public school teachers on disloyalty grounds in *Adler* v. *Board of Education of City of New York*. The law required the Board of Regents to make, after full notice and hearing (thus meeting the Supreme Court's criticism in the Joint Anti-Fascist case), a listing of organizations which it found to advocate, advise, teach, or embrace the doctrine that the government should be overthrown by force or violence or any unlawful means. Membership of a schoolteacher in any such listed organization was "prima facie evidence for disqualification for appointment to or retention in" any school position; but, before an individual was severed from or denied employment, he was to be given a full hearing with the privilege of being represented by counsel and the right of judicial review.

Before this act was passed, the *New York Times* attacked it as a "blunderbuss" bill and warned that the legislature was "enacting into law the untenable and illiberal theory of 'guilt by association.' "[31] The Vinson Court, however, upheld the law, the four justices who had voted for the federal program in the Bailey case being joined by Clark, who did not participate in the earlier decision, and Jackson, who was apparently satisfied with the procedural provisions in the New York law. For the majority, Minton contended that the "guilt-by-association" point had been disposed of by the Garner opinion, and he added:

> We adhere to that case. A teacher works in a sensitive area in a schoolroom. There he shapes the attitude of young minds toward the society in which they live. In this, the state has a vital concern. . . . That the school authorities have the right and the duty to screen the officials, teachers, and employees as to their fitness to maintain the integrity of the schools as a part of ordered society, cannot be doubted. One's associates, past and present, as well as one's conduct, may properly be considered in determining fitness and loyalty. From time immemorial, one's reputation has been determined in part by the company he keeps.

And, Minton added, it was no infringement on the rights of free speech or assembly for the state to lay down the terms on which it would employ teachers.

Justices Black and Douglas each wrote dissents.[32] Unable to cite any majority decisions upholding their views, they turned from legal precedents to argue the social unwisdom of censorship, particularly as applied to teachers. Said Douglas:

> The present law proceeds on a principle repugnant to our society—guilt by association. A teacher is disqualified because of her membership in an organization found to be "subversive." The finding as to the "subversive" character of the organization is made in a proceeding to which the teacher is not a party and in which it is not clear that she may even be heard. To be sure, she may have a hearing when charges of disloyalty are leveled against her. But in that hearing the finding as to the "subversive" character of the organization apparently may not be reopened in order to allow her to show the truth of the matter. The irrebuttable charge that the organization is "subversive" therefore hangs as an ominous cloud over her own hearing. The mere fact of membership in the organization raises a prima facie case of her own guilt. She may, it is said, show her innocence. But innocence in this case turns on knowledge; and when the witch hunt is on, one who must rely on ignorance leans on a feeble reed.
>
> The very threat of such a procedure is certain to raise havoc with academic freedom. Youthful indiscretions, mistaken causes, misguided en-

thusiasms—all long forgotten—become the ghosts of a harrowing present. Any organization committed to a liberal cause, any group organized to revolt against an hysterical trend, any committee launched to sponsor an unpopular program becomes suspect. These are the organizations into which Communists often infiltrate. Their presence infects the whole, even though the project was not conceived in sin. A teacher caught in that mesh is almost certain to stand condemned. Fearing condemnation, she will tend to shrink from any association that stirs controversy. In that manner freedom of expression will be stifled.

For the majority of the Vinson Court, however, these were matters of policy on which the appropriate legislatures were entitled to make up their minds, and they did not add up to judicially cognizable reasons for limiting legislative authority. Naturally, the Court was not unaware of the perils of this laissez faire philosophy. Justice Frankfurter said in the Rumely case: "We would have to be that 'blind' Court, against which Mr. Chief Justice Taft admonished in a famous passage . . . that does not see what 'all others can see and understand' not to know that there is wide concern, both in and out of Congress, over some aspects of the exercise of the congressional power of investigation." Since the Court's technique of denying certiorari saved it from any positive ratification of recent committee inquisitions, it is even conceivable that the way may still be open to erect First Amendment barriers to wholly irresponsible committee queries. But this entire area is one in which judicial action is bound to be circumscribed by an understandable reluctance to interfere with legislative discretion, such as was expressed by Jackson in the Eisler case: "It would be an unwarranted act of judicial usurpation . . . to assume for the courts the function of supervising congressional committees. I should . . . leave the responsibility for the behavior of its committees squarely on the shoulders of Congress."

VI. *The Rights of Denizenship*

Ignatz Mezei, born in Gibraltar of Hungarian or Rumanian parents, came to the United States in 1923 and lived in Buffalo, New York, for twenty-five years. He married and had a home there but did not become a citizen. In 1948 he sailed for Europe, without securing any re-entry papers, apparently to visit his dying mother in Rumania. Denied entry there, he remained in Hungary for nineteen months, unable to secure an exit permit. Finally, he received a quota immigration visa from the American consul in Budapest. Arriving in the United States in February, 1950, he was temporarily excluded on security grounds by an immigration inspector and shunted to Ellis Island. In May the Attorney General ordered the exclusion made permanent without a hearing, on the ground that it was based on confidential information which it would be prejudicial to the public interest to disclose. Twice Mezei was deported, but France and Great Britain both refused him permission to land. The State Department unsuccessfully negotiated with Hungary for his readmission. Mezei personally applied for entry to a dozen Latin-American countries, all of which refused to accept him.

In November, 1951, after almost two years on Ellis Island, a federal district court agreed that he was unlawfully confined there and ordered his release on a writ of habeas corpus. The court of appeals affirmed his freedom. But on March 16, 1953, the Supreme Court, by a five to four vote, held that the courts could not interfere in an exclusion proceeding grounded on danger to the national security. Mezei was returned to Ellis Island with the prospect of spending the rest of his days there, condemned to confinement without accusation of crime or judicial trial, by an exercise of unreviewed and unreviewable executive discretion. Thus executive imprisonment, "considered oppressive and lawless since John, at Runnymede, pledged that no free man should be imprisoned, dispossessed, outlawed, or exiled save by the judgment of his peers or by the law of the land,"[1] has come to the United States out of the Middle Ages.

The Mezei case starkly demonstrates the current perils in being what Justice Reed has elegantly referred to as a "denizen"[2] of the United States rather than a citizen. In fact, even a naturalized citizen is legally vulnerable to attacks from which a natural-born citizen is immune. The present chapter is concerned with the Vinson Court's stewardship in interpreting constitutional protections and statutory law affecting the status of aliens and naturalized citizens.

THE RETURN OF THE NATIVE

The political appeal of aliens in the abstract is admittedly very slight, and when the charge of radicalism is added to alien status, the public reaction is bound to be decidedly negative. "If you don't like it here, why don't you go back where you came from," is a popular and easily induced reaction. Thus deportation is always good politics.

The legal situation of the alien under threat of deportation has been correspondingly poor. His right to remain in this country is subject to legislative determination. If he is accused of violating the terms upon which continued residence is predicated, the deportation proceeding, in spite of its serious effect, is a civil proceeding and not attended by the safeguards of a criminal trial. The whole problem, moreover, is tied up with the conduct of our foreign relations, a subject which the courts recognize as belonging peculiarly to the political branches of the government, and consequently the pressure for judicial acceptance of legislative or administrative decisions is particularly strong in this field.

The administrative agency with primary responsibility for the control of aliens, the Immigration and Naturalization Service, is inevitably affected by the favorable political environment in which it operates. It is dealing with individuals who have no political status or sources of support. It is enforcing against them a popular public policy. It is consequently hardly surprising if the service interprets its statutes and arranges its procedures so as to produce the maximum number of deportations.

An administrative policy based on the philosophy that the end justifies the means, backed up by supporting legislative attitudes, is bound to produce interesting problems for a reviewing court and conflicts between justices with varying degrees of concern for the protection of individual rights as well as differing notions as to judicial responsibility for correcting legislative or administrative errors.

As would be expected, the greatest resistance to legislative and administrative policy toward aliens came from the justices who in the preceding chapters demonstrated the greatest concern for the protection of civil liberties. In its more extreme form their resistance led them to challenge the constitutionality of legislation adversely affecting aliens. Thus in a 1946 case Justices Rutledge and Murphy denied the government's power to strip a naturalized citizen of his citizenship,[3] and they repeated their challenge in a 1949 decision.[4] Though this position was presumably liquidated with their disappearance from the Court, it should be reviewed briefly.

The process of denaturalization is authorized by law in cases where citizenship has been "illegally procured." Obviously, there must be a method of canceling citizenship secured by the use of fraudulent documents or where entry into the United States was illegal.[5] But denaturalization is also a device which can be employed against naturalized citizens who hold unpopular political views. During World War I a considerable number of naturalized citizens who expressed sympathy for Germany were denaturalized, and World War II saw a denaturalization drive on both Nazis and Communists. The theory was that their naturalization had been "illegally procured" because the individual had sworn falsely that he was "attached to the principles of the United States, and well disposed to the good order and happiness of the same."

The Roosevelt Court sought to temper the World War II enthusiasm for denaturalization by insisting that in such proceedings the burden of proof was on the government and the evidence offered must be "clear, unequivocal, and convincing."[6] But where such proof was offered in the case of an active Nazi sympathizer, the Court gave its approval.[7] Murphy and Rutledge dissented. They felt that if the government had the power to denaturalize, then all naturalized persons were second-class citizens, "conditional, timorous and insecure because blanketed with the threat that some act or conduct, not amounting to forfeiture for others, will be taken retroactively to show that some prescribed condition had not been fulfilled and be so adjudged." It was this same position which they restated in the 1949 case of *Klapprott* v. *United States*, with similar lack of success.

While Justices Black and Douglas did not join Rutledge and Murphy in this challenge to the government's denaturalization powers, they more recently initiated an almost equally uncompromising attack on the government's powers to deport. In the 1952 case of *Harisiades* v. *Shaughnessy* the Court majority upheld the provision of the Alien Registration Act of 1940 authorizing deportation of legally resident aliens because of membership in the Communist party which terminated before enactment of the statute. Douglas, with Black concurring, dissented. He admitted that the Supreme Court in the 1893 case of *Fong Yue Ting* v. *United States* had held that congressional power to deport aliens was absolute and could be exercised for any reason Congress deemed appropriate. But this was a six to three decision, and he regarded Justice Brewer's dissenting opinion as sounder. Brewer wrote at that time:

> It is said that the power here asserted is inherent in sovereignty. This doctrine of powers inherent in sovereignty is one both indefinite and dangerous. Where are the limits to such powers to be found, and by whom are they to be pronounced? Is it within legislative capacity to declare the limits? If so, then the mere assertion of an inherent power creates it, and despotism exists. May the courts establish the boundaries? Whence do they obtain the authority for this? Shall they look to the practices of other nations to ascertain the limits? The governments of other nations have elastic powers. Ours are fixed and bounded by a written constitution. The expulsion of a race may be within the inherent powers of a despotism. History, before the adoption of this constitution, was not destitute of examples of the exercise of such a power; and its framers were familiar with history and wisely, as it

seems to me, they gave to this government no general power to banish. Banishment may be resorted to as punishment for crime; but among the powers reserved to the people, and not delegated to the government, is that of determining whether whole classes in our midst shall, for no crime but that of their race and birthplace, be driven from our territory.[8]

Moreover, it was Douglas' contention that the Fong Yue Ting case was inconsistent with the philosophy of constitutional law developed since 1893 for the protection of resident aliens, which has come to regard them as "persons" within the meaning of the Fifth and Fourteenth Amendments and so entitled to due process and equal protection. Specifically, resident aliens have been protected against discrimination in business or employment;[9] their property may not be taken without just compensation;[10] they are entitled to habeas corpus to test the legality of arrest,[11] to the protection of the Fifth and Sixth Amendments in criminal trials,[12] and to the right of free speech as guaranteed by the First Amendment.[13] "Those guarantees of liberty and livelihood are the essence of the freedom which this country from the beginning has offered the people of all lands. If those rights, great as they are, have constitutional protection, I think the more important one—the right to remain here—has a like dignity."

Douglas did not contend, however, that the right to remain was absolute; he agreed that some aliens by their conduct might show themselves so dangerous or hostile to the United States as to justify deportation. But the 1940 act ordered aliens deported "not for what they are but for what they once were." There was no showing that their continued presence in the country would be "hostile to the safety or welfare of the nation. . . . The principle of forgiveness and the doctrine of redemption are too deep in our philosophy to admit that there is no return for those who have once erred."[14]

While these basic constitutional attacks failed, tactics of resistance to the statutory interpretations or the procedures of the Immigration Service occasionally succeeded in winning a Vinson Court majority to abate overofficious bureaucratic zeal. *Delgadillo* v. *Carmichael* concerned a Mexican citizen, resident in the United States continuously from 1923 to 1942, who in June of that year shipped out of Los Angeles for New York as a crew member of an American merchant ship. After passing through the Panama Canal, the ship was torpedoed. Delgadillo was rescued and taken to Havana, Cuba, where the American consul took care of him for a week. He then was returned to the United States through Miami and continued to serve as a seaman in the American merchant fleet.

In March, 1944, he was convicted in California of second-degree robbery and sentenced to prison. Proceedings for deportation were begun under the statute which authorizes deportation of aliens convicted of crimes involving moral turpitude "committed within five years after the entry of the alien to the United States." This latter requirement of the statute was, of course, met only if the alien's trip from Havana to Miami was construed to be "entry" into the United States.

In a unanimous opinion the Court through Justice Douglas refused to accept this interpretation. He could not believe that Congress had intended to make an alien's right to remain in this country "dependent on circumstances so fortuitous and capricious as those upon which the Immigration Service has here seized. . . . Respect for law does not thrive on captious interpretations."

A second example is the 1950 case of *Wong Yang Sung* v. *McGrath*, where the issue was whether deportation hearings must be conducted in accordance with the procedural provisions of the Administrative Procedure Act. These hearings have in the past normally been in charge of a presiding inspector who may both prosecute and make the initial decision in the case. His job was officially described as to "conduct the interrogation of the alien and the witnesses in behalf of the Government and . . . cross-examine the alien's witnesses and present such evidence as is necessary to support the charges in the warrant of arrest."[15] He then prepares a summary of the evidence, proposed findings of fact, conclusions of law, and a proposed order. This practice constitutes a perfect example of the prosecutor-judge combination which the Administrative Procedure Act forbids. The Immigration Service in Wong Yang Sung contended that it was exempted from the act, but their argument convinced only Justice Reed.[16]

Decisions such as these were in the minority, however. More generally the Vinson Court upheld both the statutory interpretations and the procedures of the Immigration Service. In the 1950 case of *United States* ex rel. *Eichenlaub* v. *Shaughnessy* the Court rather deliberately embraced the harsher of two possible interpretations of deportation law. The case involved two aliens in almost identical circumstances. Both were natives of Germany, naturalized in the 1930's. In 1941 Eichenlaub pled guilty in federal court to acting as an agent for a foreign government without having registered with the State Department. In 1944, with his consent, a court judgment was entered canceling his citizenship on the usual ground of fraud in its procurement. Deportation proceedings were then instituted, and he was ordered deported in 1945. The circumstances in the second case were similar, except that the conviction was for violation of the Espionage Act of 1917 by transmitting to an agent of a foreign country information relating to national defense.

In both instances the government was proceeding under an act of 1920 which authorized deportation of "all aliens who since August 1, 1914, have been or may hereafter be convicted" under certain specified statutes.[17] The difficulty with the government's case was that these two men were not "aliens" at the time of their conviction; they were naturalized citizens. The government proposed that this problem be met by ruling that, since the naturalizations had been secured by fraud, they were void *ab initio*. Justice Burton for the Court suggested, however, that an easier route to the same end was to hold that the act did not mean what it seemed to say and that to satisfy its terms it was not necessary that the offenders had had the status of aliens at the time they were convicted. He felt that Congress had intended no distinction between aliens who had never been naturalized and aliens who had been denaturalized. In a very revealing sentence, Burton said: "The recognized purpose of the Act was deportation." He and his three colleagues who made up the majority here—Vinson, Reed, and Minton—obviously intended to construe the act so as to make deportations possible.

This ruling produced the interesting dissenting combination of Frankfurter, Black, and Jackson, with Frankfurter writing a short and biting dissent protesting the "ruthlessly undiscriminating construction" given to the statute. The same three justices, with Douglas again strangely missing, dissented in *Jordan* v. *De George* (1951). Here an alien twenty-nine years in the United States, with a citizen wife and son, was subject to deportation because he was twice convicted of evading federal liquor taxes. The penalty of deportation applied, according to law, only if the crimes involve "moral turpitude." The minority contended that moral turpitude was "an undefined and undefinable standard" and that Congress, warned of this fact, had nonetheless thrown on the courts the impossible burden of translating an ethical concept into a legal one. So far as this particular crime was concerned, Jackson said:

> . . . It is not particularly un-American, and we see no reason to strain to make the penalty for the same act so much more severe in the case of an alien "bootlegger" than it is in the case of a native "moonshiner." I have never discovered that disregard of the Nation's liquor taxes excluded a citizen from our best society and I see no reason why it should banish an alien from our worst.[18]

THE MEANING OF ADMINISTRATIVE FINALITY

The ruling doctrines in the field of alien control all tend toward a limitation of judicial power and responsibility. The government is acting in its capacity as a sovereign; the political branches of the government have a predominant role in the protection of the nation's security; resident aliens have no legally enforcible rights to retain their residence as against legislative judgments; deportation is not a criminal proceeding, and consequently constitutional guaranties do not apply. The scope to which these doctrines limit judicial review and establish administrative finality, not to say absolutism, can best be seen by looking into three or four relevant cases in some detail.

Ludecke v. *Watkins* was a 1948 decision concerning judicial authority to review a deportation decision. Under the regular deportation statutes, judicial review of the Attorney General's decision, though somewhat limited in scope, is readily secured through the writ of habeas corpus.[19] Ludecke, however, was being deported under the Alien Enemy Act of 1798, which gives the President, "whenever there is a declared war between the United States and any foreign nation or government," broad powers to deal with enemy aliens and provide "for the removal of those who, not being permitted to reside within the United States, refuse or neglect to depart therefrom." Ludecke had been arrested the day after Pearl Harbor and was interned for the duration of the war. Following the conclusion of hostilities with Germany, the President directed the removal from the United States of all enemy aliens "who shall be deemed by the Attorney General to be dangerous to the public peace and safety of the United States." Ludecke's removal was ordered in January, 1946, and his application for writ of habeas corpus was denied by two lower courts.

Justice Frankfurter wrote the Court's opinion refusing to restrain this exercise of presidential power. His general concern with the prevention of harshness in deportation cases, as demonstrated in the Eichenlaub case and others, was here overridden by his respect for the President's war powers and his belief that Congress had intended no judicial review in such cases. He quoted Chief Justice Marshall's comment that the act "appears to me to be as unlimited as the legislature could make it." The fact that the President was acting here through the Attorney General made no difference in his mind; it was still an unreviewable war power of the President that was being exercised. Nor did the war power cease to exist with the termination of hostilities. A "state of war" is terminated, not by the judiciary, but by action of the political branches of the government, and they had not acted to bring the war with German to an end.[20]

Justice Black in dissent was scathing and almost contemptuous of the Frankfurter opinion. In fact, the two opinions give the impression of a running duel, with Frankfurter adding rebuttal in his footnotes after reading the Black dissent and Black retaliating in footnotes of his own. Black was frankly appalled at a situation in which the Attorney General could order deportation without notice, hearing, or judicial inquiry as to the truth of the allegations on which deportation was based. He was willing to admit that the 1798 statute contemplated such action while hostilities were in progress or while there was danger of invasion. But with the unconditional surrender of Germany, the danger against which the statute was intended to guard ceased to exist, and the state of war became a "pure fiction." He closed his dissent with an invitation to Congress to "correct" the Court's decision, to which suggestion Frankfurter replied in a footnote that Congress had already indicated by a provision in a recent appropriation act that it held the view now taken by the Court—to which Black rejoined in a footnote that Congress had done no such thing.

The other three dissenters, in an opinion by Douglas, saw no reason to confine themselves to this issue of the existence of a state of war. They stood on the broader ground that it was "foreign to our system" for any officer of the government to be given discretion to "override due process," that the Attorney General was bound to give a hearing on which to base his determination (and, in fact, had done so in this case), and that the findings and the procedure of such a hearing were subject to test for due process by habeas corpus. It was this contention that Frankfurter labeled as the "doctrinaire audacity" which would hold an act "almost as old as the Constitution . . . offensive to some emanation of the Bill of Rights."

Two years later the Ludecke decision was used to deny judicial review of a particularly questionable bit of arbitrary action by the Immigration Service and the Attorney General in the case of *United States* ex rel. *Knauff* v. *Shaughnessy*. The woman concerned here was born in Germany. She left there for Czechoslovakia during the Hitler regime, and in 1939 fled to England as a refugee, where she served in the Royal Air Force. In 1946 she took civilian employment with the United States War Department in Germany. In 1948, with the permission of the commanding general at Frankfurt, she married Kurt Knauff, a naturalized citizen of the United States. He was an honorably discharged United States Army veteran, who was at the time of his marriage a civilian employee of the Army at Frankfurt. When Knauff sought to bring his wife to the United States later in 1948, she was excluded without a hearing by order of the Attorney General on the ground that her admission would be prejudicial to the interests of the United States. This procedure was duly authorized by regulations adopted under authority of the act of June 21, 1941, which provided that the President may issue "reasonable rules, regulations and orders" to govern the entrance of aliens during a period of national emergency.[21]

A four-judge majority of the Court upheld the exclusion. Justice Minton pointed out the difference between the legal situation of an alien being deported and one being excluded from the country. Admission of aliens to the United States is a privilege granted by the sovereign, and Congress can specify any conditions on admission and any procedure it wishes for determining eligibility. The alien has no right of entry, due process need not be given,[22] and determinations of the executive are not subject to judicial review "unless expressly authorized by law." The question in this case was consequently whether the executive action was in accordance with congressional authorization.

In normal times Congress does provide for a hearing in the case of aliens excluded from admission; but here the Attorney General was claiming to act under the special restriction authorized by Congress for periods of war or national emergency. However, Congress had also passed the War Brides Act, the intention of which was to ease the conditions of entry into this country for alien war brides such as Mrs. Knauff by relieving them of certain physical, mental, and documentary requirements and of the quota provisions of the immigration laws. The act did add, it is true, that war brides must be "otherwise admissible under the immigration laws," a provision which the Attorney General contended had the effect of subjecting Mrs. Knauff to screening for security reasons and to the risk of exclusion without hearing. Citing the Ludecke case, Minton concluded: "In such a case we have no authority to retry the determination of the Attorney General."

The trio of Black, Frankfurter, and Jackson was again, as in the Eichenlaub case, in dissent together. It may seem strange that Frankfurter, having approved the executive action in Ludecke, which, as a deportation proceeding, involved due process considerations, should here, in an exclusion case where the alien's legal position is much weaker, denounce the Attorney General's procedure. The explanation is that in the Knauff case he found a congressional intent which he believed the Attorney General was violating. He pointed out that the War Brides Act was "congressional beneficence" in favor of the citizen husband rather than for the alien wife, and he could not believe that, in adopting that act, Congress had meant to leave "wide open the opportunity ruthlessly to take away what it gave" by subjecting alien wives to the "hazards of an informer's tale without any opportunity for its refutation." Legislation "should not be read in such a decimating spirit unless the letter of Congress is inexorable." Justice Jackson's dissent, in which Black and Frankfurter joined, added: "Congress will have to use more explicit language than any yet cited before I will agree that it has authorized an administrative officer to break up the family of an American citizen or force him to keep his wife by becoming an exile."

Normally, with a decision of the Court, the participants pass into limbo and are never heard from again. The Knauff decision, however, set off a chain of events more interesting and better publicized than the decision itself, and worth looking into for an understanding of the working of the Immigration Service bureaucracy. In March, 1950, following the Court's decision, Mrs. Knauff was for the first time, a year and a half after her original detention on Ellis Island, given a hearing on the charges against her. Three witnesses accused her of spying for a Czechoslovak mission in Frankfurt, which she denied. The Immigration Appeals Board found against her, and her deportation was ordered. The House of Representatives had meantime passed a bill to permit her to stay in this country, and the chairman of the House Judiciary Committee notified the Attorney General that deportation while congressional action was pending would be regarded as "contemptuous" of the House. On May 17 Justice Jackson stayed the deportation twenty minutes before Mrs. Knauff's plane left for Germany and too late for her baggage to be taken off. After she gained freedom on parole in January, 1951, the Supreme Court dismissed her second appeal on March 5 because the matter was moot. But on March 27 the Immigration Service returned her to custody on Ellis

Island. On August 29 the Appeals Board reversed its earlier decision, the Attorney General approved on November 1, and Mrs. Knauff left Ellis Island, where she had been except for two months since August, 1948. She did have the manuscript of a book to show for it.[23]

Both the Ludecke and the Knauff decisions could be explained in terms of the executive's war powers, which are admittedly very broad. But the astounding doctrine of *Carlson* v. *Landon* can be blamed only on the hysteria of the cold war. The question involved in this 1952 case was whether the Attorney General, after taking into custody active alien Communists, could hold them in jail without bail at his discretion pending determination of their deportability. The statutory justification for this action was the Internal Security Act of 1950, which made membership in the Communist party grounds for deportation of aliens and which provided:

> Pending final determination of the deportability of any alien taken into custody under warrant of the Attorney General, such alien may, in the discretion of the Attorney General (1) be continued in custody; or (2) be released under bond in the amount of not less than $500, with security approved by the Attorney General; or (3) be released on conditional parole.

The liberty of five aliens was at issue in the Carlson proceeding. There was no contention by the government that if any of these aliens were admitted to bail, they would attempt to disappear or to evade possible deportation orders. The sole ground for denying bail was the allegation by officials of the Immigration Service that these aliens were security risks. The district judge said: "I am not going to turn these people loose if they are Communists, any more than I would turn loose a deadly germ in this community. If that is my duty, let the Circuit Court say so and assume the burden."

To appreciate the significance of denial of bail in a deportation case, it should be noted that such proceedings, with hearings, appeals, and reviews, may run on for years. The foreign country to which aliens are finally ordered deported may refuse to accept them. Thus a denial of bail may conceivably be a life-sentence to jail.

The Supreme Court's problem, then, was to decide whether an alien may be committed to jail for an indeterminate period because the Attorney General (actually a subordinate in the Immigration Service) alleges that he is a Communist who is too dangerous to the national security to be left at large while deportation proceedings are under way against him. Now it happens that four months before its decision in *Carlson* v. *Landon,* the Court had considered another case involving bail for Communists.[24] When twelve second-string Communist leaders were taken into custody in Los Angeles in 1951 on Smith Act indictments, bail of $50,000 was fixed for each defendant. The government's reason for asking such high bail was that four of the Communists convicted in the Dennis proceedings in New York had vanished and forfeited their bail.[25] Fixing bail of such amount was attacked as in violation of the Eighth Amendment's provision that "excessive bail shall not be required."

While disagreeing somewhat on the procedural problems involved, the Supreme Court unanimously held that in the circumstances excessive bail had been fixed. Chief Justice Vinson noted that federal law unequivocally provides that a person arrested for a noncapital offense *shall* be admitted to bail. "Unless this right to bail before trial is preserved, the presumption of innocence, secured only after centuries of struggle, would lose its meaning." He added:

> It is not denied that bail for each petitioner has been fixed in a sum much higher than that usually imposed for offenses with like penalties and yet there has been no factual showing to justify such action in this case. The Government asks the courts to depart from the norm by assuming, without the introduction of evidence, that each petitioner is a pawn in a conspiracy and will, in obedience to a superior, flee the jurisdiction. To infer from the fact of indictment alone a need for bail in an unusually high amount is an arbitrary act. Such conduct would inject into our own system of government the very principles of totalitarianism which Congress was seeking to guard against in passing the statute under which petitioners have been indicted.

Yet five justices of the Supreme Court, who had held that it would be totalitarianism not to grant reasonable bail to admitted Communists who were important officials of the party regularly indicted on a serious criminal charge,[26] held in the

Carlson case that five persons who were insignificant members of the party, if, indeed, they were functioning members of the party at all, could be detained in jail indefinitely on the request of subordinate officials in the Immigration Service.

It fell to Justice Reed to explain why alien status made this difference. First he justified congressional power to adopt the statute. Aliens are "denizens" in this country who are "subject to the plenary power of Congress to expel them under the sovereign right to determine what noncitizens shall be permitted to remain within our borders."

Second there was the problem of procedure:

> Detention is necessarily a part of this deportation procedure. Otherwise aliens arrested for deportation would have opportunities to hurt the United States during the pendency of deportation proceedings. Of course purpose to injure could not be imputed generally to all aliens subject to deportation, so discretion was placed by the 1950 Act in the Attorney General to detain aliens without bail.

Lodging such discretion in the Attorney General is not an unconstitutional delegation of legislative power, for the act states standards which are to guide its use, to wit: "When in the judgment of the Attorney General an alien communist may so conduct himself during deportation hearings as to aid in carrying out the objectives of the world communist movement, that alien may be detained."

Courts can challenge the Attorney General's judgment only on the ground that it is arbitrary, capricious, or an abuse of discretion. The government should not be expected to show in each case "specific acts of sabotage or incitement to subversive action." Reports filed by the Attorney General show that, in fact, bail has been allowed in the "large majority" of cases of deportation arrests for Communist membership.

Finally, there was the matter of the Eighth Amendment. Reed held it inapplicable and ineffective; inapplicable—because "deportation is not a criminal proceeding and has never been held to be punishment"; ineffective—because "the very language of the Amendment fails to say all arrests must be bailable." Congress can define the classes of cases in which bail shall be allowed; for example, it has provided that "in criminal cases bail is not compulsory where the punishment may be death." All that the Eighth Amendment means is that "bail shall not be excessive in those cases where it is proper to grant bail."

Reed was joined in this decision by Jackson, Vinson, Minton, and Clark. Justices Frankfurter, Burton, Black, and Douglas dissented. As usual, Frankfurter preferred to avoid any basic challenge to constitutional power but found a narrower statutory ground on which to base his dissent. He was convinced that the Attorney General had not exercised the kind of discretion which Congress had in mind when it passed the act. Congress must have meant the bailability of aliens to be based on "the danger to the public safety" of their presence within the community. This criterion must be applied individually to each alien: "In each case, the alien's anticipated personal conduct–and that alone–must be considered. Also, how expeditiously each deportation proceeding can be concluded, and therefore how long the bail in each case need be in effect, are relevant considerations."

However, instead of such individualized consideration of risk from continued freedom, the government had proceeded on the policy of denying bail "for all aliens awaiting deportation proceedings whom it deems to be present active Communists." Frankfurter concluded that all such aliens "should have the benefit of an exercise of discretion by the Attorney General, freed from any conception that Congress had made them in effect unbailable."

Burton agreed with this position, and so did Black and Douglas, but the latter two also went far beyond it into constitutional considerations. They reiterated the disbelief they had expressed in Harisiades of plenary congressional power to deport, but did not waste much time on this dry well. Black made four main charges. First, even assuming that Congress can delegate to the Attorney General "power to determine what individuals he prosecutes should be held in jail without bail," Congress did not mean this "dangerous power" to be redelegated to subordinates in the Immigration Service "entrusted with duties like those of deputy sheriffs and policemen."

Second, the courts allowed administrative officials in these cases to determine for themselves what kind of evidence was necessary to prove these aliens bad security risks. "I think that condemning people to jail is a job for the judiciary." Third, "to put people in jail for fear of their talk seems to me to be an abridgement of speech in flat violation of the First Amendment." It was also, he admitted sorrowfully, "a logical application of recent cases watering down constitutional liberty of speech"—citing the Douds, Dennis, and Feiner cases.

Fourth, he attacked Reed's idea that the Eighth Amendment was nothing but a "pious admonition" to Congress:

> Under this contention, the Eighth Amendment is a limitation upon judges only, for while a judge cannot constitutionally fix excessive bail, Congress can direct that people be held in jail without any right to bail at all. Maybe the literal language of the framers lends itself to this weird, devitalizing interpretation when scrutinized with a hostile eye. But at least until recently, it has been the judicial practice to give a broad, liberal interpretation to those provisions of the Bill of Rights obviously designed to protect the individual from governmental oppression.

As for Reed's reminder that Congress had denied bail to persons charged with capital offenses, Black failed to see "where the Court's analogy between deportation and the death penalty advances its argument unless it is also analogizing the offense of indoctrinating talk to the crime of first degree murder."

This, then, is the meaning of administrative finality, as spelled out in the Carlson case:

> Today the Court holds that law-abiding persons, neither charged with nor convicted of any crime, can be held in jail indefinitely, without bail, if a subordinate Washington bureau agent believes they are members of the Communist Party, and therefore dangerous to the nation because of the possibility of their "indoctrination of others."

This 1952 decision made less surprising, though no less frightening, the 1953 decision in the Mezei case, where the Vinson Court accepted another version of indefinite executive imprisonment. To be sure, Mezei was free to leave the United States, but no other country would take him.[27] The Court majority, speaking through Clark, rationalized the situation by treating Mezei's case as one of exclusion rather than deportation and pointing to Congress' undoubted right to exclude aliens from the United States on any grounds it sees fit.

But Jackson, dissenting along with Frankfurter, Black, and Douglas, said it was a "legal fiction" to call this an exclusion case. Rather, it was "that of a lawful and law-abiding inhabitant of our country for a quarter of a century, long ago admitted for permanent residence, who seeks to return home." Jackson granted the right of administrative detention of aliens, but he insisted that the alien detained or excluded also had rights—the basic procedural rights of due process:

> Congress has ample power to determine whom we shall admit to our shores and by what means it will effectuate its exclusion policy. The only limitation is that it may not do so by authorizing United States officers to take the life, the liberty or the property of an alien who has come within our jurisdiction without due process of law, and that means he must meet a fair hearing with fair notice of the charges.
>
> It is inconceivable to me that this measure of simple justice and fair dealing would menace the security of this country. No one can make me believe that we are that far gone.

Nor is one forced to believe that the Supreme Court will honor these five to four precedents when the hysteria of the cold war passes or that the American people will long accept such administrative powers over individual liberty as justified under a proper interpretation of the Bill of Rights. Fortunately, the judicial process can correct its mistakes, a matter on which some light is thrown by the next section.

PEARL HARBOR AFTERMATH

During World War II the Supreme Court permitted administrative finality in the form of military judgment to operate in the enforced evacuation of persons of Japanese descent from the Pacific Coast. With the wisdom and calmness of hindsight, the evacuation has been generally judged a hysterical and punitive action, unjustified by considerations of national defense.[28] The Vinson Court had no occasion to reconsider the decisions upholding this military action,[29] but two 1948 cases did something to make amends for wartime injustices by eliminating peacetime discriminations.

Oyama v. *California* involved the provisions of that state's Alien Land Law which forbids aliens ineligible for American citizenship to acquire agricultural land. Under the act, property acquired or transferred in violation of the act escheats to the state as of the date of acquisition. Kajira Oyama, an ineligible alien, had purchased in 1934 several acres of agricultural land in the name of his six-year-old son Fred, an American citizen. In 1944 the state filed a petition to declare an escheat of the land on the ground that the conveyance had been made in violation of the law.

There were several Supreme Court precedents sustaining the California act and similar laws in other states against claims that they denied aliens ineligible to citizenship their constitutional rghts.[30] Counsel for Oyama, Mr. Dean Acheson, avoided a direct challenge of these decisions by paying less attention to the rights of the alien father while stressing the denial of equal protection to his citizen son. This strategem proved successful, Chief Justice Vinson adopting this argument as the basis of his decison for a six-judge majority. He concluded that the state law discriminated against Fred Oyama and that the discrimination was based solely on his parent's country of origin. Fred Oyama had to overcome the statutory presumption that a conveyance financed by his father and recorded in his name was not a gift but a method of evading the Alien Land Law. Fred was also penalized because of the alleged failure of his father to file reports required of guardians, and thus "the father's deeds were visited on the son." An "onerous burden of proof" had to be assumed by Fred Oyama which "need not be borne by California children generally."

The state argued that this discrimination was necessary to prevent evasion of the statute. One way of countering this claim would have been to challenge the constitutionality of the law's prohibition against the ownership of agricultural land by ineligible aliens. The Chief Justice's temperament led him to seek a less drastic solution. He assumed, "for purposes of argument only," the constitutionality of the prohibition. But even so, there are constitutional limits "to the means which may be used to enforce it." Here the state's right to formulate its policy on landowning was in conflict with the right of American citizens to own land anywhere in the United States. "Where these two rights clash, the rights of a citizen may not be subordinated merely because of his father's country of origin."

The Chief Justice's 13-page opinion was merely a curtain-raiser for 42 pages of concurrence and dissent by seven of his colleagues. In fact, Justice Frankfurter was the only member of the Court to acquiesce silently in the ingenious but highly dubious reasoning of the Chief Justice. In two concurring opinions, the Black-Douglas and Murphy-Rutledge teams made it clear that they would have much preferred to arrive at Vinson's result by an unequivocal holding that the prohibition on alien landholding in the California law violated the equal protection clause and conflicted with federal laws and treaties governing the immigration of aliens and their rights after arrival in the United States. For good measure, they suggested that the Charter of the United Nations was also violated. Justice Murphy's opinion traced in detail the history of racial discrimination in California which resulted in this statute, which he characterized as "racism in one of its most malignant forms."

Justice Reed, joined by Burton, and Justice Jackson wrote dissenting opinions. Both justices rather convincingly demonstrated the illogic of the Vinson opinion. Justice Jackson summed up the case in his first paragraph:

> I am unable to see how this Court logically can set aside the judgment unless it is prepared to invalidate the California Alien Land Laws, on which it is based. If this judgment of escheat seems harsh as to the Oyamas, it is only because it faithfully carries out a legislative policy, the validity of which this Court does not question.

None of the three dissenters indicated how he would vote if the question of invalidating the land law had been reached, but clearly they would have upheld the law; for, if any one of them had considered the law unconstitutional, he could have joined with the four concurring justices to achieve a majority for that position.

From the civil liberties point of view, then, to criticize the Vinson opinon is to look a gift horse in the mouth. It assumed the constitutionality of a noxious statute, but it invalidated the only effective method of securing its enforcement, as is shown by the fact that the California Attorney General immediately after the decision canceled all statutory escheat actions under this act.[31]

That the decision had also had an important educational effect on the Supreme Court itself became evident when *Takahashi* v. *Fish and Game Commission* was decided only five months later. Here the issue was California's wartime attempt to ban Japanese from commercial fishing. A 1943 amendment to the state fish and game code prohibited the issuance of fishing licenses to "alien Japanese." In 1945 the language was changed to "any person ineligible to citizenship," in an attempt to put the ban on a less questionable constitutional footing. A seven-judge majority, speaking through Justice Black, flatly declared the prohibition unconstitutional. This result did not require the overruling of any precedents; but certainly a strong case could have been made for the code provision on the basis of a number of earlier Supreme Court decisions—and, in fact, Justice Reed did so in his dissent.

California argued that since the federal government had created a special class of aliens ineligible to citizenship, based in part on criteria of race and color, the state was free to use the same classification in its statutes. But Black pointed out the special position and powers of the federal government in relation to immigration and naturalization and the applicability of the Fourteenth Amendment and protective federal legislation to "all persons." He did not deny that a state might apply some laws "exclusively to its alien inhabitants as a class" but held that such power "is confined within narrow limits." He did have some difficulty in disposing of the analogy to the California Alien Land Law, the empty shell of which the Oyama case had left standing. Having no alternative but to assume the continued validity of that law, Black proceeded to distinguish it on the perfectly indisputable ground that it dealt with land while here the concern was with fish!

Vinson, Frankfurter, and Burton joined Black, Douglas, Murphy, and Rutledge to make up the majority in Takahashi, with no explanation for the change in their views since Oyama. Reed's dissent, in which Jackson joined, pointed out that the federal government itself gave citizens certain rights superior to those of aliens (though not particular classes of aliens) in the ownership of land and in exploiting natural resources and that the California Alien Land Law was still constitutional. All this was quite sound and helped to make clear what the Black opinion had tried not to emphasize—namely, that the Supreme Court was here adopting a new policy the support for which was to be sought not in the precedents but in the consciences of the justices and in the world situation which makes any American failure to live up to its equalitarian ideals a matter of vital concern for the future of democracy.

VII. *Separate and Unequal*

In his monumental study of the Negro problem in the United States, Gunnar Myrdal wrote:

> From the point of view of the American Creed the status accorded the Negro in America represents nothing more and nothing less than a century-long lag of public morals. In principle the Negro problem was settled long ago; in practice the solution is not yet effectuated. The Negro in America has not yet been given the elemental civil and political rights of formal democracy, including a fair opportunity to earn his living, upon which a general accord was already won when the American Creed was first taking form.[1]

The power of law to change folkways has long been in dispute. But it is clear that the Supreme Court, which should, of all federal agencies, be most sensitive to the tenets of the American Creed, has not until recently exhibited much concern over this lag in public morals or sought to use its great power to reduce the gap between theory and practice. Rather, the Court's talents and powers have historically been devoted to rationalizing the gap and reconciling it with constitutional requirements.

The most important of these rationalizations is the "separate but equal" formula by which the Court for decades justified various types of segregated treatment for Negroes. The present chapter seeks to sketch in the past development of this concept and to examine its treatment by the Vinson Court.[2]

SEGREGATION IN TRANSPORTATION

The Supreme Court has followed a tortuous and not too intellectually respectable path in its dealings with the segregation issue on public carriers. In its first case, decided in 1873, the Court upheld the damage claim of a Negro forcibly ejected from the "white" car of a railway operating into the District of Columbia.[3] The congressional authorization for this road had specified that "no person shall be excluded from the cars on account of color." By this decision the Court recognized that the provision of separate cars for whites and Negroes on a train was in itself discrimination, and it upheld the right of Congress to prohibit such discrimination, at least in the District of Columbia.

Five years later came *Hall* v. *DeCuir*. In this case an 1869 Louisiana reconstruction statute *prohibiting* discrimination on account of race or color against passengers on public conveyances traveling in the state was invoked by a Negro woman who was refused accommodations in the "white" cabin on a packet steamer running between New Orleans and Vicksburg, Mississippi. Her victory in the state court was reversed by the Supreme Court, which held the Louisiana statute unconstitutional as a burden on interstate commerce. Chief Justice Waite regarded this matter as one on which uniformity of practice was required: "No carrier of passengers can conduct his business with satisfaction to himself, or comfort to those employing him, if on one side of a State line his passengers, both white and colored, must be permitted to occupy the same cabin, and on the other be kept separate." Consequently, only Congress could adopt regulations on this subject, and, in the absence of congressional legislation, the owner of the steamboat could enforce such rules and regulations for the disposition of passengers "within Louisiana or without" as seemed to him "most for the interest of all concerned."

There was, to be sure, some congressional legislation which might have seemed relevant here. The Civil Rights Act of 1875 provided that all persons within the jurisdiction of the United States, regardless of race and color, were entitled to the enjoyment of equal accommodations and privileges of inns, public conveyances, theaters, and other places of public amusement.[4] In 1883 there came up for decision by the Supreme Court the *Civil Rights Cases*, one of which arose out of the exclusion of a Negro woman from the ladies' car on an interstate train. The rationale of *Hall* v. *DeCuir* would have seemed to approve application of the 1875 act in these circumstances, justified by congressional power to regulate interstate commerce. Instead, however, the

Court held the act unconstitutional as applied in this entire group of cases, on the ground that the Fourteenth Amendment afforded protection only against "state" action, not that of private persons, and that Congress was limited to the adoption of "corrective" legislation which would make the constitutional ban on discriminatory *state* action effective. The contention that discriminatory treatment was a badge of slave status and therefore unconstitutional under the Thirteenth Amendment was summarily rejected.

This decision still left the DeCuir case and the commerce clause as possible barriers to official state segregation attempts—but not for long. An 1888 Mississippi statute required all railways carrying passengers in the state to provide "equal but separate" accommodations for white and Negro passengers. It seemed obvious that the Supreme Court, which in DeCuir had declared a state statute *prohibiting* segregation an unconstitutional burden on interstate commerce, would have to make a similar holding against a state statute *requiring* discrimination. By a seven to two vote, however, the Court avoided the simple and honest logic of this position by acceptance of Mississippi's contention that the act applied solely to commerce within the state.[5] The fact that the journey involved in the DeCuir case was also intrastate was conveniently disregarded.

This decision left as the final possible bulwark against Jim Crow legislation the Fourteenth Amendment provisions guaranteeing equal protection of the laws. This defense fell in *Plessy* v. *Ferguson*, decided in 1896. Here a Louisiana statute requiring the segregation of the two races on public carriers was held by the Supreme Court not to violate the Fourteenth Amendment. Said Justice Brown:

> The object of the amendment was undoubtedly to enforce the absolute equality of the two races before the law, but, in the nature of things, it could not have been intended to abolish distinctions based upon color, or to enforce social, as distinguished from political, equality, or a commingling of the two races upon terms unsatisfactory to either.

The Court denied that the enforced separation of the two races stamped the colored race with a "badge of inferiority." "If this be so, it is not by reason of anything found in the act, but solely because the colored race chooses to put that construction upon it." Justice Harlan dissented, protesting that "our Constitution is color-blind, and neither knows nor tolerates classes among citizens."

Thus *Plessy* v. *Ferguson* completed the judicial foundation for state segregation statutes and gave the Supreme Court's blessing to the view that segregation was compatible with equality. "Separate but equal" was the formula for reconciling the protection of the Fourteenth Amendment with a system of state-enforced segregation.

With the Fourteenth Amendment thus eliminated, the attack on segregation in public transportation was forced to revive the argument that state action in this field constituted a burden on interstate commerce. After all, *Hall* v. *DeCuir* had not been overruled, it had merely been distinguished. It was almost half a century after *Plessy* v. *Ferguson* before this strategy won any success, however. The Court avoided the issue in a variety of ways. In a Kentucky case they did it by attributing the segregation to the regulations of an interstate carrier, conveniently disregarding the fact that the Kentucky "separate-coach" law was responsible for the carrier's regulations.[6] In another case where an injunction was sought against the Oklahoma "separate-coach" law of 1907, the Court denied that a case for relief in equity had been made out.[7] However, the decision insisted that the separate but equal standard demanded "substantial equality of treatment of persons traveling under like conditions," and the failure to supply first-class accommodations for Negroes because there was less demand for them was rebuked by Justice Hughes in the McCabe case.

In a third and unusually flagrant case, the Court avoided a consideration of the effect of the Kentucky "separate-coach" law upon interstate commerce by holding that a railroad operating from Cincinnati, Ohio, into Kentucky, carrying 80 per cent of its passengers interstate, was nevertheless an intrastate carrier so far as its operations in Kentucky were concerned.[8] This decision was reached in spite of the fact that the Court five years earlier, in a different type of case, had ruled that the same operation by the same company was interstate commerce.[9]

It remained for the Roosevelt Court to hand down the first

decision since 1873 favorable to the Negro in a Jim Crow transportation case. Arthur W. Mitchell, a Negro congressman from Illinois, was ejected from Pullman accommodations on an interstate train as it was entering Arkansas, where state law required segregation. Mitchell took the novel step of filing a complaint with the Interstate Commerce Commission alleging discriminatory action in violation of the Interstate Commerce Act. The failure of the railroad to furnish anything except second-class facilities for Negroes was held by the ICC not to constitute "unjust or undue" discrimination, but the Supreme Court upheld Mitchell's complaint that he had been denied equality of treatment.[10] The ruling, however, did not challenge the constitutionality of segregation in interstate commerce. It merely insisted that accommodations must be "substantially equal" to meet the constitutional test, and from this point of view went no further than the 1914 McCabe decision.

There was evident, however, a changed temper on the Court, which needed merely the appropriate occasion to become manifest. The opportunity came in 1946, when *Morgan* v. *Virginia* was decided. This case arose out of the prosecution of a Negro woman who was making an interstate bus trip from Virginia to Baltimore and who refused to move to the back of the bus on the request of the driver so that her seat would be available for white passengers. The Virginia supreme court affirmed her conviction. The United States Supreme Court, however, found the state Jim Crow law to be a burden on commerce in a matter where uniformity was necessary.

"It seems clear to me," said Justice Reed for the Court, "that seating arrangements for the different races in interstate motor travel require a single, uniform rule to promote and protect national travel." His decision emphasized that he was following *Hall* v. *DeCuir;* but Burton, the sole dissenter, argued that DeCuir did not require the conclusion reached by the Court here. He also noted that, in following DeCuir, the Court was not only invalidating the laws of the ten states which require segregation but also the laws of the eighteen states where segregation was prohibited. Burton contended that the record of the Morgan proceedings contained no findings of fact to demonstrate the extent of the burden on commerce resulting from the Virginia statute. The Court had therefore been unable "to make that necessary 'appraisal and accommodation of the competing demands of the state and national interests involved' which should be the foundation for passing upon the validity of a state statute of long standing and of important local significance in the exercise of the state police power."

The Court, having thus willingly rediscovered the relationship of the commerce clause to segregation, in its very next case was embarrassed to find that, as Burton had warned, the commerce clause could be invoked to protect as well as to condemn discrimination. In *Bob-Lo Excursion Co.* v. *Michigan*, a 1948 case, the Michigan Civil Rights Act was invoked against a Detroit amusement park company which operated a steamboat to an island on the Canadian side of the Detroit River. The company had refused to transport a Negro girl, who was in the company of some forty white girls, to the island on their boat, and their defense was that the state law could have no applicability to foreign commerce. The Court majority, however, resolved the dilemma by holding that this commerce, though technically foreign, was actually "highly local," the island being "economically and socially, though not politically, an amusement adjunct of the city of Detroit." The DeCuir and Morgan cases were distinguished on the ground that they did not involve such "locally insulated" situations. Moreover, in neither of those cases had complete exclusion from transportation facilities been attempted. Jackson and Vinson, dissenting, felt that the Court majority was expanding state power to include control over foreign commerce because it agreed with the state policy involved. "The Court admits that the commerce involved in this case is foreign commerce, but subjects it to the state police power on the ground that it is not very foreign."

Bob-Lo highlighted the Court's problem in attempting to achieve equalitarian goals through the cold-blooded and clumsy constitutional concept of commerce. Justice Douglas gave expression to this feeling in his concurring opinion; he would have preferred to base the decision upon the more appealing foundation of the equal protection clause. The 1950 case of *Henderson*

v. *United States* offered the Court an opportunity to abandon the "separate but equal" doctrine in favor of the clear-cut proposition that segregation, no matter how equal the facilities, is incompatible with the Constitution. The controversy concerned dining-car service for Negroes on the Southern Railway between Washington and Atlanta and arose out of the fact that ten tables in the dining car were reserved for white passengers and one table, separated from the others by a curtain, for Negro passengers. The Supreme Court solved the case by applying the Mitchell rule, holding that this arbitrary allocation interfered with equal access of passengers to facilities in violation of the Interstate Commerce Act. Thus the case was disposed of without reaching the broader constitutional issue, and the rule of "separate but equal" escaped unscathed.[11]

SEGREGATION IN EDUCATION

The fraudulent character of the protection afforded by the separate but equal rule is perhaps even more obvious in the field of education than in transportation. By any test that may be applied, Negro schools in states where segregation is the rule have been markedly inferior to white schools. For many years, however, the Supreme Court persistently avoided getting itself into situations where it would have to recognize this fact.

The story here starts in 1899, with *Cumming* v. *Richmond County Board of Education.* This case arose out of the decision of a Georgia school board to discontinue the existing Negro high school in order to use the building and facilities for Negro elementary education. No new high school for Negroes was established, though the existing white high schools were, of course, continued. Negro taxpayers sought to restrain the school board from using money to support white high schools until equal facilities for Negro students were provided. The unanimous Supreme Court decision avoided discussion of the segregation issue. It denied that discontinuance of the Negro high school was a violation of equal protection of the laws but laid more stress on the conclusion that an injunction which would close the white high schools was not the proper legal remedy and would not help the colored children. Justice Harlan concluded with a reminder that the management of schools was a state matter in which the federal government could intervene only in the case of a "clear and unmistakable disregard" of constitutional rights.

A Kentucky law requiring segregation of white and Negro students in all educational institutions, private and public, was upheld as applied to a private institution in a 1908 case, *Berea College* v. *Kentucky*. Again the Court found a way to avoid passing on the segregation issue. It argued that this was merely a matter between Kentucky and a corporation which it had created. The statute could be regarded as an amendment to the college's corporate charter, and the state could withhold privileges from one of its corporations which it could not constitutionally withhold from an individual. By separating the statutory provisions relative to corporations from the rest of the act, the Court majority escaped a discussion of the personal constitutional rights involved. Justices Harlan and Day, dissenting, contended that the Court should meet the issue head-on and not hide behind the law of corporations. They were convinced that, at least as applied to private institutions where there was "voluntary meeting" of the two races "for innocent purposes," this statute was definitely unconstitutional. The concern of the majority to localize the decision upon the corporation basis indicated that even they had doubts as to the constitutionality of enforced segregation in other circumstances.

Having successfully avoided the issue twice, the Court then felt able to act as though established practice had foreclosed discussion of the question. The 1927 case of *Gong Lum* v. *Rice* concerned a child of Chinese descent who was required to attend a Negro school in Mississippi under the state constitutional obligation that separate schools be maintained for children of "the white and colored races." As to the equal protection problem posed by this arrangement, Chief Justice Taft said for the Court: "Were this a new question, it would call for a very full argument and consideration, but we think that it is the same question which has been many times decided to be within the constitutional power of the state legislature to settle without intervention of the federal courts under the federal Constitution." The fifteen state and lower federal court decisions cited by the Chief Justice to support this conclusion could not hide the fact that there had been no Supreme Court ruling directly on the issue of segregation in educational institutions and that there had never been "full argument and consideration" by that body.

As in the transportation field, the pattern of segregation in education thus achieved a solid constitutional foundation. The more liberally oriented Court of the latter 1930's was able, however, again as in the transportation area, to effect a substantial change of direction within the confines of the doctrine by stressing the need for *equality* in segregation. Missouri refused to admit Negroes to its state law school, providing instead that the state would pay tuition fees for any of its Negro citizens who wished to attend law schools in neighboring states where segregation was not enforced. Lloyd Gaines refused this arrangement and brought suit to compel the registrar of the University of Missouri to admit him as a law student. The Supreme Court through Chief Justice Hughes upheld Gaines's position.[12] The limited demand for legal education within the state could not justify Missouri in shifting its responsibility to provide equal educational opportunities to some other state. By operating a white law school, the state was providing privileges to white students which it denied to Negroes because of their race. Equality of treatment was the only basis on which segregation was constitutionally justifiable. "The admissibility of laws separating the races in the enjoyment of privileges afforded by the State rests wholly upon the equality of the privileges which the laws give to the separated groups within the State." Justice McReynolds, dissenting along with Butler, expressed the interesting nonjudicial opinion that for Missouri to give up the practice of segregation in her schools would "damnify both races."

Missouri met this ruling by setting up a separate, and very inferior, law school for Negroes. However, the Court had given sufficient indication of its intention to insist on "substantial equality" in segregated schools to encourage further judicial tests. It was a decade later before action returned to the Supreme Court level. *Sipuel v. Board of Regents of the University of Oklahoma* (1948) involved the flat exclusion of a Negro from the Oklahoma law school and was decided by the Court in a brief per curiam opinion reaffirming the principle of the Gaines case. There followed some legal skirmishing, during which the Negro student involved, Miss Ada Sipuel, complicated the record by changing her name to Fisher by marriage. After the Supreme Court's decision, the Oklahoma courts proceeded on the assumption that a separate law school for Negroes would meet the Court's verdict. The actual order issued by the state district court was that, unless and until a separate school of law for Negroes was established, the university board of regents was either to enrol Mrs. Fisher in the first-year law class at the University or not enrol any other applicant for that class until a separate law school was established. The court order added that if a separate law school was set up, the board of regents was not to enrol Mrs. Fisher at the University of Oklahoma.

Mrs. Fisher did not regard this order as complying with the Supreme Court's mandate and asked the Court's permission to file a writ of mandamus to compel compliance. The Supreme Court refused the request, on the ground that the question whether "a state might not satisfy the equal protection clause . . . by establishing a separate school for Negroes" was not an issue in the case.[13] Thus the Court again reiterated its determination not to be drawn into a discussion of the constitutionality of enforced segregation, though Murphy thought that Mrs. Fisher was entitled to a hearing to determine whether the Oklahoma courts were evading the Sipuel decision. Rutledge went further; he was convinced that a separate law school for Negroes would not meet the Court's mandate, if for no other reason than the delay that would be involved in setting it up, and he added that "in my comprehension the equality required was equality in fact, not in legal fiction."

While this emphasis on the need for real equality was encouraging, segregation per se retained full constitutional approval. The next step was to attack this system directly and with force, as was done in two cases decided by the Court in 1950. The first, *McLaurin* v. *Oklahoma State Regents*, concerned a compromise effort made by Oklahoma to admit Negroes to white schools but on a segregated basis. The Oklahoma legislature, in pursuance to the Sipuel decision and under the compulsion of legal proceedings which McLaurin had begun to secure admission to the state university as a Ph.D. candidate in education, amended the state law to permit the admission of Negroes to institutions of higher learning in cases where such institutions offered courses not available in the Negro schools. The amendment provided, however, that the program of instruction for such Negro students should be given "upon a segregated basis." Accordingly, McLaurin was admitted to the University of Oklahoma graduate school but was required to sit apart at a designated desk in an anteroom adjoining the classroom; to sit at a designated desk on the mezzanine floor of the library, but not to use the desks in the regular reading-room; and to sit at a designated table and to eat at a different time from the other students in the school cafeteria.

McLaurin took legal action to modify these conditions as contrary to the Fourteenth Amendment, but failed in the federal district court. Before a hearing was held on his appeal to the Supreme Court, the conditions of his segregation from other students were changed. He was assigned a seat in the classroom in a row specified for colored students, was given a table on the main floor of the library, and was permitted to eat in the cafeteria like other students, though at a special table. These separations, which the state defended as "merely nominal," were declared unconstitutional by a unanimous Court. Such restrictions on McLaurin, Chief Justice Vinson wrote, "impair and inhibit his ability to study, to engage in discussions and exchange views with other students, and, in general, to learn his profession." When it was argued that white students still might refuse to associate with McLaurin even if the restrictions were lifted, Vinson replied that this consideration, if true, was irrelevant:

> There is a vast difference—a Constitutional difference—between restrictions imposed by the state which prohibit the intellectual commingling of students, and the refusal of individuals to commingle where the state presents no such bar. . . . The removal of the state restrictions will not necessarily abate individual and group predilections, prejudices and choices. But at the very least, the state will not be depriving appellant of the opportunity to secure acceptance by his fellow students on his own merits.

The second case, decided the same day, *Sweatt* v. *Painter*, was the more celebrated of the two. It involved the petition of a Negro student for admission to the University of Texas Law School, and in support of his claim a group of 188 of the nation's leading law professors filed a brief. The facts were that Sweatt had applied for admission to the law school in 1946 and had been rejected solely because he was a Negro. He then sought mandamus to compel his admission. The trial court recognized that he was entitled to the opportunity for a legal education but, instead of granting the relief asked, continued the case for six months to allow the state to supply substantially equal facilities in a separate school for Negroes. The university proceeded to set up such a school, to open in 1947. Sweatt refused to attend and secured a new hearing on the issue of the equality of facilities at the newly established school. The Texas courts ruled that the "privileges, advantages, and oportunities for the study of law" at the Negro law school were "substantially equivalent" to those available at the university law school.

This conclusion the Supreme Court held unfounded. Chief Justice Vinson's opinion contrasted the faculties, the student bodies, the libraries, the alumni, and the other facilities of the two institutions. In comparison with the University of Texas Law School, judged by the Court to be "one of the nation's ranking law schools," was the Negro law school with five full-time professors, a student body of 23, a library of 16,500 volumes, and one alumnus who had become a member of the Texas bar. Even more important, the Court went on, were

> those qualities which are incapable of objective measurement but which make for greatness in a law school. Such qualities, to name but a few, include reputation of the faculty, experience of the administration, position and influence of the alumni, standing in the community, traditions and prestige. It is difficult to believe that one who had a free choice between these law schools would consider the question close.

Finally, the Court considered that a law school limited to Negroes, a minority of the Texas population, could not be an effective "proving ground for legal learning and practice":

> The law school to which Texas is willing to admit petitioner excludes from its student body members of the racial groups which number 85%

of the population of the State and include most of the lawyers, witnesses, jurors, judges and other officials with whom petitioner will inevitably be dealing when he becomes a member of the Texas Bar. With such a substantial and significant segment of society excluded, we cannot conclude that the education offered petitioner is substantially equal to that which he would receive if admitted to the University of Texas Law School.

This language makes it clear that the Supreme Court had concluded that no law school limited to Negroes could meet the requirement of the equal protection clause. But the Court based its conclusion on the necessary and inescapable "inequality" of the education offered by such schools, not upon a condemnation of the principle of segregation. The brief of the law-school professors had sought a clear-cut re-examination of the doctrine of *Plessy v. Ferguson.* They had attempted to capitalize on the fact that there was no Supreme Court decision definitely approving the principle of segregation in education—Gong Lum had not done so directly—with the result that educational segregation could be declared unconstitutional without overruling any precedents. Chief Justice Vinson's decision announced at the outset, however, that the Court would ignore the "broader issues" which had been urged for consideration and "adhere to the principle of deciding constitutional questions only in the context of the particular case before the Court." And at the conclusion of the decision he repeated in more specific terms that the Court had not felt it necessary to "reach petitioner's contention that Plessy v. Ferguson should be reexamined in the light of contemporary knowledge respecting the purposes of the Fourteenth Amendment and the effects of racial segregation."

The Court's action in choosing the narrower rather than the broader basis for its decision was no doubt responsible for the unanimity which it achieved, and its united front in this sector was a matter of great psychological significance. Moreover, the rationale of the decision seemed definitely to condemn segregation, at least in the field of higher education, by holding that segregated schools are necessarily "unequal"; and the actual mandate in the Sweatt case was as forthright and definite as anyone could have asked for: "We hold that the Equal Protection Clause of the Fourteenth Amendment requires that petitioner be admitted to the University of Texas Law School."

On the other hand, the failure of the Supreme Court definitely to come to grips with the essential principle of segregation by a reconsideration of *Plessy* v. *Ferguson* could mean only that the Court would continue to be besieged with cases in this field. For one reason, since the constitutional status of segregation was left to depend upon actual equality or nonequality of educational facilities for the two races, there were bound to be conflicting determinations in lower courts which the Court would be asked to review. Thus only a few months after the Sweatt decision, a federal judge in North Carolina held that that state's law school for Negroes met the equal-facilities test.[14] In 1952 the Florida supreme court denied admission of Negroes to the University of Florida on the ground that the facilities at Florida A. and M. College for Negroes were equal.[15]

In the second place, on Lincoln's theory that no question is settled until it is settled right, interested parties were bound to persist in trying to get from the Court a direct holding that segregation was unconstitutional. Considering the temper of the times and the significance of the world-wide battle against racial discrimination, it was obvious that the Supreme Court could not find peaceful refuge in a doctrine which gives constitutional respectability to a policy of racial segregation.

And so the issue continued to knock on the Court's portals. In March, 1952, the Court was able to avoid the problem in a case involving the University of Tennessee. A federal judge had ruled that four Tennessee Negroes must be admitted to the state university because equal facilities were not available elsewhere in the state. They appealed this ruling, contending that its basis should have been the unconstitutionality of the state segregation law; but, because their right to admission had been granted, the Supreme Court refused to hear their case.[16]

Pressure for a decision directly on the segregation issue then shifted to several pending cases involving public education at the primary and secondary levels. All the other recent cases had concerned graduate professional or at least university education, where the breaking-down of segregation barriers presented somewhat less of a problem because of the comparatively few Negro students involved. But in 1951 a proceeding was begun in South Carolina which threatened far-reaching consequences.

A three-judge federal court there ruled that the Negro educational facilities in Clarendon County were not equal, ordered that they be made equal, and directed the school officials to report their progress within six months. The persons who instigated the suit were not satisfied with this ruling and appealed to the Supreme Court without waiting for the report to be made. In January, 1952, the Court held that until the lower court had received the report and had had an opportunity to take whatever action it deemed appropriate in light of the report, it would be premature for the Supreme Court to intervene.[17]

While the Court thus won a brief respite, the case was back before the term was over, and on June 9, 1952, the Court noted "probable jurisdiction" in the South Carolina case and also one involving segregation in the public schools of Topeka, Kansas.[18] Events thus seemed to be moving toward a climacteric in the 1952 term. In preparation for an adverse decision from the Court, Governor Byrnes of South Carolina (a former justice of the Supreme Court) announced that the state would abandon its system of public education and turn over its schools to private groups if segregation was invalidated,[19] and a state constitutional amendment to make this step possible was adopted in November, 1952.

However, the Supreme Court apparently found the issue so complex and difficult that it resorted to almost unprecedented delaying tactics. At the beginning of the 1952 term, on October 9, it postponed arguments in the cases from October 14 to December 8, which the newspapers promptly noted was after the presidential election. The reason given by the Court for the postponement, however, was to permit two additional segregation cases to be heard at the same time.[20] One of these new cases came from Virginia, where in March, 1952, a three-judge federal court had unanimously upheld the constitutionality of Virginia school segregation laws but found that facilities were not equal and ordered them to be made so.[21] The second was a case pending in the court of appeals for the District of Columbia, where a refusal to admit Negro pupils to a segregated white school was under attack.[22] In all four cases, then, the lower courts had upheld segregation laws but had demanded that educational facilities be equal.

Before the date set for the postponed hearings, a fifth case was added to the group.[23] A Delaware supreme court order admitting Negro pupils to two white high schools in Wilmington was appealed by the state of Delaware, which argued that the school authorities should be given a reasonable time to equalize Negro school facilities. The hearings on these five cases occupied three days, December 9–11, and the Court's decision was confidently anticipated before the end of the term. But on June 8, 1953, the Court announced the cases would be reargued on October 12 and set out a series of five questions to which counsel were requested to address themselves.[24] Two of the five questions related to the intent of the Congress and the state legislatures which drafted and ratified the Fourteenth Amendment and whether they understood that it would abolish segregation in public schools. Since historical evidence is not likely to prove very conclusive on this point, more interest centers on the questions which indicate that the Court had been considering the possibility of holding segregation unconstitutional but of permitting some delay in putting the new unsegregated system into effect. The actual language of question 4 (b) was, assuming that segregation is unconstitutional, "may this Court, in the exercise of its equity powers, permit an effective gradual adjustment to be brought about from existing segregated systems to a system not based on color distinctions?" Further, the Court queried whether, if it did take this approach, it should formulate detailed decrees, appoint a special master to take evidence and recommend specific terms, or remand the cases to the courts of first instance to frame the decrees. These questions indicate the care with which the Court was approaching an issue potentially more explosive than any since the Dred Scott case.

DISCRIMINATION IN HOUSING AND EMPLOYMENT

In addition to various forms of unofficial and public pressures, two legal devices have been utilized to maintain residential segregation of Negroes. The first method was adoption of municipal segregation ordinances, which appear to have been employed initially by Baltimore in 1910. Shortly afterward, the same idea was adopted by other southern cities. The Louisville ordinance came before the Supreme Court in the 1917 case of *Buchanan* v. *Warley* and was invalidated on the ground that it was an unconstitutional interference with the right of a property owner to dispose of his real estate. Thus property rights proved to be a more effective weapon against segregation than the more amorphous civil rights urged in the earlier cases, such as *Plessy* v. *Ferguson.* Attempts to circumvent the Buchanan decision were defeated in both state and federal courts, and by 1930 the unconstitutionality of municipal segregation ordinances was firmly established.[25]

The field was thus left to the second protective device—restrictive covenants entered into by property owners binding themselves not to sell or lease their property to Negroes or other racial, national, or religious groups. Because this type of agreement results from action by private persons, not by the state, it was at first generally successful in meeting constitutional tests.

The first restrictive-covenant case to reach the Supreme Court was *Corrigan* v. *Buckley*, which arose in the District of Columbia. This 1926 case saw the property owner who had broken the covenant alleging in defense that it was an infringement of the Constitution and contrary to public policy. Lower-court decisions denying these charges were upheld by the Supreme Court when it dismissed the appeal on grounds of lack of jurisdiction. Justice Sanford for the Court held that such covenants were not contrary to the Constitution or to public policy. Important in the light of later action, he added that the question whether lower-court decrees enforcing the covenants were in themselves violative of the Fifth and Fourteenth Amendments had not been properly raised by the petition on appeal but were "likewise lacking in substance." In several subsequent cases arising in the District of Columbia, which were decided by the lower courts on the authority of the Corrigan case, the Supreme Court denied certiorari.

An indication of a rift in the Court's solid front on this issue came in 1945, when Justices Murphy and Rutledge dissented from the Court's refusal to grant certiorari in another Disirct of Columbia restrictive-covenant case.[26] Events moved rapidly from that point, and in 1948 the Court handed down two unanimous decisions apparently terminating the use of restrictive covenants by denying them judicial enforcement. The first decision, *Shelley* v. *Kraemer,* concerned actions brought to enforce restrictive covenants in the states of Missouri and Michigan. Chief Justice Vinson found it relatively easy to reconcile the Court's new view with its previous decisions. *Corrigan* v. *Buckley,* he pointed out, had concerned only the right of private individuals to enter into such covenants, and he here reiterated the conclusion of the Corrigan case that

> restrictive agreements standing alone cannot be regarded as a violation of any right guaranteed . . . by the Fourteenth Amendment. So long as the purposes of those agreements are effectuated by voluntary adherence to their terms, it would appear clear that there has been no action by the State and the provisions of the Amendment have not been violated.

But in *Shelley* v. *Kraemer* the Court was willing to push beyond this point and to consider the status of action by state courts to enforce these covenants. "It cannot be doubted," said the Chief Justice, "that among the civil rights intended to be protected from discriminatory state action by the Fourteenth Amendment are the rights to acquire, enjoy, own and dispose of property." The question, then, was whether judicial enforcement of restrictive covenants amounted to "state action." The Court answered:

> We have no doubt that there has been state action in these cases in the full and complete sense of the phrase. The undisputed facts disclose that petitioners were willing purchasers of properties upon which they desired to establish homes. The owners of the properties were willing

sellers; and contracts of sale were accordingly consummated. It is clear that but for the active intervention of the state courts, supported by the full panoply of state power, petitioners would have been free to occupy the properties in question without restraint.

The fact that "the particular pattern of discrimination, which the State has enforced, was defined initially by the terms of a private agreement" made no difference. "State action, as that phrase is understood for the purposes of the Fourteenth Amendment, refers to exertions of state power in all forms." The Court concluded:

> We hold that in granting judicial enforcement of the restrictive agreements in these cases, the States have denied petitioners the equal protection of the laws and that, therefore, the action of the state courts cannot stand. . . . Having so decided, we find it unnecessary to consider whether petitioners have also been deprived of property without due process of law or denied privileges and immunities of citizens of the United States.

The second decision, *Hurd* v. *Hodge*, involved two cases arising in the District of Columbia, where the equal protection clause could not be invoked. Consequently, it was contended that judicial enforcement was forbidden by the due process clause of the Fifth Amendment. The Court, speaking again through the Chief Justice, found it unnecessary to base its decision upon constitutional grounds at all. Primary reliance was placed upon section 1 of the Civil Rights Act of 1866, which was adopted by the same Congress that initiated the Fourteenth Amendment. The statute guarantees to "all citizens" the same rights as "white citizens . . . to inherit, purchase, lease, sell, hold, and convey real and personal property." The Court held that judicial enforcement of restrictive covenants would be a violation of this section. Even in the absence of the statute, however, the Court indicated that judicial enforcement would be contrary to the public policy of the United States, which the Supreme Court would have power to correct in the exercise of its supervisory powers over the courts of the District of Columbia. These cases involved federal court action of a type which, if taken by state courts, would, as *Shelley* v. *Kraemer* had just held, violate the Fourteenth Amendment:

> It is not consistent with the public policy of the United States to permit federal courts in the Nation's capital to exercise general equitable powers to compel action denied the state courts where such state action has been held to be violative of the guaranty of the equal protection of the laws. We cannot presume that the public policy of the United States manifests a lesser concern for the protection of such basic rights against discriminatory action of federal courts than against such action taken by the courts of the States.

Justice Frankfurter, concurring in the Hurd case, would have preferred to base the decision on the special obligations of the Court in employing its discretion in an equity proceeding, such as was here involved:

> Equity is rooted in conscience. . . . In good conscience, it cannot be "the exercise of sound judicial discretion" by a federal court to grant the relief here asked for when the authorization of such an injunction by the States of the Union violates the Constitution.

Justices Reed, Jackson, and Rutledge did not participate in either of the decisions, reportedly because each of them owned property which was covered by a restrictive covenant.

By these two decisions, the Court skilfully brought itself into line with the liberal position on civil rights without harming a hair on the head of its apparently contrary precedents. The Court adhered to its earlier view that the covenants were not in themselves illegal. In doing so, it rejected without comment the novel argument urged upon it that the United States' treaty obligations under the Preamble and Articles 55 (c) and 56 of the United Nations Charter nullified such restrictive covenants. But what the Court gave by one hand it immediately took away by the other through its holding that the covenants, though valid, were not judicially enforcible.

Actually, however, it soon appeared that the decision was a little too clever. Since the Court had carefully preserved the legality of restrictive covenants, could not the signer of a covenant who breached its provisions be sued for damages by other participants in the covenant? In 1949 the Missouri supreme court took exactly this position. [27] The following year a federal district court in the District of Columbia came to precisely the opposite conclusion.[28]

In 1953 the Supreme Court in *Barrows* v. *Jackson* affirmed that the latter view was correct. A California property owner who had failed to live up to the conditions of a covenant was sued by three neighbors on the ground that the value of their property had dropped sharply since Negroes moved in. Six justices, speaking through Minton, said that the Supreme Court would not permit or require California to coerce a property owner to pay damages for failure to observe a covenant that California had no right to incorporate in a statute or enforce in equity and which federal courts could not enforce because of its being contrary to public policy.

Minton's position, while a thoroughly logical extension of the Shelley holding, was not without its difficulties; for the party who breached the covenant and "damaged" the property of her neighbors was contending that she should not be compelled to pay for that damage because the covenant unconstitutionally discriminated against non-Caucasians. But these unidentified non-Caucasians were not before the Court or directly involved in this case in any way, and the Court as a general rule does not permit a litigant to defend by invoking the constitutional rights of a third party. Minton, however, regarded this situation as "unique," justifying relaxation of the normal rule, for in no other way would it be possible to "close the gap to the use of this covenant, so universally condemned by the courts."

Chief Justice Vinson, author of the Shelley opinion, dissented by himself for the first and last time on the Court.[29] He could not see what was so "unique" about this situation that the Court should abandon its normal rules and permit a defendant to "avail herself of the Fourteenth Amendment rights of total strangers." But obviously there was no other way the Court could get out of the dilemma resulting from its failure to grasp the nettle of restrictive covenants firmly in the Shelley case. The strain of treating a morally disapproved, "unworthy" device as legal was too great for all the Vinson Court except Vinson.[30]

A somewhat comparable impact of social policy on judicial decision can be seen in the 1952 case of *Brotherhood of Railroad Trainmen* v. *Howard*. This brotherhood, which refused to accept Negroes as members, had for years used its influence to try to eliminate Negro trainmen and get their jobs for members of the brotherhood. In 1946 the brotherhood induced one road to discharge its colored "train porters," who actually performed brakemen's duties, and fill their jobs with white men who would do less work but get more pay. Complaint was brought charging that this discriminatory action violated the train porters' rights under the Railway Labor Act and the Constitution.

A rather similar case had come up in 1944, *Steele* v. *Louisville & Nashville Rr. Co.*[31] There the Brotherhood of Locomotive Firemen and Enginemen had forced the railroads to enter into contracts discriminatory to nonmember Negro firemen. The Court unanimously held that a labor union acting as statutory representative of a craft under the Railway Labor Act was obligated "to represent the entire membership of the craft." In the Howard case, however, there was a difference. The "train porters" had never been regarded as belonging to the craft of brakemen; they had been treated for forty years as a separate class for representation purposes and had their own union. Consequently, it was argued that the brotherhood was merely using its statutory bargaining power against other employees to protect its own members, not discriminating against minority members of its craft.

Justice Black, for the majority, rejected this distinction, saying: "Bargaining agents who enjoy the advantages of the Railway Labor Act's provisions must execute their trust without lawless invasions of the right of other workers." This wholly praiseworthy sentiment cannot conceal the fact, however, that the Court was taking a long jump forward from the Steele case. The jump was too much for Minton, Vinson, and Reed, dissenting. The brotherhood here had never purported to represent the train porters, so it could not be condemned on Steele grounds of failure to represent the entire craft. Instead, Black held the contract negotiated by the union illegal because discriminatory against another craft. But what makes a discriminatory contract illegal? Federal and state governments cannot discriminate, but is there any federal law which says that private parties may not? Is it not, in fact, to fill this gap that a federal FEPC has been urged? Black's opinion professed to find such a code of fair employment practices implicit in the Railway Labor Act: "The Federal Act . . . prohibits bargaining agents it authorizes from using their position and power to destroy colored workers' jobs in order to bestow them on white workers. And courts can protect those threatened by such an unlawful use of power granted by a federal act." What this holding amounts to is that a private organization given privileges by federal legislation becomes subject to the limitations which would affect the federal government itself, a rather striking piece of judicial legislation.

All in all, the liberal record of the Vinson Court in racial discrimination cases stands out in sharp contrast to the generally antilibertarian trend of its decisions in other fields. Moreover, a comparison of the 1948 and 1953 restrictive-covenant decisions, as well as the 1944 Steele and the 1952 Howard decisions, reveals a progressively developing boldness in the handling of discrimination issues. The pending school segregation cases, which may well have been decided before this book is published, will demonstrate whether, as seems probable, and in what fashion this trend is to continue on the Warren Court.

VIII. *Trials and Errors*

One of the Supreme Court's most important functions is to maintain acceptable standards in the criminal prosecutions conducted in both federal and state courts throughout the country. The Roosevelt Court, with its general concern for libertarian principles, took a greater interest in this area than had any of its predecessors. But at the same time, and perhaps because it was breaking new ground, it developed some startling divisions, as to both basic theories and their application. These divisions may have seriously limited the Court's effectiveness in securing recognition for the standards it supported.

The principal source of the standards by which the Court judges the procedures in criminal prosecutions is the Fourth through the Eighth Amendments. While the meaning to be read into these constitutional provisions is by no means free from doubt, there is at least no question that the amendments do apply in federal prosecutions. But for state trials there is vigorous controversy as to whether these Bill of Rights requirements are even applicable, or whether the Court must deduce the relevant rules from other sources. Because of this difference in constitutional theory as to federal and state prosecutions, the discussion of the present chapter will examine the two areas separately.

FEDERAL SEARCHES AND SEIZURES

While the Vinson Court had something to say on coerced confessions,[1] right to counsel,[2] and jury trial[3] in the federal courts, its primary problem was to determine the extent of the protection afforded by the Fourth Amendment against unreasonable searches and seizures.[4] The difficulties encountered led Justice

Black to say in 1950 that "in no other field has the law's uncertainty been more clearly manifested."[5]

Before we attempt to thread our way through this tangle, the language of the amendment should be firmly in mind:

> The right of the people to be secure in their persons, houses, papers, and effects, against unreasonable searches and seizures, shall not be violated, and no warrants shall issue, but upon probable cause, supported by oath or affirmation, and particularly describing the place to be searched, and the persons or things to be seized.

The relationship of a warrant to the legitimizing of a search, as Justice Murphy summarized it,

> rests upon the desirability of having magistrates rather than police officers determine when searches and seizures are permissible and what limitations should be placed upon such activities. . . . In their understandable zeal to ferret out crime and in the excitement of the capture of a suspected person, officers are less likely to possess the detachment and neutrality with which the constitutional rights of the suspect must be viewed.[6]

It was the 1946 decision in *Harris* v. *United States* which got the Supreme Court into the most trouble in this field. Prior to that time the law was fairly clear that, in the course of a proper arrest, a search without a warrant could reach only objects in plain sight of the arresting officers. In the Harris case, however, FBI agents, equipped with warrants of arrest for mail fraud, had conducted a five-hour search of the four-room apartment in which Harris was arrested, in the hope of finding materials used in his check-forging operations. Instead, they stumbled on some selective service classification cards and registration certificates which were unlawfully in his possession, and he was subsequently convicted on this evidence.

The Court, by a five to four vote, with Chief Justice Vinson writing the opinion, held that this was not unconstitutional search and seizure. The division was a strange one, for the libertarians Black and Douglas voted along with Reed and Burton in the majority, while the dissenters protesting the validity of such a "general exploratory crusade" were Murphy, Rutledge, Frankfurter, and Jackson. It seems unlikely that Black and Douglas could have been too much at ease on Vinson's side of the fence;

and, in fact, when the opportunity presented itself in the next term, Douglas switched over, thereby turning the Harris dissenters into a majority. Black, however, maintained his position.

The first victory for the new majority in the 1947 term was actually achieved by a seven to two vote, for the facts in *United States* v. *Di Re* converted not only Douglas but also Reed and Burton. Here evidence of possession of counterfeit gasoline ration coupons had been secured by search of the defendant's person without a warrant of any kind. One month later, however, in *Johnson* v. *United States*, Douglas' vote was the deciding one in a five to four division. Federal agents had demanded admission without a warrant into a hotel room from which the odor of burning opium was issuing and had made the arrest after admission and search. The government contended that the search without warrant was valid because incident to the arrest, but had to admit that there was no probable cause for the arrest until the room had been entered. "Thus the Government is obliged to justify the arrest by the search and at the same time to justify the search by the arrest. This will not do," said Justice Jackson.

The principal decision resulting from the new lineup, however, was *Trupiano* v. *United States*. The crime here was operation of a still on rented farm property in New Jersey. The farm owner, suspecting the use to which his property was being put, reported to government agents, who had the operations under surveillance from the time they began. Indeed, a government agent posing as a "dumb farm hand" was engaged to help run the still, and he reported on activities to his superiors by two-way radio. A raid was eventually made, with the farm owner's co-operation, but no warrant was secured. The odor of fermenting mash and the sound of a gasoline motor were plainly noticeable as the agents approached the building containing the still. Through the open door they saw one of the operators of the still at work. An agent entered and arrested him. A number of cans containing alcohol and vats containing fermenting mash, as well as the distillery equipment, were in plain sight within the building, and some of the cans could be seen from outside. Other members of the gang were arrested outside the building.

Justice Murphy for the five-judge majority held that the failure of the government agents to secure a warrant for the search of this building, when one could have been obtained so easily, invalidated the seizure. He agreed that the arrest of the still operator was justified, even without a warrant, because of the well-established right of law-enforcement officers to arrest without a warrant for a felony committed in their presence. But there was also a long line of cases "recognizing that an arresting officer may look around at the time of the arrest and seize those fruits and evidences of crime or those contraband articles which are in plain sight and in his immediate and discernible presence." Over against this rule, however, Murphy placed the principle that search warrants must be secured and used "wherever reasonably practicable"; and he could here see no conceivable reason for the agents' failure to get a warrant "except indifference to the legal process for search and seizure which the Constitution contemplated." As for the justification that the person arrested was actually surrounded by the contraband property at the time of his arrest, Murphy said this was a "fortuitous circumstance." He might have been out in the farmyard, and then the case for seizure would have collapsed. Recognizing that this decision was incompatible with Harris, Murphy chose to distinguish the two cases on the basis of factual differences, "leaving it to another day to test the Harris situation by the rule that search warrants are to be obtained and used wherever reasonably practicable."

Chief Justice Vinson wrote the dissenting opinion, his first since joining the Court. To him it was absurd doctrine to hold that the absence of a search warrant prevented an arresting officer from making

> a valid seizure of contraband materials located in plain sight in the structure in which the arrest took place. . . . To insist upon the use of a search warrant in situations where the issuance of such a warrant can contribute nothing to the preservation of the rights which the Fourth Amendment was intended to protect, serves only to open an avenue of escape for those guilty of crime.

As for Murphy's claim that the proximity of the felon to the contraband was "purely fortuitous," Vinson drily observed:

"Criminals do not normally choose to engage in felonious enterprises before an audience of police officials."[7]

The net result of Douglas' switch in the 1947 term was thus to swing the Court from one extreme to the other on the search and seizure issue and to leave the Court as far as ever removed from a workable rule. Subsequent developments were consequently awaited with interest. The 1948 term brought two decisions, *Brinegar* v. *United States* and *McDonald* v. *United States*, the first supporting and the second condemning a search without warrant, but neither getting to the vitals of the dispute.[8] But in the 1949 term the Court, with two new Truman appointees, moved back toward the Harris doctrine, liquidating Trupiano in the process.

The occasion was *United States* v. *Rabinowitz*, a 1950 decision involving the crime of selling postage stamps fraudulently overprinted to give them a higher value for philatelists. Informed that Rabinowitz, a stamp dealer, had secured a quantity of such counterfeits, a government agent purchased four of the stamps from him. With this evidence, a warrant of arrest was secured. The arrest was made in the dealer's office, and the officers then proceeded, over his objection, to search his desk, safe, and file cabinets for an hour and a half. This search turned up 573 of the counterfeits, which were identified as such by experts whom the officers had brought along with them.

This search was upheld by the four Truman justices plus Reed, with Minton writing the opinion. Obviously, the search was a more limited one than that in Harris, which consequently furnished "ample authority" for it. But what about the Trupiano doctrine that failure to secure a warrant when it was "practicable" to do so invalidated what might otherwise be a valid seizure incident to an arrest? Minton met this problem by overruling Trupiano, to the extent that it required "a search warrant solely upon the basis of the practicability of procuring it rather than upon the reasonableness of the search after a lawful arrest. . . . The relevant test is not whether it is reasonable to procure a search warrant, but whether the search was reasonable." In this case the trial court had ruled the search reasonable, and Minton affirmed this conclusion, because the room was a business office open to the public, small, and under the immediate control of the occupant.

Justice Frankfurter, dissenting for himself and Jackson, recapitulated the now familiar arguments for a strict interpretation of the Fourth Amendment. His rebuttal to the majority dealt largely with what he regarded as their misinterpretation of the precedents. Their true teaching, he maintained, was that "the warrant of arrest carries with it authority to seize all that is on the person, or in such immediate physical relation to the one arrested as to be in a fair sense a projection of his person." There is a "right to search an arrested person and to take the stuff on top of the desk at which he sits." But if the right extends beyond this, where does it stop? If a small room, why not a large room? If one room, why not an entire house?

Frankfurter did not place major reliance on Murphy's Trupiano rule, but he did make such capital as he could out of its overruling. He contended that "the presence or absence of an ample opportunity for getting a search warrant [was] very important" and had been recognized prior to Trupiano. "It is not a rule of those who came on this Court in recent years." Overruling Trupiano also attacked Di Re, Johnson, and McDonald, leaving them "derelicts on the stream of the law." And he concluded, with some bitterness:

> These are not outmoded decisions eroded by time. Even under normal circumstances, the Court ought not to overrule such a series of decisions where no mischief flowing from them has been made manifest. Respect for continuity in law, where reasons for change are wanting, alone requires adherence to Trupiano and other decisions. Especially ought the Court not reinforce needlessly the instabilities of our day by giving fair ground for the belief that Law is the expression of chance—for instance, of unexpected changes in the Court's composition and the contingencies in the choice of successors.

A third dissent to Rabinowitz was supplied, strangely enough, by Black (Douglas did not participate). Black had been one of those objecting to Trupiano when it was announced, and he still believed that it "added new confusions 'in a field already replete with complexities.'" But overruling Trupiano would merely aggravate existing uncertainty, he felt, by casting doubt on the three recently decided cases mentioned by Frankfurter (two of the three also having received Black's dissent). "In my judgment it would be wiser judicial policy to adhere to the Trupiano rule of evidence, at least long enough to see how it works." This rather unusual concern for *stare decisis* on Black's part suggests that he had finally been persuaded that the Fourth Amendment enjoyed a "preferred" position along with the First.

Out of this confusion, the only certainty that seemed to emerge was that the Roosevelt Court's left and right wings had now finally coalesced into a four-judge minority on the Vinson Court on the search and seizure issue. But even this certainty was dissolved in a 1952 decision, when Jackson, long the most vociferous champion of the Fourth Amendment, deserted to write the majority opinion in *On Lee* v. *United States*. Here the government had secured evidence against a man who combined operation of a Chinese laundry with opium peddling, through a supposed friend who entered the laundry and engaged On Lee in conversation, in the course of which incriminating statements were made. The friend was "wired for sound," and the laundryman's statements were broadcast to a Narcotics Bureau agent stationed outside the laundry with a receiving set. The agent subsequently testified as to the substance of the conversation at the trial.

For the majority Jackson said this was simply a case of "eavesdropping on a conversation, with the connivance of one of the parties" and was unrelated to genuine cases of search and seizure. Frankfurter, Douglas, and Black dissented, but Burton also joined them. Frankfurter and Douglas contended that this practice was analogous to wire tapping, which Justice Holmes had attacked in the famous Olmstead case as a "dirty business."[9]

The net result of these rather confusing developments was unquestionably to give federal law-enforcement officers greater leeway in making searches without warrants and to leave reviewing courts with rather vague notions as to the grounds on which searches might be declared unreasonable. Murphy's Trupiano rule that a warrant had to be secured if there was time to do so had at least the virtue of definiteness. Now the Court is back again grappling with the undefined test of "reasonableness."

However, this test did retain protective value even on the Vinson Court. During the same term as the On Lee case, the government lost by a seven to two vote in *United States* v. *Jeffers*. Federal law officers had entered a hotel room rented to two elderly ladies and found some narcotics which had been stored there without their knowledge by their nephew. The search was clearly unlawful as to the two aunts, and there was not the slightest reason why a search warrant could not have been secured. A guard could have been posted at the door to prevent destruction or removal of the narcotics. But the government argued that the nephew's privacy had not been invaded, since it was not his room, and that consequently he lacked the necessary standing to claim constitutional protection. The Court majority rejected this claim as a "quibbling distinction." Vinson and Reed dissented.[10]

STANDARDS FOR STATE PROSECUTIONS

When we turn from an examination of search and seizure, coerced confession, or right to counsel in federal prosecutions to consider the same issues in state trials, we immediately encounter some overriding constitutional differences. The Supreme Court's historic position, as first stated in *Barron* v. *Baltimore* in 1833, has been that the Bill of Rights applied to the federal government only, not to the states. Under this interpretation the Supreme Court would have no basis for reviewing the practices employed in state criminal prosecutions. However, the adoption of the Fourteenth Amendment did supply such a basis. The Supreme Court initially interpreted the due process requirement to impose two fundamental obligations upon state courts—they must have jurisdiction over the defendant, and the defendant must be tried in an orderly manner before an impartial tribunal. But that the more specific provisions of the Fourth through the Eighth Amendments were made effective against the states by the due process clause, the Court consistently refused to admit. In such basic decisions as *Hurtado* v. *California* (1884), *Maxwell* v. *Dow* (1900), *Twining* v. *New Jersey* (1908), and *Palko* v. *Connecticut* (1937) the Court held that indictment by grand jury, trial by jury, and protection against self-incrimination and against double jeopardy were not such fundamental attributes of a fair trial as to be protected against state action under due process. These procedural protections, said Justice Cardozo in the Palko case, have "value and importance" but "are not of the very essence of a scheme of ordered liberty. To abolish them is not to violate a 'principle of justice so rooted in the traditions and conscience of our people as to be ranked as fundamental.' "

The Court might have been thought to be weakening in this position when in 1925, as already noted, the Gitlow case held that the "liberty" protected by the Fourteenth Amendment against state violation included all the liberties of the First Amendment. If the First Amendment was incorporated into the Fourteenth, why were not the Fourth through the Eighth incorporated likewise? If there is a single standard which both federal and state governments must respect in civil liberties, why is there a double standard where criminal prosecutions are concerned? Is it logical that practices which would be unconstitutional in the federal courts do not constitute grounds for Supreme Court reversal of state convictions?

To the left wing of the Roosevelt Court, this double standard seemed neither logical nor required by the Fourteenth Amendment. Their position was best stated by Justice Black in the noteworthy 1947 case of *Adamson* v. *California;* but, by a five to four vote, they failed to carry the Court with them. Black's case rested on two main points. First, he contended that the framers of the Fourteenth Amendment had definitely announced their intention to incorporate the entire Bill of Rights into the amendment, and he cited historical evidence to support this conclusion, which he felt had been overlooked by the Supreme Court in the Hurtado and subsequent decisions.

Second, he contended that the Court's failure to accept the standards of the Fourth through the Eighth Amendments as its guide in reviewing state convictions threw it back on vague "natural-law" standards which would periodically expand or contract "to conform to the Court's conception of what at a particular time constitutes 'civilized decency' and 'fundamental principles of liberty and justice.' " He doubted whether the Court was wise enough "to improve on the Bill of Rights by substituting natural law concepts."

But the Court majority preferred to stand by the precedents of over sixty years. Frankfurter was not alarmed at the obligations which the Court thus had to assume in determining appropriate standards for state courts; reviewing courts should not expect to find the "standards of justice . . . authoritatively formulated anywhere as though they were prescriptions in a pharmacopoeia." He repudiated Black's "notion that the Fourteenth Amendment was a covert way of imposing upon the States all the rules which it seemed important to Eighteenth Century statemen to write into the Federal Amendments," and he denied that the historical evidence cited by Black proved any such conclusion to be correct.

On this latter point, Frankfurter's position has been upheld by a most careful examination of the evidence made by Charles Fairman and Stanley Morrison.[11] Their findings as to the intent of the framers of the Fourteenth Amendment render Black's contentions extremely dubious on historical grounds.[12] But, as Professor Morrison points out, if Black's research was "inadequate and misleading," at least his logic is superior to that of the Court majority, which must justify incorporation in the Fourteenth Amendment of the First Amendment, while denying such status to the rest of the Bill of Rights.

The argument of the Adamson opinion continued on the Vinson Court; but, with the passing of Rutledge and Murphy, any chance of ultimate victory for the full incorporation theory was lost. The Vinson Court, then, without recourse to the standards supplied by the Bill of Rights, had to decide on the basis of the facts in individual cases which came up to it whether "fundamental canons of decency and fairness" had been observed. Marked differences of opinion were evident in these cases.

So far as the unreasonable search and seizure requirement is concerned, that provision has passed the Supreme Court's test and has been accepted as an essential element in the concept of "ordered liberty." In the 1949 case of *Wolf* v. *Colorado*, the Court through Justice Frankfurter unanimously held that "the security of one's privacy against arbitrary intrusion by the police . . . is basic to a free society." But the Court then proceeded to split, six to three, on the matter of enforcing the Fourth Amendment provision in state prosecutions. In the federal courts it is enforced by judicial refusal to accept evidence secured by unreasonable search and seizure methods, the Supreme Court having derived this practice directly from the Fourth Amendment in the 1914 case of *Weeks* v. *United States*. But the Court majority in *Wolf* v. *Colorado* decided that this was merely a rule of evidence which the states were not constitutionally obliged to adopt. Justices Murphy, Rutledge, and Douglas dissented, for they were convinced that the search and seizure requirement without the sanction of excluding testimony illegally secured would be a "dead letter."[13]

The 1951 case of *Stefanelli* v. *Minard* did nothing to prove they were wrong. Here a conviction for bookmaking in New Jersey had been secured with the aid of evidence obtained in a fashion contrary to the Fourth Amendment. Since *Wolf* v. *Colorado* had said that freedom from arbitrary intrusion by the police is a basic freedom, counsel in the Stefanelli case argued that the search amounted to deprivation of a right, privilege, or immunity secured by the Constitution under the federal Civil Rights Act, and brought a suit in equity in a federal district court to suppress the evidence in order to bar its further use in state criminal proceedings. Justice Frankfurter, who in the Wolf case had given assurance that there were several effective sanctions against illegal search and seizure other than barring use of evidence in the trial,[14] here held that going to the federal courts for an injunction to suppress the evidence was not one of them. Opening up state criminal proceedings to collateral attack in the federal courts by injunction would, he cogently argued, be disastrous. He convinced Black, but not Douglas, who invoked the ghosts of Rutledge and Murphy in support of his contention that "any court may with propriety step in to prevent the use of . . . illegal evidence."[15]

Next we turn to cases where denial of the right to counsel is alleged. The Sixth Amendment guarantees this right in federal prosecutions. At the state level, however, the Court is willing to admit the essentiality of counsel only in capital cases. With lesser crimes the constitutional necessity for counsel varies with the circumstances. The Roosevelt Court's principal statement of its position in this field was made in 1942 in what Justice Black has referred to as the "ill-starred" decision of *Betts* v. *Brady*, which pointed out that a number of state constitutions do not recognize right to counsel as fundamental and that it is not required by the common law. Thus the Court has assured itself of a continuing job of reviewing state court practices with respect to counsel. Twelve such cases were decided by the Vinson Court between 1946 and 1953; in six of them it ruled that absence of counsel had, in fact, been fatal to the fair-trial requirement.[16] The Court's difficulty in interpretation of its own standards is shown by the fact that only one of the twelve decisions was unanimous.[17]

First we may look briefly at types of situations in which the Court majority said counsel is required in order to prevent a defendant from being prejudiced in his rights. In *Townsend* v. *Burke*, the twenty-nine-year-old defendant was something of a veteran in encounters with the law. Without counsel or an offer of counsel, he pleaded guilty to charges of burglary and armed robbery. The trial judge, before passing sentence, reviewed the crimes with which the defendant had been previously charged. Apparently seeking to enliven the proceedings, the judge, after referring to the charge of receiving a stolen saxophone in 1937, interjected: "What did you want with a saxophone? Didn't hope to play in the prison band then, did you?"

The Supreme Court was obviously not favorably impressed by this judicial facetiousness just prior to imposition of a sentence of ten to twenty years in the penitentiary. But the real fault lay in the fact that the 1937 charge had actually been dismissed and that on two of the other charges which the court had recited the defendant had been found not guilty. Whether the prosecutor had misinformed the court or whether the judge had misread the record, the Supreme Court concluded that the defendant had been sentenced on the basis of assumptions concerning his criminal record which were "materially untrue" and that he had been seriously disadvantaged by lack of counsel, who could have kept the court from proceeding on false assumptions. For this decision,

Justices Jackson and Frankfurter joined the Four, with Vinson, Reed, and Burton dissenting.[18]

Another example is the 1951 case of *Palmer* v. *Ashe*. A twenty-one-year-old, with a record of prior confinement to an institution for imbecility as well as a record of various minor crimes, had a one-minute trial in 1931, at which he pleaded guilty to what he allegedly thought was a charge of breaking and entering. He had no counsel, nor was he offered one. After he got to prison he learned he had been convicted on a robbery charge. Justice Black held that absence of counsel had made it possible for officers to deceive the prisoner and had prevented the plea of guilty from being an "understanding" one. A minority of Vinson, Minton, Reed, and Jackson believed that the findings of the Pennsylvania courts should not be reversed on the basis of "improbable allegations" about a trial which had taken place eighteen years previously.

In the six cases in which absence of counsel was approved, the first five saw vehement dissents by the Four.[19] The last case, decided in 1950, found Black the sole dissenter, for Douglas was absent and Murphy and Rutledge were dead. *Bute* v. *Illinois* can be used to illustrate these decisions. Bute, fifty-seven years old, pleaded guilty to two indictments charging the taking of indecent liberties with children. The Court's holding, in so far as it can be untangled from Burton's verbosities, is that these were noncapital, "elementary" offenses and that the "special circumstances" were not sufficient to make counsel necessary. Justice Douglas' dissent for the Four was a restatement of the case against *Betts* v. *Brady:*

> The basic requirements for fair trials are those which the Framers deemed so important to procedural due process that they wrote them into the Bill of Rights and thus made it impossible for either legislatures or courts to tinker with them. . . . I think that the Bill of Rights is applicable to all courts at all times.

As for the facts of this particular case, it was easy to say that the offense was a "simple and uncomplicated one"; but in a "repulsive crime" of this sort feeling is likely to be strong against the defendant, and many issues will arise "which only a skilled lawyer can consider intelligently." He would be sure Bute had a fair trial "only if counsel had stood at his side and guided him across the treacherous ground he had to traverse."

In another group of state cases the allowable limits on the use of confessions in criminal cases have been examined. Here again the tendency of the Vinson Court to weaken the protective doctrines of the Roosevelt Court is noteworthy. The uncompromising position with respect to the use of coerced confessions in state criminal cases taken by the Roosevelt Court can be illustrated by two decisions. In the first, *Chambers* v. *Florida*, decided in 1940, four young Negroes charged with the murder of a white man were kept in custody and questioned, one by one, with no opportunity between grillings to obtain rest or sleep, for five days and nights until they made confessions. A burning opinion by Justice Black for a unanimous Court reversed the convictions.

Then in a 1944 case, *Ashcraft* v. *Tennessee*, a somewhat more restrained type of coercion was also condemned. Ashcraft was a white man whose confession of murder was elicited by thirty-six hours of continuous questioning under powerful electric lights by relays of officers, investigators, and lawyers. Such a situation, the Court said in an opinion also by Justice Black, is "so inherently coercive that its very existence is irreconcilable with the possession of mental freedom by a lone suspect against whom the full coercive force is brought to bear." But Justices Jackson, Roberts, and Frankfurter dissented in Ashcraft on the ground that questioning, "even if persistent and prolonged," was not in the same category as violence. Thus the Court, while unanimous in condemning confessions secured through actual physical coercion, was less agreed in adopting a similar view as to situations only "inherently coercive."

In four subsequent state cases while Murphy and Rutledge were still on the bench, the Vinson Court stood by the principles of these decisions, though by the narrowest of margins.[20] The first case was *Haley* v. *Ohio* (1948). Haley, a fifteen-year-old Negro boy suspected of murder in the holdup of a store, was arrested at midnight and questioned for five hours by relays of police, with no friend or counsel present. He then signed a confession. Evidence as to whether he was beaten was disputed. He was not formally charged with the crime until three days later.

During that period he was held incommunicado, and a lawyer was denied admission. It was five days before his mother was allowed to see him.

Justice Douglas, speaking for the Four, wrote the Court's opinion. He felt that the proceedings here would have merited "careful inquiry" if a mature man had been involved, but for an adolescent to be worked over in this way was in "disregard of the standards of decency" and contrary to the constitutional requirements of due process. He cited Chambers and Ashcraft in support of the ruling.

Justice Frankfurter supplied the fifth vote needed to make Douglas' opinion the view of the Court, but he did not join in that opinion. It will be recalled that Frankfurter dissented in the 1944 Ashcraft decision; when the case came back to the Supreme Court again in 1946 after a retrial, he noted that he felt bound by the earlier decision and so did not repeat his dissent. In the Haley case, however, his separate opinion failed to mention either Chambers or Ashcraft, and he made it clear that he was proceeding on grounds peculiar to himself. It was, in fact, in this opinion that Frankfurter made his widely quoted statement that he did not personally believe in capital punishment but added that, as a judge, he could not force his views upon the states by claiming that "due process" forbade the extreme penalty. As a judge he had to be alert to keep from reading his own biases into the Fourteenth Amendment. Yet whether a confession was voluntary or coerced could not be "a matter of mathematical determination." It was a "vague and impalpable" issue, to be determined by "psychological judgment" based on the "deep, even if inarticulate, feelings of our society." With this elaborate apologia for the judicial function and with the assurance that it was the "deeply rooted feelings of the community" that dictated his decison, he voted to reverse the conviction.

In concluding that a statement is not voluntary which results from pressures such as were exerted in this case to make a lad of fifteen talk when the Constitution gave him the right to keep silent and when the situation was so contrived that appreciation of his rights and thereby the means of asserting them were effectively withheld from him by the police, I do not believe I express a merely personal bias against such a procedure.

Justices Burton, Vinson, Reed, and Jackson dissented. Burton's long opinion contended that the issue was purely a factual one as to how the confession was secured. The widely differing stories that were told made it clear that someone had committed perjury. The trial judge and the jury were in the best position to determine the facts in such a controverted situation, and the Supreme Court, relying upon "conjecture" or "suspicion," should not substitute its judgment for theirs.

In the following term confession cases came up from three different states.[21] In each instance a suspect had been taken into custody by police officers and questioned intensively for periods of several days, with confessions as the eventual result. Admittedly, there had been intense psychological pressure in all three cases, and there was some contention that force had been used in one.

By the same five to four vote as in Haley, the Court held the confessions to have been illegally secured.[22] This time Justice Frankfurter, the swing man on this issue, wrote the Court's opinions, though only Rutledge and Murphy concurred in them. Again, as in Haley, Frankfurter was careful to preface his invalidation of state action by recognizing that the Court's power to review state administration of criminal justice was of "such delicacy and import" that it must "be exercised with the greatest forbearance." But on the basis of the uncontroverted facts in these cases Frankfurter was clear that the confessions had not been the result of "free choice." He said: "A statement to be voluntary of course need not be volunteered. But if it is the product of sustained pressure by the police it does not issue from a free choice. When a suspect speaks because he is overborne, it is immaterial whether he has been subjected to a physical or a mental ordeal." This statement clearly represented a considerable change from Frankfurter's views in the 1944 Ashcraft decision, which is perhaps why he did not refer to that case except to cite it in a footnote, but preferred to support his position by discussion of the difference between the inquisitorial system of criminal justice of the Continent and the Anglo-Saxon accusatorial system.

Vinson, Reed, Burton, and Jackson dissented. The latter challenged the majority view forcefully, though in a confused opinion, which even he must have found unsatisfactory. Jackson's basic complaint was that the American legal system gives criminals too much protection for the good of society. These cases grew out of the dilemma of police officers who had reasonable ground to *suspect* an individual but not enough legal evidence to charge him with guilt. How else could a crime be solved in such cases than by taking the suspect into custody for questioning? "The alternative was to close the books on the crime and forget it, with the suspect at large. This is a grave choice for a society in which two-thirds of the murders already are closed out as insoluble."

So Jackson would preserve the right to arrest on suspicion and to interrogate. But must counsel be present during interrogation? Here is another dilemma. If no counsel is present, Jackson admits that the result is "a real peril to individual freedom." But if counsel is allowed, then the crime will not be solved, for "any lawyer worth his salt will tell the suspect in no uncertain terms to make no statement to police under any circumstances." Jackson confessed his own uncertainty as to the proper answer to these problems, but his final inclination was that "for the present, I should not increase the handicap on society." The final evidence of his dilemma was that he listed himself as concurring with the majority in the Watts case and dissenting in the other two, although the three cases were basically identical and he gave no explanation for treating them differently.

With the personnel changes of 1949, Jackson's belief that criminals were being given too much protection for the good of society tended to become the Court's majority view. Post-1949 decisions seem to have canceled out the Roosevelt Court's rulings on coerced confessions and self-incrimination in three important respects.

First, the Vinson Court denied that confessions secured while a suspect is unlawfully detained in jail are automatically invalid. In the 1943 case of *McNabb* v. *United States*, the Roosevelt Court, with only Reed dissenting, had voided a federal court conviction because of delay in taking the prisoners before the nearest judicial officer for hearing or commitment, as required by federal statute. The Court's ruling was understood to mean that any conviction secured as a result of confession during such a period of unlawful detention, regardless of the voluntary nature of the confession, was invalid. There was considerable criticism of the McNabb rule as placing a substantial impediment in the path of law-enforcement officers, and the House of Representatives formally condemned the decision.[23] But in 1948 the Court, by a five to four vote, reiterated the McNabb rule in the case of *Upshaw* v. *United States*. These, of course, were federal cases, and under the doctrine of *Adamson* v. *California* the Court was not obliged to apply the same rule in state proceedings. Only Black and Douglas dissented when it upheld confessions secured between arrest and arraignment in *Gallegos* v. *Nebraska* (1951) and *Stroble* v. *California* (1952).[24] Frankfurter joined them in the 1953 case of *Brown* v. *Allen*, where a preliminary hearing was not given until eighteen days after the arrest.

Second, the Vinson Court in the 1953 case of *Stein* v. *New York* substantially modified the standards laid down for determining the existence of psychological coercion in the Ashcraft case. In Stein, two murder suspects were questioned intermittently for twelve hours of a thirty-two-hour period. Jackson for the majority pointed out that they were mature and experienced men and that one at least was sufficiently self-possessed to bargain as to the terms on which he would confess. But Frankfurter, who had originally opposed the Ashcraft view, was here convinced that the confessions were "the product of coercive police pressure. I cannot believe that these confessions . . . would be admitted in a criminal trial in England, or in the courts of Canada, Australia or India." Naturally, Black and Douglas agreed with him.

Third, the Vinson Court, by its ruling in the same case, adopted the view that, even if a defendant has been deprived in his trial of constitutional rights, he is not entitled to a new trial if the state can show that there is sufficient evidence, apart from that unconstitutionally admitted, to justify the jury in finding guilt. Frankfurter replied: "An impressive body of opinion, never questioned by any decision or expression of this Court, has established a contrary principle." Douglas, with Black's concurrence, itemized these cases, involving denial of counsel, use of perjured testimony, secret trial, mob domination of a trial, and discrimination against Negroes in selection of juries. In none of them, he said, had "the weight of the evidence against the defendant been deemed relevant to the issue of the validity of the conviction." The Court's question in each case had been solely whether constitutional rights had been preserved or infringed. But in the Stein case, Jackson and the majority held that there was enough evidence apart from the confessions "so that it could not be held constitutionally or legally insufficient to warrant the jury verdict"; and he concluded: "We are not willing to discredit constitutional doctrines for protection of the innocent by making of them mere technical loopholes for the escape of the guilty. . . . The people of the State are also entitled to due process of law."

A final group of problems in state standards of justice resulted from discrimination against Negroes in the selection of jurors in various southern states. Since 1935, when the "second Scottsboro case," *Norris* v. *Alabama*, was decided, the Supreme Court has been clear that the systematic exclusion of Negroes from grand or trial juries is unconstitutional.[25] This principle has been so well accepted that in four decisions from 1947 to 1953 the Vinson Court unanimously voided convictions in cases where such discrimination was established.[26] But two developments indicated even in this field a weakening of protective standards in the hands of the Vinson Court.

The first was Jackson's dissenting opinion in the 1950 case of *Cassell* v. *Texas*. To be sure, he was the sole dissenter, and the Court majority reversed the conviction for racial discrimination in the selection of the grand jury. But the influence which Jackson has had on the Court in this area makes his position worthy of special attention. Basically, his view was that discrimination in the selection of a grand jury is without significance, provided that the trial jury is properly constituted. Convictions should not be set aside for errors not affecting the substantial rights of the accused. In this case, he felt that any discrimination there might have been was harmless to the defendant. "To conclude otherwise is to assume that Negroes qualified to sit on a grand jury would refuse even to put to trial a man whom a lawfully chosen trial jury found guilty beyond a reasonable doubt."

Jackson was disturbed by "the spectacle of a defendant putting the grand jury on trial before he can be tried for a crime," and he found it illogical that, as a result of the Court's holding here, "the crime of discrimination offsets the crime of murder and . . . the State must start over again, if death of witnesses, loss of evidence or other conditions wrought by time do not prevent." Jackson would prefer a method of moving against discrimination which did not identify "the right of the most worthy Negroes to serve on grand juries with the efforts of the least worthy to defer or escape punishment for crime." He suggested methods for direct enforcement of the right of qualified Negroes to sit on juries, such as injunction or mandamus against state officers responsible for discrimination.

So far as we are aware, no other justice agrees with Jackson's proposal to strip federal constitutional protections from the grand jury, though the philosophy of the Stein decision, just discussed, would yield comparable results if generally adopted. However, in the 1953 decision of *Brown* v. *Allen*, Jackson plus Reed and the four Truman justices did let two apparent systems of discrimination get by without constitutional challenge. In one North Carolina county, jurors were selected, apparently by an impartial process, but only from a list of the county's taxpayers. Reed for the Court majority recognized that such lists would have "a higher proportion of white citizens than of colored, doubtless due to inequality of educational and economic opportunities," but held that the Court "should not condemn good faith attempts to secure competent juries merely because of varying racial proportions."

In a second North Carolina county, dots were shown to have been placed on all the scrolls in the jury box bearing the names of Negroes. Here the Court majority agreed that the evidence showed that no Negro had ever served on a jury in that county prior to this case but concluded that the county had turned over a new leaf. For this proceeding there were some names of Negroes in the jury box, and, since the venire was drawn by a five-year-old child, the dots on the scrolls could not have resulted in actual discrimination. Reed concluded: "Such an important national asset as state autonomy in local law enforcement must not be eroded through indefinite charges of unconstitutional actions."[27]

FEDERAL-STATE COURT RELATIONS

Some special problems of federal-state court relationships in administration of criminal law came to a head on the Vinson Court. The Court has generally enforced, for obvious reasons, a rule that all appropriate state remedies must be exhausted before persons held in prison under state convictions can appeal to the Supreme Court on writ of certiorari[28] or to a federal district court on writ of habeas corpus.[29] Beginning about 1944, however, the Court encountered difficulties in applying its rule, particularly in the case of petitioners from Illinois. During the three terms from 1944 through 1946, 1,260 petitions for certiorari *in forma pauperis* were received by the Court, of which 638 came from Illinois. These petitions were denied by the Court "with mechanical regularity."[30] But by the 1947 term the Court's experience with Illinois cases led it to suspect that the process of exhausting remedies in that state was such a complicated "merry-go-round" that attempts to enforce compliance with the exhaustion requirement would constitute a denial of justice. In *Marino* v. *Ragen*, where the Illinois attorney-general confessed error in the trial and consented to reversal of a conviction, Rutledge, with the concurrence of Douglas and Murphy, took occasion to excoriate "the Illinois procedural labyrinth . . . made up entirely of blind alleys, each of which is useful only as a means of convincing the federal courts that the state road which the petitioner has taken was the wrong one."

The following term the Court ran out of patience and granted eight petitions for certiorari from Illinois, saying: "If there is now no post-trial procedure by which federal rights may be vindicated in Illinois, we wish to be advised of that fact."[31] The Illinois legislature subsequently passed a post-conviction hearing act,[32] but even this failed to terminate the problems. The act authorized the court in which the original conviction took place to receive petitions setting forth the respects in which the prisoner claimed his constitutional rights were violated and to receive oral testimony or documentary proof. The court's action on the petition was reviewable in the Illinois supreme court on writ of error. After some twenty-five cases under this act had come to the Supreme Court, where the convicting courts had denied relief without inquiring into the verity of the allegations and where it appeared that the state's failure to provide indigent defendants with a transcript of their trial proceedings had prevented the Illinois supreme court from reviewing the cases on writ of error, the Supreme Court became suspicious that Illinois still had no adequate post-conviction remedy.[33] The end of the Illinois story is not yet in sight, but in any event these cases gave the Vinson Court an opportunity to demonstrate the potentialities of direct intervention to review past state convictions. However, considering the fact that the Court must, of necessity, consider rather superficially the great mass of petitions for certiorari which it receives and must deny the great majority of them, other methods of protection against alleged state infringements on federal rights are bound to be sought.

Application for writ of habeas corpus from the appropriate federal district court is the other practicable method of review in such cases. In 1867 Congress authorized federal courts to issue writs of habeas corpus to prisoners "in custody in violation of the Constitution or laws or treaties of the United States."[34] Up to that time the writ, the historic purpose of which had been to challenge detention by executive authorities without judicial trial, had not been available against any sentence imposed by a court of competent jurisdiction. This provision in the 1867 act, however, opened up the way for federal judges to entertain collateral attacks on state court criminal judgments.[35]

The increased concern which the Roosevelt Court manifested over standards of state criminal prosecution caused the number of applications for habeas corpus to grow by leaps and bounds. In 1941 the federal district courts received 127 such petitions; 269 in 1943; 543 in 1948; and 541 in 1952. Naturally, few of these petitions actually resulted in discharge of the prisoner.[36]

On the issue as to what standards the Fourteenth Amendment required federal courts to enforce on the states in habeas corpus proceedings, the discussion of the preceding section is sufficient. But these habeas corpus cases presented some interesting procedural matters for the Vinson Court which have not yet been noted. In 1944 the Court summed up its notions as to the rule of comity which should govern federal and state court relations in *Ex parte Hawk:*

> Ordinarily an application for habeas corpus by one detained under a state court judgment of conviction for crime will be entertained by a federal court only after all state remedies available, including all appellate remedies in the state courts and in this Court by appeal or writ of certiorari, have been exhausted.

But in 1948 a bare majority of the Court, composed of the Four plus Frankfurter, held in *Wade* v. *Mayo* that it was proper for a federal district court to entertain a habeas corpus petition filed by a state prisoner who had failed to seek a writ of certiorari from the Supreme Court, Justice Murphy saying that there should be no "hard and fast rule" on this subject.

The passing of Rutledge and Murphy from the Court led to the reversal of this holding in the 1950 case of *Darr* v. *Burford* and a return to the Hawk view that state remedies which must be exhausted include application to the Supreme Court for certiorari. Justice Frankfurter, with the concurrence of Black and Jackson (Douglas not participating), wrote a masterful dissent. In insisting that certiorari be sought from the Supreme Court before habeas corpus could be asked from a district court, the majority was impaled on the horns of a dilemma. Either the Supreme Court's denial of certiorari embodied a finding on the merits of the legal issue involved, or it did not. The former view was completely contrary to the general understanding, repeated time and time again by the Supreme Court, that its refusal to grant certiorari "has no legal significance whatever bearing on the merits of the claim. The denial means that this Court has refused to take the case. It means nothing else."

Yet Justice Reed, who wrote for the Court in *Darr* v. *Burford*, appeared to imply that the denial of certiorari might be given some weight in a later application for habeas corpus in lower federal courts. If he meant to say this, he was not speaking for the majority, for Burton and Clark added a reservation specifically disclaiming any such view. Thus *Darr* v. *Burford* combined maintenance of the Court's historic rule that denial of certiorari means nothing, with an insistence that application for certiorari was an essential procedural step. To Frankfurter and the minority this was a "meaningless multiplication of steps in the legal process."

This curious situation in which the Court accepted Frankfurter's view as to the meaning of denial of certiorari but denied its consequences was repeated three years later in the grand mixup of *Brown* v. *Allen*. In each of the three cases decided by this 1953 opinion, in all of which the death sentence had been passed, certiorari had been sought from the Supreme Court and denied prior to initiation of the habeas corpus action. Justice Reed, writing the Court's opinion and joined by Minton and Vinson, stuck to his *Darr* v. *Burford* guns; he could see no reason why a district court "should not give consideration to the record of the prior certiorari in this Court and such weight to our denial as the District Court feels the record justifies." But Frankfurter's dissent, stating the contrary view, again won majority support on this point.

The only change in lineup between Darr and Brown concerned Jackson. In the earlier case he had supported Frankfurter's view, as the better of two "unsatisfactory courses open to us." In Brown he was no longer so sure. With characteristic pithiness he observed: "The Court is not quite of one mind on the subject. Some say denial means nothing, others say it means nothing much. Realistically, the first position is untenable and the second is unintelligible." He agreed that the Court passed upon these applications "so casually or upon grounds so unrelated to their merits that our decision should not have the weight of finality." But because "no one knows all that a denial means, does it mean that it means nothing?" What Jackson was searching for was some method of preventing convicts from litigating "again and again exactly the same question on the same evidence." He believed that the federal courts had been subjected to such a multiplicity of habeas corpus petitions, "so frivolous, so meaningless, and often so unintelligible that this worthlessness of the class discredits each individual application." He proposed to reduce this deluge to "manageable proportions" by certain procedural safeguards.[37]

Black and Douglas, who were part of the Frankfurter majority on this point, warned against any such "attempts to confine the Great Writ within rigid formalistic boundaries." But it was Frankfurter who made the most careful rejoinder:

> Surely it is an abuse to deal too casually and too lightly with rights guaranteed by the Federal Constitution, even though they . . . may be invoked by those morally unworthy. Under the guise of fashioning a procedural rule, we are not justified in wiping out the practical efficacy of a jurisdiction conferred by Congress on the District Courts. Rules which in effect treat all these cases indiscriminately as frivolous do not fall far short of abolishing this head of jurisdiction.

His opinion sought for a middle way which would not supply mechanical rules for the district courts but which would also not "leave them free to misuse the writ by being either too lax or too rigid in its employment."

JUDICIAL REVIEW OF MILITARY COURTS

The system of military justice, working through courts-martial and other commissions and tribunals, normally operates completely outside the purview of the Supreme Court. Occasionally, however, a conviction before a military court is appealed to the regular courts by writ of habeas corpus. In general, where such review is sought, the Supreme Court limits itself very strictly to a determination as to whether the tribunal was legally constituted and had jurisdiction to impose punishment for the conduct charged.

For example, in the 1952 case of *Madsen* v. *Kinsella* the Court considered the jurisdiction of the United States Court of the Allied High Commission for Germany, over the wife of a United States Air Force officer who killed her husband while living with him in the American Zone of Germany. The tribunal had not been established or authorized by Congress but had been set up under presidential authority to govern areas occupied by United States military forces. The Supreme Court, with only Black dissenting, upheld the jurisdiction of these "common law courts."[38] But in *United States* ex rel. *Hirshberg* v. *Cooke* (1949) a court-martial was unanimously held to have been without jurisdiction under naval law.

Efforts of the more liberal members of the Court to go beyond problems of jurisdiction into the procedures of military courts have been uniformly unsuccessful. In 1949 the Court refused to invalidate two convictions by courts-martial which were attacked on grounds of double jeopardy and failure to provide a pretrial investigation as required by the Articles of War, though Murphy, Douglas, and Rutledge dissented in both cases.[39] Again in 1953 the Court majority refused to reverse two convictions allegedly secured with the use of coerced confessions, with Black and Douglas dissenting.[40]

Somewhat more complicated are situations involving appeals by non-Americans against military punishment. The Roosevelt Court had handled two important cases of this sort–*Ex parte Quirin*, involving eight German saboteurs who were tried by a presidentially appointed military commission, and *Application of Yamashita*, testing the conviction of a Japanese general for violation of the laws of war by an American military commission set up by General MacArthur in the Philippines.[41] In both cases the Court confined itself narrowly to an examination of the commissions' jurisdiction and upheld the convictions.

Hirota v. *MacArthur*, decided in 1948, differed from the Yamashita case, in that the Japanese generals involved had been tried for war crimes before a military tribunal set up by General MacArthur "as the agent of the Allied Powers" which had defeated Japan. The generals sought to file habeas corpus petitions directly with the Supreme Court. In a three-paragraph per curiam opinion their motions were denied, on the ground that, because of its international status, "the courts of the United States have no power or authority to review, to affirm, set aside or annul the judgments and sentences imposed" by the tribunal.

The starkness of this ruling was somewhat relieved by the concurring opinion of Justice Douglas, filed six months later, to which we are indebted for the only judicial analysis of the interesting problems presented by this case.[42] He differed with the view of the per curiam opinion that the international character of the tribunal precluded judicial review by the Supreme Court, an issue which, he remarked with considerable understatement, the Court's opinion did not "adequately analyze." But he also felt it necessary to deal with a prior problem, one which the per curiam opinion completely passed over—whether there was any jurisdictional basis for American courts to consider these habeas corpus applications. It had been contended for the government that the cases could not be filed originally in the Supreme Court, whose original jurisdiction is strictly limited by the Constitution. Douglas appeared willing to accept this position. But it was also contended that no federal district court had jurisdiction over the case either, and this Douglas would not admit.[43] He contended that a habeas corpus petition could be filed in any judicial district where there was a respondent responsible for the custody of the petitioners. Here that district was the District of Columbia, where MacArthur's superiors were located. He would consequently have remitted the parties to the district court for the District of Columbia, and let the case come to the Supreme Court on certiorari. The majority, however, had been "unwilling to take that course, apparently because it deems the cases so pressing and the issues so unsubstantial that the motions should be summarily disposed of."

Since the Court had thus insisted on considering the merits of the case, though in absurdly brief fashion, Douglas passed on to his reasons for disagreement with the majority position that the international character of the tribunal precluded judicial intervention. He was willing to concede that the Supreme Court had "no authority to review the judgment of an international tribunal"; but he was extremely unhappy about it, for it would leave "the power of those tribunals absolute." There was, he felt, a way out of the dilemma. If the court could not be reached, the jailer could:

> If as a result of unlawful action, one of our Generals holds a prisoner in his custody, the writ of *habeas corpus* can effect a release from that custody. It is the historic function of the writ to examine into the cause of restraint of liberty. We should not allow that inquiry to be thwarted merely because the jailer acts not only for the United States but for other nations as well.

The judicial review which Douglas would thus provide would be limited to an examination of the jurisdiction of the international tribunal. It would "ascertain whether, so far as American participation is concerned, there was authority to try the defendants for the precise crimes with which they are charged. That is what we should do here."

And that is what Douglas proceeded to do in the remainder of his opinion. His conclusion was that the Tokyo tribunal had been set up by the executive branch of the government acting within its constitutional military powers:

> . . . It did not therefore sit as a judicial tribunal. It was solely an instrument of political power. Insofar as American participation is concerned, there is no constitutional objection to that action. For the capture and control of those who were responsible for the Pearl Harbor incident was a political question in which the President as Commander-in-Chief, and as spokesman for the nation in foreign affairs, had the final say.

While the Hirota case disposed of the claims for judicial reviewability of judgments against enemy aliens by international tribunals, it did not cover appeals from enemy aliens against purely American military courts or commissions. The American occupation of Germany brought a flood of cases of this type. In something over a two-year period from January, 1948, the Supreme Court received habeas corpus petitions on behalf of over two hundred German enemy aliens confined by American military authorities abroad. The Court denied the motions in every case, usually by a four to four vote during the 1947 and 1948 terms. The standard formula was that Vinson, Reed, Frankfurter, and Burton would indicate there was "want of jurisdiction," citing Article III, section 2, clause 2, of the Constitution,[44] while Black, Douglas, Murphy, and Rutledge would note their opinion "that the motion for leave to file the petition should be granted and that the case should be set for argument forthwith," while Jackson would not participate. These cases were variously styled, in one of them the respondent named being none other than "Harry S. Truman, Commander in Chief of the Armed Forces of the United States."[45]

Eventually, one of these cases reached the Supreme Court by

way of the District of Columbia courts in 1950, when Rutledge and Murphy were no longer on the Court. *Johnson* v. *Eisentrager* was originated by twenty-one German nationals in the service of the German government who were located in China during World War II. After the unconditional surrender of Germany, which obligated all forces under German control to cease active hostilities at once, they were alleged to have continued hostile operations by furnishing intelligence concerning American forces to the Japanese. After the Japanese surrender they were taken into custody and tried and convicted by a wholly American military court sitting in China. The prisoners were repatriated to Germany to serve their sentences, under custody of the United States Army. This case was initiated by habeas corpus petition to the district court of the District of Columbia, with the Secretary of Defense and top army officers named as respondents. The district court dismissed the petition,[46] but the court of appeals reversed, holding that "any person, including an enemy alien, deprived of his liberty anywhere under any purported authority of the United States is entitled to the writ if he can show that extension to his case of any constitutional rights or limitations would show his imprisonment illegal."

Justice Jackson, in rejecting this conclusion for a six-judge majority, said: "We are cited to no instance where a court, in this or any other country where the writ [of habeas corpus] is known, has issued it on behalf of an alien enemy who, at no relevant time and in no stage of his captivity, has been within its territorial jurisdiction." The remainder of Jackson's fairly long and vigorous opinion was a defense of this state of affairs. Residence within the country was in his opinion essential to qualify an alien for judicial protection by American courts. Aliens resident in the United States are in most respects as fully entitled to constitutional rights and the judicial enforcement thereof as are citizens. In wartime enemy aliens resident in the United States suffer a considerable loss of status and become constitutionally subject to summary arrest, internment, and deportation, but they can still resort to the courts for a review of jurisdictional questions raised by the executive action. In general, resident enemy aliens retain their right to bring suits except where the litigation would hamper our war effort or give aid to the enemy. But nonresident enemy aliens have, according to the law of nations, the common law, and American practice, no right to maintain an action during the period of hostilities.

Black, along with Douglas and Burton, dissented. He said that since enemy alien belligerents had been permitted to contest convictions for war crimes in both the Quirin and the Yamashita cases, the majority view rested solely on the fact that the capture, trial, and imprisonment took place outside American territory. If these prisoners had been brought to the United States, they would admittedly have had access to our courts, which means that a prisoner's right to test legality of a sentence depends upon where the government chooses to imprison him. "The Court is fashioning wholly indefensible doctrine if it permits the executive branch, by deciding where its prisoners will be tried and imprisoned, to deprive all federal courts of their power to protest against a federal executive's illegal incarcerations." The constitutional guarantee against illegal imprisonment should extend to any land governed by the United States:

> Conquest by the United States, unlike conquest by many other nations, does not mean tyranny. . . . Our nation proclaims a belief in the dignity of human beings as such, no matter what their nationality or where they happen to live. Habeas corpus, as an instrument to protect against illegal imprisonment, is written into the Constitution. Its use by courts cannot in my judgment be constitutionally abridged by Executive or by Congress.

The range from local police courts to international tribunals is a big one but, as this chapter has indicated, the Supreme Court has responsibilities running the entire gamut. The divisions of opinion on the Vinson Court were in part as to whether the Constitution obliges the Court to enforce uniform procedures and standards of prosecution at all levels. However, under this jurisdictional guise much deeper motivational differences appear to be at work, grounded in varying conceptions of justice.

It is an index of this fact to note how Jackson and Frankfurter, whose premises in numerous areas bring them out with the same results, have been in increasing disagreement as to the Court's role with respect to state criminal procedure. Jackson's motivation has been to strengthen the hand of society in its dealings with crime. Frankfurter, though he starts with a bias against undue federal interference in state administration of justice, has none the less a respect for procedural protections which he will not permit even the claims of state autonomy to override. These procedural protections must be provided, he sums up, "not out of tenderness for the accused but because we have reached a certain stage of civilization"—a civilization which, Douglas adds, "by respecting the dignity of the least worthy citizen raises the stature of all of us."[47]

IX. *Patterns of Division*

In this review of the Vinson Court's principal civil liberties decisions an attempt has been made, so far as possible, to note the positions taken by individual justices in support of, or in opposition to, the doctrines which have been announced by the Court. However, identification of personal views has necessarily been subordinated to following the main lines of tendency. Now the time has come to see what can be done toward accounting for the positions taken by the members of the Court—to concentrate upon the individual participants in the judicial process rather than upon its institutional product.

The difficulties in the path of any such effort have already been alluded to in the first chapter. But at least a beginning can be effected by way of a study of judicial voting behavior. One of the most useful things to know about a justice is where he is located on the Court in relationship to his colleagues. Is he seldom or usually in disagreement with the decisions of the Court? Does he dissent often by himself? This, of course, would be an indication of a generally unorthodox state of mind. Do his dissents in company with other justices seem to be simply random associations, or is some pattern of alignment indicated? That blocs of opinion exist on the Court has long been recognized. Some three decades ago the phrase "Holmes and Brandeis dissenting" was a famous one. Persons who follow the decisions of the Court with any care will be acquainted with the general alignment of justices; but a more systematic method of analyzing these associations is clearly desirable, particularly in recent years, which have seen such a remarkable proliferation of dissenting opinions.

Data on judicial voting behavior can be effectively presented by a graphical arrangement, as in Table 2, giving for any period the number of cases in which each pair of justices was in dissent together. In addition, the table indicates in parentheses the number of cases, if any, in which a justice was the sole dissenter from a Court decision, and the top line in the table shows the total number of dissents for each justice for the period. The location of the justices in the table is such as to bring out the bloc relationships by placing each justice as close as possible to those with whom he dissented most often and farthest from those with whom he had the fewest common dissents.

TABLE 2

PARTICIPATION OF AND AGREEMENTS AMONG SUPREME COURT JUSTICES IN DISSENTING OPINIONS, 1931–35 TERMS*

	Stone	Cardozo	Brandeis	Hughes	Roberts	Van Devanter	Sutherland	Butler	McReynolds
No. dissents	67	55	57	15	15	17	23	36	33
Stone	(4)	51	53	12	6	......	......	1	......
Cardozo	51	(3)	40	12	2	1	......	1	......
Brandeis	53	40	(1)	10	8	......	1	3	......
Hughes	12	12	10	(2)	1	1	......	......	......
Roberts	6	2	8	1	(1)	......	5	7	3
Van Devanter	......	1	......	1	......	(1)	13	13	11
Sutherland	......	......	1	......	5	13	(1)	19	13
Butler	1	1	3	......	7	13	19	(5)	17
McReynolds	......	......	......	......	3	11	13	17	(13)

* Justice Holmes, who served part of the 1931 term, is excluded from the table.

Such a table provides a kind of X-ray insight into opinion on the Court.[1] The total number of dissents for each justice is an index to the *intensity* of his disagreement with the Court's predominant trends. Thus Stone, with 67 dissents for the 1931–35 term, can be thought of as roughly twice as disaffected as McReynolds, who was pushed into disagreement only 33 times during the same period.

The charting of interrelationships in the dissenting votes enables us to discover the *direction* of dissent and makes it clear that in the same period there were two separate blocs of dissenters pulling away in opposite directions from the Court majority. One bloc, composed of Stone, Cardozo, and Brandeis, entertained a common body of opinions which led it to take a position on one side of the Court on numerous occasions, while another group composed of Van Devanter, Sutherland, Butler, and McReynolds existed on the other side of the Court. In order to accord with usual political designations, the former bloc is given a position on the left of the table, and the latter on the right. Chief Justice Hughes and Justice Roberts were in the center of the Court, though the former, on the relatively few occasions when he did dissent, tended to join his colleagues on the left, while Roberts' dissents were rather evenly divided between justices of the two wings.

TABLE 3

AGREEMENT AMONG SUPREME COURT JUSTICES IN NONUNANIMOUS OPINIONS, 1931–35 TERMS*

(In Percentages)

	Stone	Cardozo	Brandeis	Hughes	Roberts	Van Devanter	Sutherland	Butler	McReynolds
Stone	......	89	83	54	43	33	29	20	22
Cardozo	89	......	79	59	42	36	31	21	26
Brandeis	83	79	......	60	55	41	39	31	30
Hughes	54	59	60	......	77	77	71	60	62
Roberts	43	42	55	77	......	74	78	71	67
Van Devanter	33	36	41	77	74	......	93	82	79
Sutherland	29	31	39	71	78	93	......	87	78
Butler	20	21	31	60	71	82	87	......	75
McReynolds	22	26	30	62	67	79	78	75	......

* Justice Holmes, who served part of the 1931 term, is excluded from the table.

A second method of using this same information, and one which has some advantages over the first type of table, is to reduce the data on agreements and disagreements among the justices to a percentage basis. In Table 2, only the interagreements in dissenting opinions were shown. But in Table 3, agreements in nonunanimous opinions between every pair of justices, whether on the majority or the minority side, are reflected in percentage figures. For example, during the 1931–35 terms Justices Stone and Cardozo agreed with each other in 98 of the 110 nonunanimous opinions in which both participated, for an agreement rate of 89 per cent. On the other hand, Stone and McReynolds were on the same side in only 27 of the 125 disputed cases in which both participated, so their agreement rate is only 22 per cent.

Table 3 brings out even more clearly than Table 2 the blocs on either side of the Court. Stone, Cardozo, and Brandeis had interagreement rates of 79–89, while the Van Devanter-Sutherland-Butler-McReynolds bloc was almost as cohesive, with agreement rates ranging from 75 to 93 per cent. The reason for the predominance of this four-judge group during the period is found in the fact that the two center justices, Hughes and Roberts, tended to agree with them more than with the three-judge group, though in Hughes's cases this tendency was comparatively slight.

Such tables are effective in revealing at any one time the anatomy of opinion on the Court, quite irrespective of the issues over which disagreement arose. By preparing tables of alignments for each term over a period of years, it is possible, in addition, to trace shifts of judicial positions and the realignments resulting from the appointment of new justices to the Court.

Application of this technique to the Roosevelt Court has yielded interesting results, which need be only briefly summarized here.[2] The initial Roosevelt appointees tended to vote together, and they quickly took over control of the Court. During the 1939 term, for example, dissent came primarily from a right-wing group of Hughes, Roberts, and McReynolds. But by the 1941 term, when Roberts was the only non-Roosevelt-appointed justice remaining, the Roosevelt justices were beginning to form their own left, center, and right wings. These orientations, however, were much less distinct than the comparable divisions had been during the 1931–35 period, for example.

This was the situation which existed when Vinson became Chief Justice. The fact that the composition of the Court was unchanged during the 1946, 1947, and 1948 terms makes it possible to use a single table to show the voting alignments for that period. Table 4 reveals, first of all, the existence of a reasonably firm bloc of four justices on the left side of the Court, their deviation from the Court majority being evidenced by the fact that they dissented in from 85 to 103 of the cases decided. This bloc had its beginnings in the 1938 term, when Douglas joined the Court and promptly revealed a strong affinity for Black's general position. Murphy and Rutledge subsequently affiliated with the group, though their ties with each other were closer than to either Black or Douglas.

During the 1946–48 period, Jackson and Frankfurter were dissenting at about the same rate as the left wing (95 and 96 dissents, respectively); but their deviation from the Court majority was for the most part in a different direction and over different issues from those which led the Four to dissent. There was some meeting of minds in dissent between Frankfurter and Jackson from the one side and Douglas, Rutledge, and Murphy from the other;

TABLE 4

PARTICIPATION OF AND AGREEMENTS AMONG SUPREME COURT JUSTICES IN DISSENTING OPINIONS, 1946–48 TERMS

	Douglas	Rutledge	Murphy	Black	Reed	Vinson	Burton	Jackson	Frankfurter
No. dissents	103	103	92	85	52	50	69	95	96
Douglas	(10)	56	55	55	8	7	8	12	13
Rutledge	56	(5)	72	61	8	3	10	12	15
Murphy	55	72	(4)	58	2	5	3	13	18
Black	55	61	58	(2)	6	6	6	5	6
Reed	8	8	2	6	(3)	21	27	25	16
Vinson	7	3	5	6	21	......	27	26	22
Burton	8	10	3	6	27	27	(6)	33	29
Jackson	12	12	13	5	25	26	33	(7)	58
Frankfurter	13	15	18	6	16	22	29	58	(8)

but typically they were not on the same side of the fence. The 58 joint dissents of Frankfurter and Jackson evidence a substantial common area of agreement between them.

The center of the Court during this three-year period was composed of the two Truman appointees plus Reed. Vinson and Reed had 50 and 52 dissents, respectively, while Burton was a little more active in dissent, with 69. The pattern of their dissenting alignments shows that the leanings of all three were much more definitely toward the right of the Court than toward the left.

The rather complex pattern of alignments demonstrated by Table 4 calls for the additional clarification which can be supplied by translating these voting data into percentage figures. Table 5 gives the percentage of agreements in disputed cases during the three-year period for every pair of justices. It brings out again very clearly the four-judge left, the three-judge center, and the two-judge right. The internal cohesion of each of these three groups was almost identical, their average interagreement rates being 73.5, 76, and 74, respectively. As for the relationships between particular pairs of justices, eight pairs had agreement rates of better than 70 per cent, the highest being Murphy-Rutledge at 82, and seven pairs were below 40 per cent. All seven of the latter were pairs of one left- and one right-wing justice, Murphy-

TABLE 5

AGREEMENT AMONG SUPREME COURT JUSTICES IN NONUNANIMOUS OPINIONS, 1946–48 TERMS

(In Percentages)

	Douglas	Black	Murphy	Rutledge	Reed	Vinson	Burton	Frankfurter	Jackson
Douglas	......	71	68	66	47	47	42	35	33
Black	71	......	78	76	53	53	47	37	34
Murphy	68	78	......	82	45	48	40	42	37
Rutledge	66	76	82	......	47	44	42	36	33
Reed	47	53	45	47	.....	78	75	57	63
Vinson	47	53	48	44	78	......	76	62	65
Burton	42	47	40	42	75	76	.....	61	64
Frankfurter	35	37	42	36	57	62	61	.....	74
Jackson	33	34	37	33	63	65	64	74	......

Frankfurter at 42 being the only left-right pair to get higher than a 37 per cent rate of agreement.

The death of Murphy and Rutledge in the summer of 1949 and their replacement by Clark and Minton was bound to cause a reorientation on the Court. The expectation was that the two new appointees would generally align themselves with the Court's center group, though it was thought that Minton might move somewhat into Black's orbit, since they had been closely associated in the Senate. The voting alignments on the Court as remade in 1949 are covered by Table 6. It shows clearly how the four Truman justices, with the assistance of Reed, dominated the Court. Dissents of the four Truman appointees during the period ranged from 15 to 47, and total 146 (an average of 9 per term). The five Roosevelt justices dissented a total of 518 times (an average of 26 per term). The Court's decisions, it will be noted, were most satisfactory to Clark, who dissented only 15 times in four years.

Under the pressure of the Vinson majority, justices on the two wings of the Court showed increased tendencies toward fraternization. In fact, the data seem to justify transferring Frankfurter and Jackson from their former positions on the right of the Court and placing them with Black and Douglas. In almost half of his dissents (49 out of 101) Frankfurter had the company of Black, while Black and Jackson attacked the majority together on 27 occasions.

TABLE 6

PARTICIPATION OF AND AGREEMENTS AMONG SUPREME COURT JUSTICES IN DISSENTING OPINIONS, 1949–52 TERMS

	Black	Douglas	Frankfurter	Jackson	Reed	Minton	Burton	Vinson	Clark
No. dissents	148	130	101	80	59	47	44	40	15
Black	(27)	79	49	27	11	16	16	13	6
Douglas	79	(18)	33	18	21	14	16	14	7
Frankfurter	49	33	(8)	46	13	10	13	2	1
Jackson	27	18	46	(13)	16	11	9	5	3
Reed	11	21	13	16	(6)	17	11	15	2
Minton	16	14	10	11	17	(3)	10	16	4
Burton	16	16	13	9	11	10	(2)	7	4
Vinson	13	14	2	5	15	16	7	(1)	8
Clark	6	7	1	3	2	4	4	8	......

With this interesting development, it is particularly important that we turn to a percentage table for verification. The first thing to be noted in Table 7 is the close relationship between the four Truman justices, whose agreement rates ran from 75 to 83 per cent. Reed was only a slightly less devoted member of the group, and the average interagreement rate for these five justices of the Vinson majority was the high one of 77.3 per cent.

For the other four members of the Court, the story is different. The Black-Douglas pair dropped from an agreement rate of 71 per cent for the 1946–48 period to only 61 per cent for 1949–52. The Frankfurter-Jackson relation similarly declined from 74 to 68 per cent. Moreover, the *rapprochement* between the Black-

Douglas and Frankfurter-Jackson wings of the Court which Table 6 seemed to show is revealed by Table 7 as rather limited. The Douglas-Jackson ratio was actually down one point, from 33 to 32. The other agreement rates were up from the 1946–48

TABLE 7

AGREEMENT AMONG SUPREME COURT JUSTICES IN NONUNANIMOUS OPINIONS, 1949–52 TERMS

(In Percentages)

	Douglas	Black	Frankfurter	Jackson	Reed	Minton	Burton	Vinson	Clark
Douglas	......	61	40	33	42	36	42	39	40
Black	61	......	49	39	34	41	43	42	47
Frankfurter	40	49	.....	69	51	52	58	51	59
Jackson	33	39	69	.....	62	61	61	62	67
Reed	42	34	51	62	......	75	71	76	75
Minton	36	41	52	61	75	......	75	81	80
Burton	42	43	58	61	71	75	......	75	80
Vinson	39	42	51	62	76	81	75	......	83
Clark	40	47	59	67	75	80	80	83	......

TABLE 8

DISSENTING RECORDS OF JUSTICES 1946–52 TERMS

(In Percentages)

	1946	1947	1948	1949	1950	1951	1952
Black	21	23	24	33	39	42	37
Douglas	21	28	34	30	38	34	51
Murphy	24	23	27	....	....	....	....
Rutledge	30	22	29	....	....	....	....
Frankfurter	23	25	27	32	24	22	27
Jackson	20	25	33	27	19	18	22
Reed	12	14	16	16	12	22	10
Burton	14	22	18	8	14	13	10
Vinson	9	13	18	2	6	14	18
Clark	....	....	....	0	10	1	6
Minton	....	....	....	5	14	18	14

period—Black-Frankfurter from 37 to 49, Black-Jackson from 34 to 39, and Douglas-Frankfurter from 35 to 40. Nevertheless, these four justices obviously fail to qualify as a bloc, their average interagreement rate being 48.5 per cent.

Finally, one additional table will help to clarify the relation of individual justices to the Court since the 1946 term. Table 8 presents the record of dissents registered by each justice as a proportion of the total number of cases he participated in during each term. Several different reaction patterns are evident. Black and Douglas had a generally rising curve of dissent over the entire period, with a slight recession for Black in 1952 and a sharp increase for Douglas the same term. His figure of 51 per cent dissents established a record high on the Court.

Reed and Frankfurter were fairly consistent over the period, Frankfurter's rate being roughly twice that of Reed's, except in 1951. Vinson, Burton, and Jackson, the remaining justices to serve for the entire seven years, showed a tendency for their rates of dissent to rise through the 1948 term and then to drop as the Court's composition changed. In Vinson's case the drop was dramatic, from 18 per cent in 1948 to 2 per cent in 1949, a striking indication of the extent to which the addition of Minton and Clark strengthened Vinson's hand. However, his rate subsequently began to push back up, and during his last term on the Court he again reached a figure of 18 per cent dissents.

X. *Libertarian Activism: The Four*

The tables of the preceding chapter, which cover not only the civil liberties cases but all nonunanimous decisions of the Vinson Court, give an accurate picture of alignments on the Court, but they do not relate the divisions to issues or throw any light on why the justices voted as they did. Consequently, we now turn more specifically to an examination of the alignment of the justices on civil liberties problems.

JUDICIAL DECISION-MAKING

The theory as to the relationship between a judge's decisions and his personal convictions on which this analysis proceeds needs to be made clear at the beginning. There is no naïve assumption that justices in deciding cases are completely free to vote their own preferences or that a voting record necessarily mirrors a justice's inner convictions. On the other hand, there is no assumption, which would be even more naïve, that a Supreme Court justice merely "looks up the law" on a subject and applies it to the case in hand. Certainly, at the level of high policy with which the Supreme Court deals, selection from among the courses of decision open to the Court is a process in which personal choice plays a deciding role. The great early American judge, Chancellor Kent, once explained how he arrived at his decisions. He first made himself "master of the facts." Then, he continued, "I saw where justice lay, and the moral sense decided the court half the time; I then sat down to search the authorities. . . . I might once in a while be embarrassed by a technical rule, but I almost always found principles suited to my view of the case."[1]

The important thing is to understand the operating conditions under which the judge makes his choice. In many respects his situation is quite comparable to that of any individual who must make decisions on important matters within an institutional framework which brings to him questions for decision and provides mechanisms for making those decisions effective. Appellate courts share with legislatures the problems of decision-making in a collectivity of equals, as opposed to decision-making in a hierarchy. We may tend to think of legislators as having greater freedom than judges in arriving at policy choices, and of their votes as definite expressions of their personal convictions. But upon reflection it becomes obvious that legislators, too, are not able to vote as free agents. They must think about what is good for their party. They must take some account of how their constituency feels on the subject and the effect of their vote on the prospects for re-election. They may decide to vote for something they do not want, in order to get support for something which they want very much. They may decide to vote for less than they want, because their practical judgment tells them that that is all they can get.

For example, a few years ago, an amendment was offered in the House of Representatives to a public housing bill, forbidding segregation in the housing for which it provided. This amendment was a purely tactical move by opponents of public housing, who wanted to strip the measure of its southern support. In these circumstances, many liberal supporters of public housing felt compelled to oppose the antisegregation amendment in order to save the bill. They would never have voted this way if they had been free agents. But they were not free. The institutional framework in which they operated had presented them with two choices—they could stand on principle and lose public housing through a political trick, or they could get public housing at the cost of a temporary desertion of their principles. Their choice was personal. The alternatives were imposed.

A Supreme Court justice finds himself in much the same situation, though operating within a judicial rather than a legislative framework does make for some differences. He does not have a constituency of electors or a party position to consider. But the rules and traditions of the Court supply institutional preferences with which his own preferences must compete. One of these institutional preferences, for example, is "stare decisis," the rule of precedent. The individual judge may think that the precedents are wrong or outmoded. If so, he may follow his personal preference and state his reasons for voting to change the law. He is free to do that. He is not free to ignore the precedents, to act as though they did not exist. He has free choice, but among limited alternatives and only after he has satisfied himself that he has met the obligations of consistency and respect for settled principles which his responsibility to the Court imposes upon him. His private views as an individual help to form and may be incorporated into his public views as a justice, but they are not the same thing.

What this means, in more concrete terms, is that when a civil liberties case comes to the Supreme Court, the justices are not asked whether they are more or less in favor of civil liberties. They are asked how the Court, consistently with its role as the highest judicial body in a federal system, should dispose of a proceeding, the basic facts in which have been found and the form of which has been given by lower judicial bodies. Under these circumstances some justices may not even choose to think of the civil liberties issue in the case. They may see the controlling problem as adherence or nonadherence to the precedents. They may think of the issue as judicial respect for legislative action. As participants in the judicial process, they have a perfect right to choose from among the alternatives presented the ones which determine their view of the case.

This background should be helpful in preventing misunderstanding of the next statistical device to be employed. Table 9 is a "box score" made up on the votes of the Vinson Court justices in 113 of the principal nonunanimous civil liberties decisions since 1946. The intention has been to include all such decisions which fall into the categories covered by chapters iii–viii, whether or not they were actually discussed in those chapters. Cases in both the free speech and the criminal-defendant categories are divided according to whether they were federal or state prosecutions. The free speech classification is a rather loose one, including not only the area covered in chapters iii and iv but also the loyalty and congressional inquiry cases of chapter v. It may be noted that all but one of the federal free speech cases involved Communists in some way. Table 9 gives, for each category, the percentage of cases which the Court as a whole, and each individual justice, decided favorably to the particular civil liberties claim involved.

The immediately arresting fact about this table is that it gives a somewhat different picture of judicial alignments than the preceding tabular presentations. The justices are divided very clearly into two groups, those more favorable and those less favorable than the Court as a whole to civil liberties claims. The familiar four-judge libertarian group, voting favorably in from 87 to 100 per cent of the cases, is joined by Frankfurter, with a 61 per cent record. On the other side of the Court, Jackson was slightly below the Court's position, with 31 per cent, while the four Truman justices plus Reed have records ranging from 24 to 13 per cent.

Considering the complicated character of the judicial decision-making process, the value or meaning of such a box score may be disputed. Tables of this sort, used by a good many analysts of the Court since they were first developed by the author a decade ago,[2] have been subjected to criticism on several grounds. The controversy is probably best summed up in two *Atlantic Monthly* articles by Irving Dilliard and Mark De Wolfe Howe.[3] For purposes of his article, Dilliard had compiled a box score on the votes of the justices in civil liberties cases. Howe in rebuttal flatly doubted "whether the statistical analysis of Supreme Court opinions can, under any circumstances, be fruitful." Box scores cannot "record the impalpable factors in a process as subtle and complex as that of constitutional adjudication." The *Washington Post* editorialized: "We hope that Mr. Howe's expose of this shallow thinking about the judicial process will hasten the relegation of box scores to the sports pages—where they belong."[4]

Admittedly, such statistical devices cannot be used as a principal reliance in explaining the decisions of the Supreme Court. A box score is no substitute for the process of careful analysis of judicial writing by trained minds using all the established methods for coaxing meaning out of language. The results of such analysis can be presented only in more language, not in mathematical symbols. There is no method "by which an IBM machine can be used as a substitute for scholarship."[5] But when all this is

TABLE 9

VOTING RECORD OF SUPREME COURT JUSTICES IN CERTAIN NONUNANIMOUS CIVIL LIBERTIES CASES 1946–52 TERMS*

(In Percentages)

	FOR ALIEN CLAIMS	FOR NEGRO CLAIMS	FOR CRIMINAL DEFENDANTS' CLAIMS		FOR FREE SPEECH CLAIMS		TOTAL
			State	Federal	State	Federal	
No. cases....	23	4	37	21	16	12	113
Murphy........	100	100	100	100	100	100	100
Rutledge........	100	100	100	85	100	100	96
Douglas.........	63	100	97	84	100	100	89
Black...........	100	100	86	62	94	100	87
Frankfurter......	82	75	46	85	13	83	61
Court...........	39	75	35	43	25	17	35
Jackson.........	50	33	14	55	6	45	31
Clark...........	14	67	32	14	10	....	24
Burton..........	35	75	19	14	19	8	22
Minton.........	19	33	12	0	27	0	14
Vinson..........	30	0	16	0	19	0	14
Reed...........	9	33	14	10	31	0	13

* The cases included in Table 9, classified according to the six headings used in the table, are as follows:

Aliens (23): For alien claims (9): *Oyama* v. *California* (1948); *Takahashi* v. *Fish and Game Commission* (1948); *U.S.* ex rel. *Johnson* v. *Shaughnessy* (1949); *Wong Yang Sung* v. *McGrath* (1950); *McGrath* v. *Kristensen* (1950); *Bindczyck* v. *Finucane* (1951); *Mandoli* v. *Acheson* (1952); *Kwong Hai Chew* v. *Colding* (1953); *Bridges* v. *U.S.* (1953). Against alien claims (14): *Ludecke* v. *Watkins* (1948); *Ahrens* v. *Clark* (1948); *Klapprott* v. *U.S.* (1949); *Savorgnan* v. *U.S.* (1950); *U.S.* ex rel. *Knauff* v. *Shaughnessy* (1950); *U.S.* ex rel. *Eichenlaub* v. *Shaughnessy* (1950); *Ackermann* v. *U.S.* (1950); *Jordan* v. *De George* (1951); *Harisiades* v. *Shaughnessy* (1952); *Carlson* v. *Landon* (1952); *U.S.* v. *Spector* (1952); *Kawakita* v. *U.S.* (1952); *Heikkila* v. *Barber* (1953); *Shaughnessy* v. *U.S.* ex rel. *Mezei* (1953). The Klapprott decision was against the alien, in the sense that the dissenting opinion would have been more favorable to his claims.

Negroes (4): For Negro claims (3): *Bob-Lo Excursion Co.* v. *Michigan* (1948); *Brotherhood of Railroad Trainmen* v. *Howard* (1952); *Barrows* v. *Jackson* (1953). Against Negro claims (1): *Briggs* v. *Elliott* (1952).

State criminal defendants (37): For defendants' claims (13): *Haley* v. *Ohio* (1948); *Wade* v. *Mayo* (1948); *Townsend* v. *Burke* (1948); *Uveges* v. *Pennsylvania* (1948); *Watts* v. *Indiana* (1949); *Turner* v. *Pennsylvania* (1949); *Harris* v. *South Carolina* (1949); *Cassell* v. *Texas* (1950); *Keenan* v. *Burke* (1951); *Palmer* v. *Ashe* (1951); *Jennings* v. *Illinois* (1951); *Dixon* v. *Duffy* (1952); *Daniels* v. *Allen* (1953). Against defendants' claims (24): *Carter* v. *Illinois* (1946); *Louisiana* ex rel. *Francis* v. *Resweber* (1947); *Gayes* v. *New York* (1947); *Foster* v. *Illinois* (1947); *Fay* v. *New York* (1947); *Adamson* v. *California* (1947); *Bute* v. *Illinois* (1948); *Gryger* v. *Burke* (1948); *Moore* v. *New York* (1948); *Taylor* v. *Alabama* (1948); *Wolf* v. *Colorado* (1949); *Quicksall* v. *Michigan* (1950); *Darr* v. *Burford* (1950); *Gallegos* v. *Nebraska* (1951); *Stefanelli* v. *Minard* (1951); *Leland* v. *Oregon* (1952); *Stroble* v. *California* (1952); *Schwartz* v. *State* (1952); *Sweeney* v. *Woodall* (1952); *Edelman* v. *California* (1952); *Brock* v. *North Carolina* (1953); *U.S.* ex rel. *Smith* v. *Baldi* (1953); *Brown* v. *Allen* (1953); *Stein* v. *New York* (1953).

Federal criminal defendants (21): For defendants' claims (9): *Ballard* v. *U.S.* (1946); *Upshaw* v. *U.S.* (1948); *Lustig* v. *U.S.* (1949); *McDonald* v. *U.S.* (1948); *Von Moltke* v. *Gillies* (1948); *U.S.* v. *Di Re* (1948); *Johnson* v. *U.S.* (1948); *Trupiano* v. *U.S.* (1948); *U.S.* v. *Jeffers*. Against defendants' claims (12): *Harris* v. *U.S.* (1947); *Frazier* v. *U.S.* (1948); *Humphrey* v. *Smith* (1949); *Wade* v. *Hunter* (1949); *Brinegar* v. *U.S* (1949); *Dennis* v. *U.S.* (1950); *U.S.* v. *Rabinowitz* (1950); *On Lee* v. *U.S.* (1952); *Lutwak* v. *U.S.* (1953); *Burns* v. *Wilson* (1953); *U.S.* v. *Grainger* (1953); *Rosenberg* v. *U.S.* (1953).

State free speech claims (16): For free speech claims (4): *Craig* v. *Harney* (1947); *Saia* v. *New York* (1948); *Terminiello* v. *Chicago* (1949); *Kunz* v. *New York* (1951). Against free speech claims (12): *Fisher* v. *Pace* (1949); *Kovacs* v. *Cooper* (1949); *International Brotherhood of Teamsters* v. *Hanke* (1950); *Breard* v. *City of Alexandria* (1951); *Feiner* v. *New York* (1951); *Tenney* v. *Brandhove* (1951); *Garner* v. *Board of Public Works* (1951); *Beauharnais* v. *Illinois* (1952); *Adler* v. *Board of Education* (1952); *Montgomery Building Trades* v. *Ledbetter Erection Co.* (1952); *Local Union No. 10.* v. *Graham* (1953); *Poulos* v. *New Hampshire* (1953).

Federal free speech claims (12): For free speech claims (2): *Christoffel* v. *U.S.* (1949); *Joint Anti-Fascist Refugee Committee* v. *McGrath* (1951). Against free speech claims (10): *United Public Workers* v. *Mitchell* (1947); *American Communications Assn.* v. *Douds* (1950); *Osman* v. *Douds* (1950); *U.S.* v. *Bryan* (1950); *U.S.* v. *Fleischman* (1950); *Dennis* v. *U.S.* (1951); *Rogers* v. *U.S.* (1951); *Bailey* v. *Richardson* (1951); *Sacher* v. *U.S.* (1952); *In re Isserman* (1953). *Bailey* v. *Richardson* was a tie, but it had the effect of upholding the unfavorable lower court decision.

said, a place remains for a properly prepared box score used to highlight or summarize or put in shorthand form findings which support and give additional meaning to the results of more orthodox inquiry.

The data of Table 9, then, cannot be accepted as an index of personal attachment to libertarian values on the part of the justices. These votes were cast not in their personal but in their judicial capacity and represented their resolution of situations where many legitimate values may have been competing for attention. What the table does establish is the degree to which each member of the Court found it desirable or possible *as a judge* to prefer libertarian values over others present in the proceedings. These are what Mark De Wolfe Howe calls "relational statistics"; and, although Howe is a bitter critic of the statistical method as applied to judicial decisions, he is willing to admit that, if interpreted on this basis, box scores may be acceptable.[6] But he adds the warning that relational statistics "have significance only when discriminating account is taken of all the values which are brought into relationship."

Obviously, it is impossible to identify all the values which each justice may have related to the decision of a case. But the working hypothesis suggested by the material of the preceding chapters is that a decision involving civil liberties questions will be primarily influenced by the interaction of two factors. One is the direction and intensity of a justice's libertarian sympathies, which will vary according to his weighting of the relative claims of liberty and order in our society. Theoretically, positions on a liberty-order attitude scale could range from an individualistic anarchism at one extreme to rigid authoritarianism on the other. The orthodoxy required for a Supreme Court appointment insures, however, that the spread of opinion among members of that body will be much narrower.

The second factor is the conception which the justice holds of his judicial role and the obligations imposed on him by his judicial function. Every justice in deciding a case must give some thought to what is appropriate for him as a judge to do. The pressures which bear upon him are many, and they are mostly toward a pattern of conformity—conformity with precedents, conformity with the traditions of the law, conformity with public expectations as to how a judge should act, conformity toward established divisions of authority in a federal system based on the principle of separation of powers. While no justice can be oblivious to these pressures, they are not self-enforcing, and he is free to make his own interpretations of their requirements in guiding his own judicial conduct. The attitude scale involved may be thought of as ranging from an expansionist to a contractionist judicial philosophy, from broad to narrow judicial review, from judicial activism to judicial restraint.

Any attempt to rank justices on these two scales in an absolute fashion would be hopeless, but it should not be so difficult to locate them relatively to each other, and particularly by reference to their deviation from the Court's majority position at any one time. Table 9 shows that five members of the Vinson Court—Murphy, Rutledge, Douglas, Black, and Frankfurter—voted for libertarian claims substantially more often than the Court majority. In terms of our hypothesis, the extremely high rate of support for libertarian claims registered by the first four of these justices suggests that they are strongly positive on both scales; their personal preferences must be strongly libertarian, and they must have a conception of their judicial function which permits, or even requires, them to give judicial effect to these preferences. Without assuming any absolute identity of views on their part, the motivation of these four justices can be characterized as "libertarian activism."

THE SIGN OF FOUR

"The law," said Justice Murphy in the Falbo case, "knows no finer hour than when it cuts through formal concepts and transitory emotions to protect unpopular citizens against discrimination and persecution."[7] This one sentence seems to capsulate much of the motivation of the libertarian activist. There is implicit, first of all, a judgment as to the relative worth of the different values which the Court may be called upon to protect. The libertarian holds with intense conviction to the general principles of an open society and the essentiality of the basic human liberties to the democratic way of life. The whole preferred-position argument, as developed in chapter ii, is built upon such a ranking of values. Black's words are very telling:

> I view the guaranties of the First Amendment as the foundation upon which our governmental system rests and without which it could not continue to endure as conceived and planned. Freedom to speak and write about public questions is as important to the life of our government as is the heart to the human body. In fact, this privilege is the heart of our government. If that heart be weakened, the result is debilitation; if it be stilled, the result is death.[8]

The height of the pedestal on which the libertarian activist places First Amendment freedoms gives them, in fact, a preference which is very nearly unassailable. As a practical matter, he is willing to concede that there is no absolute right to free speech, save for a Robinson Crusoe. Murphy said in the Chaplinsky case: "it is well understood that the right of free speech is not absolute at all times and under all circumstances." But in the heat of argument the activist periodically forgets these qualifications and is swept into defense of an absolutist position. Thus in *Wieman* v. *Updegraff* Black preached the necessity for an "uncompromising interpretation of the Bill of Rights" and insisted that the First Amendment invalidated "the slightest suppression of thought, speech, press or public assembly." And in *Poulos* v. *New Hampshire* Douglas said that "even a reasonable regulation of the right to free speech is not compatible with the First Amendment."

Associated with these absolutistic interpretations in the opinions written by the libertarian activists is a high degree of sympathetic identification with litigants whose civil liberties have allegedly been violated. No adventure in content analysis will be attempted here, but the case of *Carlson* v. *Landon* well illustrates the difference between neutral and sympathetic judicial treatment. Justice Reed's majority opinion veiled the impact of the deportations at issue by impersonal and colorless references to petitioners' "many years residence spent in this country" and "their integration into community life through marriage and family connections." Black, on the other hand, set forth in detail the personal circumstances of the aliens involved. From his dissent we learn that Mrs. Stevenson, one of the candidates for deportation, has a son who "has long been subject to attacks of undulant fever"; that the son and his seventy-year-old grandmother need Mrs. Stevenson's help; and that her husband is doing the housework while she is "detained in jail as dangerous to our national security." As for two other deportees, we learn that Mr. Carlisle's health is bad; that Mr. Zydok is fifty-six years old, has two American-born sons who served in World War II, sold $50,000 worth of war bonds during the war while working as a waiter, and donated blood on seven occasions to the Red Cross.

Are these personal details recounted by Black irrelevant appeals to sympathy? Do such data merely obscure the basic legal issue as to whether Congress had intended to give the Attorney General discretion to detain suspect aliens without bail? Or is it possible that these glimpses of the kind of people against whom the Attorney General had chosen to exercise his legislatively delegated powers give some useful perspective for judicial review?

The emotional overtones present in numerous libertarian dissents give some hint of the sense of personal involvement in the controversy experienced by these justices. Of the many illustrations which could be given, the indignant finale of Rutledge's dissent in *Foster* v. *Illinois*, an alleged denial-of-counsel case, has been selected:

> When men appear in court for trial or plea, obviously without counsel or so far as appears the means of securing such aid, under serious charges such as were made here involving penalties of the character imposed, it is altogether inconsistent with their federal constitutional right for the court to shut its eyes to their apparently helpless condition without so much as an inquiry concerning its cause. A system so callous of the rights of men, not only in their personal freedom but in their rights to trial comporting with any conception of fairness, as to tolerate such action, is in my opinion wholly contrary to the scheme of things the nation's charter establishes. Courts and judges, under that plan, owe something more than the negative duty to sit silent and blind while men go on their way to prison, for all that appears, for want of any hint of their rights.
>
> Adding to this blindness a "presumption of regularity" to sustain what has thus been done makes a mockery of judicial proceedings in any

sense of the administration of justice and a snare and a delusion of constitutional rights for all unable to pay the cost of securing their observance.

It is, of course, possible for emotion to be so strongly experienced as to overbear reason. Perhaps this happened to Justice Murphy in the Hirota case, where, as already noted, the Court said it was powerless to review the conviction by an international tribunal. Murphy dissented, but without giving any reason, creating what John Frank calls a "mysterious intellectual episode": "The dissent presumably means that he felt the petition should have been received; but it is impossible, for this commentator at least, even to conceive of a theory on which the Supreme Court might have had jurisdiction, and it would have been interesting to know what Justice Murphy had in mind."[9]

Almost by definition, the sympathies of the libertarian are principally aroused by the "unpopular citizens" of whom Murphy spoke, the weak and friendless, the minorities, the victims of all kinds of discrimination, suppression, or brutality. The activist is "an automatic defender of the underdog."[10] The discussion of the preceding chapters should have made clear the extent of libertarian support of such notable underdogs as aliens, racial and religious minorities, and defendants in criminal trials. Another underdog with whom Murphy especially was in sympathetic rapport was the American Indian. In five elaborate treaty disputes between 1942 and 1947, Murphy was always on the side of the Indians; and the opinions he wrote in these cases required an immense amount of digging through old treaties, legislative debates, executive agency records, and maps.[11] His attitude is well illustrated by a quotation from one of his dissenting opinions:

> As a people our dealings with the Indian tribes have been too often marked by injustice, neglect and even ruthless disregard of their interests and necessities. As a nation we have incurred moral and political responsibilities toward them and their descendants which have been requited in some measure by treaties and statutes framed for the protection and advancement of their interests. Those enactments should always be read in the light of this high and noble purpose, in a manner that will give full scope and effect to the humane and liberal policy that has been adopted by the Congress to rectify past wrongs.[12]

Another group of cases with considerable appeal for libertarian justices on underdog grounds are workmen's compensation proceedings, which in the federal courts typically pit an injured railroad or maritime worker against his employer. The Federal Employers' Liability Act is an archaic method of acknowledging the responsibility of society for railroad accidents. The fact of negligence on the part of the carrier must be established, usually by jury trial. The original reception of the act by the courts was not favorable. Numerous restrictive interpretations were grafted on to the statute, and doubtful questions of fact were often taken from the jury and resolved by the courts in favor of the employer. The Supreme Court itself was active in overturning jury verdicts rendered for employees.

Congress undertook to correct the first of these conditions by amendatory legislation in 1939,[13] and the Roosevelt Court sought to correct the second by granting certiorari in a considerable number of cases in which jury verdicts for the employee had been set aside by the courts. On the Vinson Court this activity continued, the activist bloc having within itself the four votes needed to grant certiorari. In 1949 Justice Frankfurter noted that during the previous decade 30 petitions for certiorari had been granted to review a judgment denying recovery under the Employers' Liability Act in a case turning solely on jury issues, while in the same period only one similar petition on behalf of a carrier had been granted. In rebuttal, Douglas argued that the Court in these cases was helping to undo the mischief it had originally caused and restoring "the historic role of the jury . . . in this important class of cases."[14]

The principal religious minority before the Court in recent years has been Jehovah's Witnesses, and the greater part of their troubles with the law occurred prior to the Vinson Court.[15] In the 1940 flag-salute case, the libertarians—then only a trio—had not fully awakened to the implications of the issue, and they did not support Stone, who was the lone dissenter against the decision upholding the flag salute as a compulsory exercise for public school children.[16] But within two years the three had joined Stone in a four-judge dissent to the first municipal license tax case, and they took advantage of the opportunity to confess that they had been wrong about the flag salute.[17] With Rutledge's addition to the Court for the 1942 term, the libertarians were seldom thereafter divided in a Jehovah's Witnesses case or unfavorable to the contentions of the sect.[18] Black showed his underdog sentiments very clearly in this sentence from the Jehovah's Witnesses case of *Martin* v. *Struthers:* "Door to door distribution of circulars is essential to the poorly financed causes of little people."

Sympathy for the underdog can seldom be given effect without a corresponding rejection of the claims of the upperdog. A decision that Jehovah's Witnesses can operate their loud-speaker in a small park on Sunday devalues the claims of those who just want to sit in the park and relax. The right of a Fascist to harangue his followers involves some conflict with the right of the community to be free from riots. The activist "infracaninophile"[19] consistently favors the injured few over the allegedly suffering many.

There is one element in Murphy's Falbo statement which seems inconsistent with libertarian interests, and that is his derogation of "formal concepts." In fact, examination of activist decisions reveals that they are much concerned with matters of form and procedure and often rely on formal concepts to achieve libertarian victories. This strategy is particularly apparent in the Court's review of criminal prosecutions. The libertarian typically insists upon strict and literal adherence to the procedural safeguards surrounding the administration of justice. Thus in the controversy over application of the Bill of Rights to state criminal prosecutions, the four libertarian activists were united in preferring the relatively specific constitutional standards to the vaguer "standards of civilized decency" which were all that the Court majority was prepared to make effective in state trials.

Other areas of disagreement further demonstrate this rigorous libertarian insistence on procedural protection. One essential of fair procedure is due notice, and notice is not given if the statute under which prosecution is proceeding defines the crime vaguely or indefinitely. Libertarian application of the "void for vagueness" rule controlled the decision in the 1948 case of

Winters v. *New York*, where the four libertarians plus Reed and Vinson invalidated a New York statute which, as interpreted, forbade the "massing" of stories of bloodshed and lust in magazines in such a way as to incite to crime against the person. The clause, "so massed as to incite to crime," the Court said, "is not an effective notice of new crime. The clause has no technical or common law meaning." "Void for vagueness" is certainly a "formal concept."

A final illustration of libertarian use of formal concepts to protect unpopular persons is supplied by the appeal of the Japanese general, Yamashita, against his war-trial conviction. Yamashita's trial by an American military commission for violation of the laws of war was held by the Court majority not to be subject to judicial review; but Murphy and Rutledge both insisted on examining and condemning the procedures which General MacArthur had authorized for the trial. Murphy believed that Yamashita was "rushed to trial under an improper charge, given insufficient time to prepare an adequate defense, deprived of the benefits of some of the most elementary rules of evidence and summarily sentenced to be hanged."[20]

What, then, is the explanation of Murphy's apparent inconsistency of attitude toward formal concepts? Perhaps we find an answer in his reaction to the 1946 case of *Carter* v. *Illinois*. The Court majority, in considering the fairness of a state trial, had declined to go behind the "common law record," although there were known facts outside that record indicating that the trial had been improper. Murphy said:

> Legal technicalities doubtless afford justification for our pretense of ignoring plain facts before us, facts upon which a man's very life or liberty conceivably could depend. Moreover, there is probably legal warrant for our not remanding the case . . . to allow those facts to be incorporated in the formal record. . . . But the *result* certainly does not enhance the high traditions of the judicial process.[21]

For the judicial activist, the *result* is the test of a decision. The validity of formal concepts depends upon whether their use gives the right answer. The activist appears to experience a deep sense of personal responsibility for the immediate consequences of his judicial decisions. This incubus can be avoided by a conception that the Court is operating within limits and manipulating its powers according to external standards provided by the legal system. This view was well stated by Justice Gibson in 1825, when he argued that justices are in the situation of jurors in capital cases, who "do not deprive a prisoner of life by finding him guilty of a capital crime; [they] but pronounce his case to be within the law, and it is therefore those who declare the law . . . who deprive him of life."[22] But the activist cannot accept this limited role. He cannot rid himself of the notion that the Court does have a range of discretion, that there are choices open to him. Consequently, he must make the choice which will give the right result. He cannot reconcile himself to the idea that there can be a wrong without a remedy—and a judicial remedy, not merely a legislative or electoral remedy.

Consistency for the libertarian activist is the consistency of seeking, wherever possible, the libertarian result. In one case this may require loose construction of a statute, in another strict construction. Take two illustrative situations. Federal legislation covering railroad injuries, as already noted, is hopelessly old-fashioned; railroads are liable only for accidental injuries to employees resulting from the negligence of other employees. The activist reaction is to bring the legislation up to date and protect the underdog by broadly interpreting its standards. Thus a fireman who had contracted silicosis by breathing silica dust from sand that was used in locomotive sanding boxes alleged faultily to release excessive amounts of sand was held to have suffered an "injury" under the Federal Employers' Liability Act and an "accident" within the meaning of the Boiler Inspection Act.[23]

Contrariwise, narrow construction was the libertarian reaction of Justice Black in *United States* v. *Alpers*, involving a conviction for shipping obscene phonograph records in interstate commerce. Black dissented from the conviction, because the statute covered shipment of obscene books, pamphlets, pictures, films, "or other matter of indecent character," but did not mention phonograph records specifically. "Censorship in any field may so readily encroach on constitutionally protected liberties that courts should not add to the list of items banned by Congress," he said.

Similarly, the libertarian activist's attitude toward procedural requirements varies according to the results achieved. Where procedure is a restraint on interference with liberties, it is welcomed and even treated as a constitutional requirement. Thus in *Trupiano* v. *United States*, Murphy's majority opinion insisted that a search warrant was necessary to justify seizure of moonshining equipment, even though the operator of the still was lawfully arrested in the midst of the implements of his crime. This is the same justice who believed in cutting through formal requirements if they stood in the way of libertarian results.

These reflections, which obviously fall far short of "explaining" the motivations characterized here as libertarian activism, are not to be interpreted as expressing either praise or dispraise for the judicial practices described. Some effort in this direction will be made in the final chapter. But at this point it is well to suggest that, even if the analysis of the present chapter is correct, no implication should be drawn that these judicial reactions or practices are unique or characteristic of only a few members of the Court. It would, indeed, be a very irresponsible or unrealistic justice who was not concerned about the consequences of his decisions and who did not test his reasoning by the kind of results it produced. Jackson has admitted his concern with results as frankly as Murphy. In the Mezei case he said: "Despite the impeccable legal logic of the Government's argument on this point, it leads to an artificial and unreal conclusion." If there are differences between the justices classified as libertarian activists and other members of the Court, they are, of course, differences of degree. The nature of some of these differences is the subject of the next chapter.

XI. *Libertarian Restraint*

Justice Frankfurter

The Vinson Court's fifth libertarian, according to the evidence of Table 9, was Justice Frankfurter. However, the substantially lesser degree of support for libertarian claims shown by his record indicates that he was either less libertarian or less activist or both than the four justices who outranked him. There is a widespread impression that Frankfurter has not acted like a liberal on the Court. It derives from the position he has taken in such important controversies as the two flag-salute cases, the two sound-truck cases, *Dennis* v. *United States*, *Feiner* v. *New York*, *International Brotherhood of Teamsters* v. *Hanke*, and numerous others. It derives also from the bitter campaign he has waged against the use of the clear-and-present-danger test, with or without preferred-position amplification, as a guide for judicial decisions in the civil liberties field.

These apparently antilibertarian doctrines and results, however, can be at least partially explained on the basis of a libertarian theory—the theory that the primary responsibility of a liberal justice is to restrain the exercise of judicial power. This theory sees the Court not as crusader or advocate but as one of the instruments of political and social accommodation and adjustment in a complicated governmental system. As opposed to the goal-orientation of the activists, this view might be called functionally oriented. Its announced emphasis is not on securing a result conforming to the jurist's own scheme of values but upon adherence to appropriate judicial standards and proper manipulation of judicial techniques.

Standards for determining the appropriateness of judicial reactions are derived from considerations of the position of an appellate court within the federal judicial system and of the position of the entire judicial branch vis-à-vis the legislature and executive in a system based on the separation of powers. This point of view will be much concerned with fixing the boundaries of judicial power and will conceive that it is the justice's primary responsibility to stay within the confines of those boundaries.

In application, this concern about judicial limitations has been responsible for strict construction of the Court's jurisdiction over "cases and controversies," for the doctrine of "political questions" which are immune to judicial review, for the various rules protecting acts of Congress from being declared unconstitutional, for the "reasonable-man" theory of review of state legislation. Where the Court has in the past divided on application of these principles of judicial limitation, it has typically been the liberal justices who have stressed the necessity for judicial self-restraint, as opposed to the conservative practice of broad judicial review. It was a liberal minority which spoke through Justice Stone during the New Deal constitutional crisis with the now classic warning that "the only check upon our own exercise of power is our own sense of self-restraint."[1] And it was in *Ashwander* v. *TVA* that the liberal trio of Brandeis, Stone, and Cardozo reformulated the general principles of limited judicial review of constitutional questions.

This liberal doctrine of judicial restraint was a direct heritage for the Roosevelt Court, which found it effective in protecting progressive social legislation from invalidation, but somewhat less well adapted to the uses of crusading liberal justices confronted with legislative assaults on basic civil liberties. Thus the Roosevelt Court, though composed almost entirely of "liberals," quickly split apart on the issue of judicial restraint, and the division has continued on the Vinson Court. Frankfurter's attempts to apply these principles of libertarian restraint clearly account for many of the antilibertarian results he has achieved.

JUDICIAL RESTRAINT AND THE SEPARATION OF POWERS

The doctrine of judicial self-restraint, as it affects and has been developed by the Supreme Court, has been in large part an outgrowth of the system of separation of powers. The President,

Congress, and the Supreme Court have separate bases in the Constitution for their status and functions, but in operation they are interconnected and interdependent. The members of the Court are appointed by the President, with Senate confirmation. The Court relies upon the executive for enforcement of its decisions; the only enforcement officers under its own control are a few marshals. The Court's very jurisdiction depends upon the sufferance of Congress, which under the Constitution could cut off Supreme Court review of all cases except those which arise under the original jurisdiction of the Court, such as cases in which a state is a party. Statutory interpretations handed down by the Court can be reversed by congressional amendment of the statutes. A basic adjudication like that in the off-shore oil cases[2] can be nullified, as Congress did in 1953, by legislation quit-claiming the lands to the coastal states ousted by the Court's decisions. A declaration of unconstitutionality imposes a more substantial bar, but it can be overridden by the more complicated amendment process.

Under these circumstances, ordinary political prudence, if nothing more, must suggest to the Supreme Court the desirability of avoiding contests with the other two branches. For Justice Frankfurter, considerations of prudence are reinforced by his strong belief that the Court is the least representative or democratically responsible of the three branches. In *Dennis* v. *United States* he wrote: "Courts are not representative bodies. They are not designed to be a good reflex of a democratic society. Their judgment is best informed, and therefore most dependable, within narrow limits." And on another occasion he went so far as to say that "the powers exercised by this Court are inherently oligarchic."[3]

Frankfurter consequently feels under great pressure to yield to both Congress and the executive in cases of conflict. The sharpest challenge the Court can direct at Congress is to declare unconstitutional a law it has passed. On numerous occasions Frankfurter has spelled out his conception of the Court's obligation to use this power with "humility" and to base its judgments of constitutionality not on "feelings" but on "rational standards" which are "impersonal and communicable."[4] But application of such principles of restraint does not, of necessity, preclude him from discovering limitations on legislative powers. In each of the following three cases, his reasoning achieved at least a short-run libertarian result, but in each case his premises in challenging legislative action were narrower than those of the activists and revealed the effectiveness of his restraint philosophy.

United States v. *Lovett*, decided in 1946, held, as already mentioned, that appropriation language cutting off pay to three named federal employees was a bill of attainder. But Frankfurter (along with Reed) proposed to give these three employees their back salary on a technical ground without reaching the constitutional question. For, he said, "a decree of unconstitutionality by this Court is fraught with consequences so enduring and far-reaching as to be avoided unless no choice is left in reason."

Then there was the 1948 case of *United States* v. *C.I.O.*, which grew out of the Taft-Hartley Act's restriction on expenditures in political campaigns. The provision seemed to outlaw any comment on or participation in elections by labor newspapers if they were supported by general union funds—in fact, Senator Taft so stated when the bill was under consideration. The four activists held this "indiscriminate blanketing of every expenditure made in connection with an election" to be a prior restraint which could not be squared with the First Amendment. But Frankfurter was part of a five-judge majority which cleared the statute by holding that Congress had not intended to prohibit political comment by union newspapers.

The third example is *United States* v. *Rumely*, where Frankfurter for the Court ruled that the House of Representatives had not authorized an investigating committee to look into the distribution of literature by a lobbying organization, and thus again avoided a "grave constitutional question." Since the House had specifically voted approval of the committee's action, Black and Douglas could not follow Frankfurter's reasoning or avoid the constitutional issue.

When we turn to judicial-executive relations, the same inclination to bend over backward to avoid conflicts is evident. Here the principal issues have arisen in the foreign-affairs field; and on such matters the Court has traditionally been very reluctant to intervene because of the President's broad constitutional authority and the practical reasons which make quick and authoritative executive action essential.

Frankfurter wrote the Court's decision, to which the activists dissented, in *Ludecke* v. *Watkins.* There, as already noted, he upheld the power of the President, under the Alien Enemy Act of 1798, to deport alien enemies in wartime without provision for judicial review. He said:

> Such great war powers may be abused, no doubt, but that is a bad reason for having judges supervise their exercise. . . . Accordingly, we hold that full responsibility for the just exercise of this great power may validly be left where the Congress has constitutionally placed it—on the President of the United States. The Founders in their wisdom made him not only the Commander-in-Chief but also the guiding organ in the conduct of our foreign affairs. He who was entrusted with such vast powers in relation to the outside world was also entrusted by Congress, almost throughout the entire life of the nation, with the disposition of alien enemies during a state of war. Such a page of history is worth more than a volume of rhetoric.

Frankfurter expressed a similar philosophy, though in a minority, in the Hawaiian martial law case of 1946, *Duncan* v. *Kahanomoku.* With the Japanese attack on Pearl Harbor, martial law had been declared in Hawaii by the governor, an action which the President approved two days later. Civil and criminal courts were forbidden to try cases, and military tribunals were set up to replace them. The Supreme Court majority, composed of the Four plus Stone and Reed, ruled in this test case that when Congress had granted the governor of Hawaii power to declare "martial law," it had not "intended to authorize the supplanting of courts by military tribunals." Murphy would have gone further and held that such trials were unconstitional.

Burton and Frankfurter were the only justices who believed that the Court was impinging on executive territory. They felt that "the conduct of war under the Constitution is largely an executive function," in which "executive discretion to determine policy is . . . intended by the Constitution to be supreme," at least on the battlefield. The original declaration of martial law after the Pearl Harbor attack was clearly justified, and the executive authorities should be allowed a reasonable period in which "to decide when and how to restore the battle field to its peace time controls." They feared that the Court in condemning, from the safe vantage point of 1946, the military decisions made in 1941 and 1942, might be establishing a precedent "which in other emergencies may handicap the executive branch of the Government in the performance of duties allotted to it by the Constitution."

ACTIVISM AND RESTRAINT IN THE STEEL CASE

So far as the Supreme Court's interpretation of separation of powers goes, however, all other cases pale into insignificance compared with the Court's ruling in the famous 1952 steel seizure case, which invalidated President Truman's seizure of the nation's steel industry. Opinions may well differ as to whether this was a civil liberties decision. The constitutional issues it dealt with did not grow out of the Bill of Rights, and its immediate impact was upon property rights rather than freedom of speech, thought, or person. Yet some of the Supreme Court justices and a large part of the press certainly related the issue to a broader civil liberty framework. In any case, the decision is extremely important for the light it casts on current judicial practice relative to the doctrines of self-restraint.[5]

Briefly, the facts in the case of *Youngstown Sheet and Tube Co.* v. *Sawyer* were as follows: In the latter part of 1951 a dispute arose between the steel companies and their employees over terms and conditions of employment. On December 18 the steel workers' union gave notice of intention to strike when the existing agreements expired on December 31. On December 22 President Truman referred the dispute to the Federal Wage Stabilization Board, and the strike was called off, but the board's subsequent report produced no settlement. On April 4, 1952, notice of a strike for April 9 was issued. A few hours before the strike was to begin, the President issued Executive Order 10340, directing the Secretary of Commerce to take possession of and operate the steel mills of the country. The President based his action on a contention that the work stoppage would jeopardize the national defense, particularly in Korea. The next morning he sent a message to Congress reporting his action, and a second message on April 21. The steel companies obeyed the Secretary's orders under protest and brought suit for injunction against him in the District of Columbia district court. On April 30 Judge Pine granted a preliminary injunction restraining the Secretary from continuing the seizure. On the same day the court of appeals stayed the injunction. The Supreme Court accepted the case on May 3 and heard arguments beginning May 12. The decision was rendered June 2, the Court holding by a six to three vote that the President had exceeded his constitutional powers.

The doctrine of judicial self-restraint rigorously applied in this situation would call for upholding the President's action if at all possible or, alternatively, for finding some reason for judicial nonintervention. There were procedural grounds available for the latter purpose.[6] The case could have been remanded to the district court with directions to make findings on the facts as they bore on the constitutional issue. Judge Pine had made no finding as to whether the President was justified in his claim that a national emergency existed, having treated the existence of such an emergency as irrelevant to the constitutional issue.[7] Or the Court could have found several technical reasons for invalidating the injunction. Before a judge issues an injunction, he is supposed to determine that there is no remedy at law and that the damages from which injunctive relief is sought are irreparable. He is supposed, in using this time-honored equitable remedy, to balance the equities, and particularly in the case of a public official claiming to act in the public interest, when the issue is a broad question of constitutional power, he should be very reluctant to issue a preliminary injunction prior to a full trial. Judge Pine, however, simply assumed the damages were irreparable and said that more facts would not alter his "fixed conclusion . . . that defendant's acts are illegal."

The Supreme Court did not choose to base its decision on technical grounds, either, but met the substantive issue head-on. Given this approach, was there any basis on which a justice dedicated to self-restraint could have upheld the President's action? The answer is that there was and that Chief Justice Vinson wrote such an opinion, which was concurred in by Reed and Minton.

Vinson's theory of the President's seizure was that its purpose was "to faithfully execute the laws by acting in an emergency to maintain the status quo, thereby preventing collapse of the legislative programs [military procurement and anti-inflation] until Congress could act." In the message sent to Congress immediately after the seizure, the President explained this reason for his action "and expressed his desire to co-operate with any legislative proposals approving, regulating or rejecting the seizure of the steel mills." His action was intended "only to save the situation until Congress could act."

Vinson argued that action for this purpose was constitutional, for two reasons. First, the relevant statutes in effect at the time gave the President free choice as to what remedy, if any, he should attempt to apply in averting a steel strike. There were on the statute books three laws which might be considered available for use by the President. The first was the Selective Service Act of 1948, which specifically gave the President authority to seize plants which fail to produce goods required by the armed forces or the Atomic Energy Commission for national defense purposes.

The second was the Taft-Hartley Act, which includes provisions adopted for the purpose of dealing with nation-wide strikes. Under this act the President was authorized to appoint a board of inquiry and thereafter, in proper cases, seek injunctive relief for an eighty-day period against a threatened work stoppage. The President can invoke that procedure whenever, in his opinion, "a threatened or actual strike . . . affecting an entire industry . . . will, if permitted to occur or to continue, imperil the national health or safety." The act contains no seizure provisions.

The third was the Defense Production Act of 1950, Title II of which delegates to the President power to acquire by condemnation property needed for national defense, when the need is immediate and all other means of securing the property on a fair basis have been exhausted. This provision was obviously not thought of as a way of dealing with strikes, for Title V covered the mediation of labor disputes affecting national defense, though it created no sanctions for the settlement of such disputes. Under this latter authority the President had created the Wage Stabilization Board, and he later added disputes functions to its duties.[8]

Among the four alternatives available under these three acts, President Truman chose the last by referring the dispute to the Wage Stabilization Board to investigate and make recommendations for fair and equitable terms of settlement. By using this method, he actually secured a ninety-nine-day delay of the strike call, compared with the eighty-day cooling-off period under Taft-Hartley. The WSB was also able to check the recommended wage settlement against its own wage stabilization regulations, which a Taft-Hartley board of inquiry could not have done.

But the objection was that the Taft-Hartley Act procedure, which made no provision for seizure, was the one Congress had developed specifically to deal with nation-wide strikes. Now it may well have been a vindictive hostility to that act, which was passed over his veto, which led President Truman to ignore it; but the fact is that the provisions of the statute leave its invocation within the discretion of the President. He used his discretion and chose the alternative remedy of the WSB. In Vinson's opinion, "Taft-Hartley was a route parallel to, not connected with, the W.S.B. procedure." Having exhausted the WSB procedure, the President was under no obligation to try Taft-Hartley as well.

This brings us to Vinson's second point, which is that the President, having exhausted the statutory remedy he chose to use, was justified in seizing the mills as a temporary means of averting a strike, pending congressional action. Admittedly, there was no statutory authorization for the seizure,[9] but Vinson regarded the constitutional grant of "executive power" to the President and his constitutional responsibility to "take care that the laws be faithfully executed" as providing inherent power for such presidential action. There were two contrary positions on the Court—that the President had no such inherent power or that the inherent power which the President might otherwise have had, had been eliminated in this situation when Congress refused to include seizure authority in the Taft-Hartley Act.

Judge Pine's decision had adopted the first point of view. He denied that the President had any "inherent" powers not traceable to an express grant in the Constitution. As his sole authority for this position, he cited a passage from the book which William Howard Taft wrote after he had been President and before he was Chief Justice:

> The true view of the Executive functions is, as I conceive it, that the President can exercise no power which cannot be fairly and reasonably traced to some specific grant of power or justly implied and included within such express grant as proper and necessary to its exercise. Such specific grant must be either in the Federal Constitution or in an act of Congress passed in pursuance thereof. There is no undefined residuum of power which he can exercise because it seems to him to be in the public interest . . . his jurisdiction must be justified and vindicated by affirmative constitutional or statutory provision, or it does not exist.[10]

Taft's position was in direct contradiction to the so-called "stewardship" theory of Theodore Roosevelt, who contended that the President could "do anything that the needs of the Nation demanded unless such action was forbidden by the Constitution or by the laws."[11] But Judge Pine dismissed the stewardship theory as one which does not "comport with our recognized theory of government." The numerous instances in American history where presidents have acted on a theory of inherent powers he dismissed as "repetitive, unchallenged, illegal acts."

While Judge Pine's action in enjoining the steel seizure was upheld by the Supreme Court, it is important to understand that his denial of inherent powers to the President was not ratified by the Court. Only Black and Douglas approved the Pine position that the President was limited to expressly granted powers, and even they made no specific reference to the Taft statement. Frankfurter and Burton found a consideration of inherent powers unnecessary to decision of the case. Clark fully accepted the doctrine of inherent powers, and Jackson substantially did so. Thus there were at least five votes against Pine's constitutional interpretation; and Vinson's opinion, speaking for

Reed and Minton as well, stands as the most authoritative statement on the general nature of presidential power to emerge from the confusion of the steel seizure decision.

How, then, does it happen that the government lost the case? The answer to this question requires some analysis of the position taken by the six majority justices, each of whom wrote an opinion. Black wrote the opinion of the Court, in which Douglas concurred. True to their activist inclinations and undeterred by any sense of judicial self-restraint, they, like Judge Pine, took up dogmatic positions based on a hard-and-fast interpretation of the separation of powers. Black's statement of this theory, in its rigor and naïveté, is probably without precedent in Supreme Court history. He disposes of the entire controversy in thirteen paragraphs, and his argument is on such a plane of lofty moral and constitutional generalities that he does not bother to cite a single Supreme Court decision bearing on the substantive issue.[12] Actually, no one else but Douglas accepted Black's separation of powers dogma.[13] Frankfurter specifically attached a paragraph to Black's opinion for the Court in order to warn that "the considerations relevant to the legal enforcement of the principle of separation of powers seem to me more complicated and flexible than may appear from what Mr. Justice Black has written."

Consequently, we must turn away from Black and Douglas to the other four majority justices in a search for the real doctrine of the steel decision. All four of their decisions contrast favorably with those of Black and Douglas in their humility and in their recognition that the American Constitution is a pragmatic affair. Jackson stresses the folly of any rigorous notions about strict separation of the branches of government. Successful operation of our system requires a combination of "separateness" with "interdependence," "autonomy" with "reciprocity." He says that "presidential powers are not fixed but fluctuate, depending upon their disjunction or conjunction with those of Congress." He finds that when the President "takes measures incompatible with the expressed or implied will of Congress, his power is at its lowest ebb"; and because he was convinced that the President had done that here, he found the action unconstitutional.

Justice Clark explicitly affirmed that "the Constitution does grant to the President extensive authority in times of grave and imperative national emergency. In fact, to my thinking, such a grant may well be necessary to the very existence of the Constitution itself." But he joined the majority because he believed that Congress had provided a statutory method of seizure in the Selective Service Act which the President had ignored.

It is Frankfurter's opinion, however, which holds greatest interest, as a careful and conscientious effort to reconcile judicial self-restraint with an adverse judgment on presidential action. He started his concurring opinion with another long disquisition about the judiciary not being "the overseer of our government" and the necessity for the judiciary to avoid constitutional questions, if at all possible. He rebuked Judge Pine for his indecent haste to get at the constitutional issue, which led the lower court to start at the "wrong end" of the case. But Frankfurter, after starting at the right end, made a surprisingly brief and superficial excursion through the jurisdictional issues and then concluded that he, too, must deal with the constitutional issue, though "with the utmost unwillingness" and "without attempting to define the President's powers comprehensively." "The judiciary may as this case proves have to intervene in determining where authority lies as between the democratic forces in our scheme of government. But in doing so we should be wary and humble. Such is the teaching of this Court's role in the history of the country."

Thus Frankfurter approached the problem, not as a matter of laying down the law to the President, but as a matter of balancing the equities in this particular instance between the two democratic branches of the government, to both of which the Supreme Court owed deference. Examination of congressional actions pertaining to the use of presidential seizure powers from 1916 to the passage of the Taft-Hartley Act convinced Frankfurter that Congress had "deemed seizure so drastic a power as to require it to be carefully circumscribed whenever the President was vested with this extraordinary authority. The power to seize has uniformly been given only for a limited period or for a defined emergency, or has been repealed after a short period."

When considering the Taft-Hartley bill, Frankfurter went on, Congress gave careful attention to the seizure device and on "a balance of considerations . . . chose not to lodge this power in the President." It is true that Congress did not write into the act a statutory prohibition on presidential seizure, but it

> expressed its will to withhold this power from the President as though it had said so in so many words. The authoritatively expressed purpose of Congress to disallow such power to the President and to require him, when in his mind the occasion arose for such a seizure, to put the matter to Congress and ask for specific authority from it, could not be more decisive if it had been written into . . . the . . . Act.

What happened in this case was that Frankfurter, the apostle of self-restraint, was caught in a crossfire between Congress and the President and could not be deferential to both. He chose Congress, but his opinion nonetheless gave respectful consideration to the case for the President, and he even wound up with the suggestion that a very minor change in the presidential seizure formula might have legitimized the action.[14] The careful restraint of his approach, contrasted with the activist, not to say reckless, dogmatism of the Black opinion, supplies an instructive lesson in judicial behavior which has a direct bearing on civil liberties problems.

SELF-RESTRAINT AND FEDERALISM

The existence of two levels of governmental authority in the American federal system and judicial responsibility for maintaining the constitutional allocation of functions between the two levels supply another system of restraints which Supreme Court justices may feel impelled to observe. This motivation can be seen clearly at work in Frankfurter's review of criminal convictions coming up from the state courts. Whereas the activist argues that in such cases the Court should take whatever action is necessary to achieve a just result for the individual defendant, the advocate of self-restraint holds that the Court can undertake to remedy injustices only in so far as its action is compatible with recognition of a wide measure of autonomy for state systems of justice and substantial presumptions of regularity in state procedures.

The contrast can best be brought out by specific situations. A 1948 case, *Taylor* v. *Alabama*, involved a nineteen-year-old Negro sentenced to execution for rape. The defendant had been ably represented by counsel, and confessions he had made were admitted without contention that they were in any way coerced. The day before the execution was to take place, new counsel for Taylor petitioned the Alabama supreme court to order the trial court to reopen the proceedings in order that affidavits might be presented as to physical violence allegedly suffered by Taylor in jail prior to his confessions. The state court refused, holding that the charges were "unreasonable and that there is no probability of truth contained therein." The Supreme Court, by a five to three vote, ruled that the Alabama court acted within its constitutional authority. The dissenters were Murphy, Douglas, and Rutledge, with Black not participating. Frankfurter's concurring opinion, in its strictures on Murphy's dissent, makes clear the former's standards for the relations between the Supreme Court and state courts:

> The dissenting opinion is written as though this Court were a court of criminal appeals for revision of convictions in the State courts. It is written as though we were asked to consider independently, and as a revisory appellate tribunal which had power to do so, whether a conviction in the courts of Alabama was based upon a coerced confession.

Again, in *Uveges* v. *Pennsylvania*, Frankfurter expressed a similar attitude of respect for state courts, this time in dissent along with Jackson and Burton. The majority had held that the defendant had been denied his constitutional right to counsel, and the minority might have agreed with them on the substantive issue. But what they objected to was the fact that the allegations on the basis of which the Supreme Court had granted certiorari had not been before the Pennsylvania supreme court when it denied an appeal in the case. Frankfurter consequently felt it to be quite improper for the Supreme Court to grant relief without allowing the state courts opportunity to correct their own errors. "After all," he concluded, "this is the Nation's ultimate judicial tribunal, not a super-legal-aid bureau."

One final illustration is found in the Terminiello case, where the Court majority had, by its own independent research, discovered a federal ground for reversing the conviction which had never been argued by the parties. Frankfurter saw this action as a rude upsetting of the "delicate" balance between federal and state courts. The Supreme Court had no authority to review state judgments unless some claim under the Constitution or laws of the United States had been made before the state court and denied by it. In this proceeding, "how could there have been a denial of a federal claim by the Illinois courts . . . when no such claim was made? . . . This is a court of review, not a tribunal unbounded by rules. We do not sit like a kadi under a tree dispensing justice according to considerations of individual expediency."[15]

A second civil liberties situation with potentialities of federal-state conflict arises out of application of the post–Civil War federal civil rights statutes. During the Reconstruction period Congress, under the domination of the Radical Republicans, passed numerous acts intended primarily to guarantee the civil rights of the newly freed Negroes. Some of this legislation was subsequently declared unconstitutional, and Congress repealed other parts. But certain provisions remained in effect and have supplied a basis for direct federal prosecution of state officials or even in some cases private citizens whose acts have infringed the rights guaranteed. During his tenure as Attorney General, Frank Murphy set up a Civil Rights Section in the Department of Justice, which has sponsored a more or less active program of enforcement based on these statutes.[16]

In 1945 the case of *Screws* v. *United States* required the Court to interpret this legislation as applied to a Georgia peace officer who had murdered a Negro whom he had under detention.[17] For the majority of the Roosevelt Court, including the activists, there was no federalism issue here. Their problem was whether or not this criminal statute was "void for vagueness," a matter which we have already noted as a characteristic libertarian concern. It was a three-judge minority of Roberts, Frankfurter, and Jackson which raised the federalism issue. They considered this to be a "patently local crime" and questioned "whether the States should be relieved from responsibility to bring their law officers to book for homicide, by allowing prosecutions in the federal courts for a relatively minor offense carrying a short sentence." This particular federal statute, born of the "vengeful" Reconstruction period, had been a "dead letter" for years. Its language was "shapeless and all-embracing," and it could serve as "a dangerous instrument" of political intimidation and coercion.

> The presuppositions of our federal system, the pronouncements of the statesmen who shaped this legislation, and the normal meaning of language powerfully counsel against attributing to Congress intrusion into the sphere of criminal law traditionally and naturally reserved for the States alone. . . . If it be significantly true that crimes against local law cannot be locally prosecuted, it is an ominous sign indeed. In any event, the cure is a re-invigoration of State responsibility. It is not an undue incursion of remote federal authority into local duties with consequent debilitation of local responsibility.

In 1951 the Court by a five to four vote upheld the principle of the Screws decision in *Williams* v. *United States*, where a Florida police officer had beaten theft suspects to secure confessions.[18] But in another case, decided the same day and arising out of the same Florida violence, *United States* v. *Williams*, Frankfurter and Jackson turned their Screws dissent into the Court's majority view.[19] At issue here was section 19 of the Criminal Code, a companion to section 20, which had been upheld in the Screws and first Williams decisions. The difference is that section 19 covers conspiracies of two or more persons against an individual's civil rights, while section 20 covers substantive offenses by persons acting "under color" of law. Rutledge had maintained in the Screws case that the basic rights guarded by both sections were identical, but Frankfurter was able in the second Williams case to impose a much more limited interpretation on section 19, restricting its protection to rights which Congress could constitutionally secure against interference by private individuals, such as the right to vote in congressional elections, and denying its coverage to those rights which Congress merely guarantees from interference by a state. Thus Frankfurter and Jackson won a partial victory in limiting the impact of federal civil rights legislation on the states.[20]

The same refusal to extend the protection of federal civil rights legislation was evident in *Collins* v. *Hardyman.* Members of the American Legion had broken up a meeting in California which intended to discuss the Marshall Plan and to adopt a resolution opposing it. The resolution was to be forwarded to federal officials in the form of a petition for redress of grievances, a type of communication guaranteed by the Constitution. A damage suit was brought against the persons who broke up the meeting under the so-called Ku Klux Act, alleging invasion of plaintiffs' civil rights. Frankfurter was part of a Court majority which denied that this was a conspiracy of such scope as to justify the application of federal protective legislation. It was simply a "lawless political brawl," Jackson said. "California courts are open to plaintiffs and its laws offer redress for their injury and vindication for their rights." Activists Black and Douglas, along with Burton, dissented, contending that the right to petition the federal government for a redress of grievances had been violated and that Congress had meant to protect such rights by this legislation.[21]

Finally, we can see the federalism issue as a restraint on the Court in its handling of certain election cases. Elections for federal offices under the American Constitution present a curious picture of divided federal-state responsibilities. Composition of the electorate is determined by the states, but within the limitations of the Fifteenth and Nineteenth Amendments. State officials set up and conduct the elections at which members of Congress are chosen, but subject to the overriding power of Congress to make or alter any such regulations as to the "times, places, and manner" of holding those elections. In such a setting of divided authority, the Supreme Court is bound to be called on repeatedly to exercise its adjudicatory functions.

On the whole, the Court has not been reluctant to implement the Constitution's supervisory controls over state election operations. Two illustrative cases from the period of the Roosevelt Court may be noted. One is *United States* v. *Classic*, decided in 1941, in which the Court ruled that Congress' authority to regulate elections extended to primaries, where "they are a step in the exercise by the people of their choice of representatives in Congress." The 1944 case of *Smith* v. *Allwright* ruled that the Democratic party in Texas was violating the Fifteenth Amendment by excluding Negroes from its party primaries, even though this exclusion was accomplished by party resolution rather than by state law.[22]

Aside from racial discrimination situations, however, the more recent Court under Frankfurter's leadership has been extremely reluctant to assert any authority over electoral matters. The key case was *Colegrove* v. *Green*, decided in 1946 after Stone's death and before Vinson's appointment. This proceeding was brought to test the legality of Illinois's failure since 1901 to redistrict the state for purposes of representation in the House of Representatives. As a result of this inaction, a great inequality had developed among the various congressional districts, with some almost nine times as populous as others. The Court was asked to declare the districting plan invalid, but it refused by a four to three vote. Frankfurter's opinion for the Court held that this was "an appeal to the federal courts to reconstruct the electoral process of Illinois," an issue which was "of a peculiarly political nature and therefore not meet for judicial determination." If there was any authority in the federal government to compel such reconstruction (and Frankfurter's opinion inferred that there was), it belonged to Congress and not to the courts. Moreover, Congress could handle the matter affirmatively, while all that the courts could do was the negative job of invalidating the existing system. Justices Black, Douglas, and Murphy dissented.

This same disposition was controlling in the 1948 case of *MacDougall* v. *Green*. The proceeding arose out of the efforts of Henry Wallace's Progressive party to get on the Illinois ballot for the presidential election in 1948. Illinois law requires that a petition to form and to nominate candidates for a new political party must be signed by 25,000 qualified voters, including 200 voters in each of at least 50 counties within the state. The Illinois election officials found that the Progressive party's petitions did not meet this requirement. Party officials then turned to the federal courts, alleging that the statute amounted to a denial of the due process, equal protection, and privileges and immunities clauses of the Fourteenth Amendment. Their argument was based on the peculiarities of population distribution in Illinois, where 87 per cent of the people reside in the 49 most populous counties, and only 13 per cent are residents of the 53 least populous counties.

By a per curiam opinion, with Douglas, Black, and Murphy dissenting, the Supreme Court refused relief. Unlike the decision in *Colegrove* v. *Green*, which denied the competence of the federal courts to pass judgment on such political matters, the Court in the MacDougall opinion definitely upheld the constitutionality of the statute. "It is allowable state policy," said the Court, "to require that candidates for state-wide office should have support not limited to a concentrated locality." The statutory provision here was not regarded as unreasonable, for of the 25,000 signatures, only 9,800, or 39 per cent, need be distributed, while the other 61 per cent could come from a single county. The opinion called attention to the unequal representation of population found in the United States Senate, and added:

> It would be strange indeed, and doctrinaire, for this Court, applying such broad constitutional concepts as due process and equal protection of the laws, to deny a State the power to assure a proper diffusion of political initiative as between its thinly populated counties and those having concentrated masses, in view of the fact that the latter have practical opportunities for exerting their political weight at the polls not available to the former.

Colegrove v. *Green* inflicted a considerably more serious casualty in 1950, when in *South* v. *Peters* the Court dismissed an attack upon the county unit system of voting in Georgia as applied in primary elections.[23] The system allots each county a number of unit votes, ranging from six for the eight most populous counties to two for most of the counties. A gross discrimination in favor of the smaller and rural counties results. On the average, each vote in Fulton County, in which Atlanta is located, has about one-eleventh the weight of votes cast in the rest of the state, and in one rural county votes were worth 120 times the votes in Atlanta. Wrapped up in the discrimination against urban counties was discrimination against Negroes, who normally did not vote in Georgia except in the cities.

The Supreme Court dismissed the suit contesting the constitutionality of this system in a per curiam opinion whose reasoning was confined to this single sentence: "Federal courts consistently refuse to exercise their equity powers in cases posing political issues arising from a state's geographical distribution of electoral strength among its political subdivisions." *Colegrove* v. *Green* and *MacDougall* v. *Green* were cited in support. Douglas and Black, dissenting, protested that the unit vote was a clear violation of the equal protection clause. The device Georgia was employing was "as deeply rooted in discrimination as the practice which keeps a man from the voting booth because of his race, creed, or color or which fails to count his vote after it has been cast," and for the Supreme Court to fail to move against it "undermines the advances made by the . . . *Classic* and *Allwright* cases."

JURISDICTIONAL LIMITATIONS

Finally, we may note the jurisdictional guise in which the self-restraint philosophy sometimes presents itself. Frankfurter, the keeper of the Court's jurisdictional conscience, has manifested great concern about the technicalities of jurisdiction; he has insisted that parties have a real and substantial interest in the litigation they inaugurate and has demanded that the Court protect itself from accepting cases which for any reason are not fully ripe for judicial review.

Take, for example, Frankfurter's position in *United States* v. *C.I.O.*, already discussed. During the oral argument in the case, Frankfurter, by his line of questioning, had appeared to charge that the government had connived with the CIO to get this test case into the courts.[24] His thought as formulated and clarified by his concurring opinion was not that the litigation had "been contrived by pre-arrangement of the parties" or that there were "derogatory implications of collusion." Rather his position was that both parties were so eager

> to elicit from this Court a decision at the earliest possible moment, [that] each side was at least unwittingly the ally of the other in

> bringing before this Court far-reaching questions of constitutionality under circumstances which all the best teachings of this Court admonish us not to entertain. . . . The questions involving the power of Congress come before us not so shaped by the record and by the proceedings below as to bring those powers before this Court as leanly and as sharply as judicial judgment upon an exercise of congressional power requires.

Consequently, he would have preferred to dismiss the proceedings as not fulfilling the spirit of the "case or controversy" requirement. Since the rest of the Court found that the case called for adjudication, however, he joined with the majority in construing the statute so as to avoid the constitutional issue.

This same attitude was even more forcefully stated in *Adler* v. *Board of Education of New York*, the 1952 case concerning the loyalty of public school teachers. Six members of the Court upheld the statute in question, while Black and Douglas considered it unconstitutional. Frankfurter alone took the position that the Court should have declined jurisdiction in the case, which had begun as a declaratory judgment action seeking to have the New York statute declared unconstitutional. He doubted whether the persons who had brought the suit—parents and teachers—had a sufficient legal interest to invoke judicial protection. Parents might prefer to have their children educated in a system where teachers did not feel restrained by such statutory limitations on their freedom.

> But it is like catching butterflies without a net to try to find a legal interest, indispensable for our jurisdiction, in a parent's desire to have his child educated in schools free from such restrictions. The hurt to parents' sensibilities is too tenuous or the inroad upon rightful claims to public education too argumentative to serve as the earthy stuff for a legal right judicially enforceable.

As for the teachers who were parties to the suit, none of them alleged that they had engaged in the proscribed types of activities or that they were threatened under the law.

But more important in Frankfurter's estimation than the standing of the parties was the fact that the Supreme Court was being asked to pass on the constitutionality of "a complicated statutory scheme . . . aligned with a complex system of enforcement," the machinery for which had not yet been set in motion.

All of it is still an unfinished blueprint. We are asked to adjudicate claims against its constitutionality before the scheme has been put into operation, before the limits that it imposes upon free inquiry and association, the scope of scrutiny that it sanctions, and the procedural safeguards that will be found to be implied for its enforcement have been authoritatively defined. I think we should adhere to the teaching of this Court's history to avoid constitutional adjudications on merely abstract or speculative issues and to base them on the concreteness afforded by an actual, present, defined controversy, appropriate for judicial judgment, between adversaries immediately affected by it. In accordance with the settled limits upon our jurisdiction I would dismiss this appeal.

In contrast with this penchant for avoiding Supreme Court involvement in controversies, the activist resolves any jurisdictional doubts in favor of granting review in civil liberties cases, as is illustrated in two 1953 decisions. *Edelman* v. *California* involved a very loosely worded vagrancy statute which had apparently been invoked because of speeches Edelman had made in a public park. The majority dismissed the writ of certiorari, believing that the conviction had been based on adequate state grounds; but Black and Douglas, scenting a case of persecution for speech, protested that the Court should declare such "dragnet legislation" unconstitutional. Again, in *Albertson* v. *Millard*, the majority refused to review the Michigan Communist Control Act on the ground that there had been no interpretation of the statute by the state courts. Douglas and Black felt that the meaning of the act was quite clear and opposed postponing the litigation.

The controversy between Frankfurter and the four activists over the granting of certiorari in workmen's compensation cases is also instructive. According to the Supreme Court's rules, certiorari is to be granted only in "cases involving principles the settlement of which is of importance to the public, as distinguished from that of the parties." By the 1948 term, Frankfurter was convinced that the activists were using their four votes to bring up on certiorari workmen's compensation cases which had no general interest or importance, merely because they wanted to reverse decisions which had gone against the employee.[25] "The

Court," he said, "should save its energy for cases it necessarily must adjudicate in order to adjudicate them with due regard for the needs of the deliberative process."[26] Suiting the action to the words, he began in these cases to vote to dismiss the writ of certiorari as having been improvidently granted.[27]

Frankfurter was able to cite some precedents for this procedure,[28] but there is an inherent fallacy in his position. When Congress, at the request of the Court, gave the Court almost complete discretion as to cases it would accept by the Judiciary Act of 1925, the congressional committees were assured that the Court would grant certiorari on the vote of four justices. Now in these workmen's compensation cases four justices, fully informed as to the kind of issues they raised, believed them to be of public importance and voted to grant certiorari. What Frankfurter was proposing to his colleagues, consequently, was that, having placed a case on the docket by four votes, they should take it off by five.[29]

Finally, it is significant to observe that Frankfurter's characteristically conscientious and restrained approach to the judicial function has occasionally been carried to the point of complete immobilization, leaving him unable to reach any decision at all in a case. The most notable instance was, of course, the Rosenberg case, where he protested, with much justification, that the pressure put on the Court for an immediate review of Justice Douglas' order staying the execution prevented an adequate opportunity for considering the serious legal problems involved. But equally indicative of a significant character trait was his stand in another 1953 proceeding, *Burns* v. *Wilson*, also involving the death sentence. He concluded in this case that he could not "assume the responsibility, where life is at stake, of concurring in the judgment of the Court. Equally, however, I would not feel justified in reversing the judgment. My duty, as I see it, is to resolve this dilemma by doing neither." He wanted the case set down for reargument, because of the issues of far-reaching import that were at stake.

A different kind of dilemma which he solved in much the same way was presented by *Radio Corp. of America* v. *United States*, where the Federal Communications Commission's approval of the Columbia Broadcasting System's method of color television was up for review. Here Frankfurter's disapproval of judicial intrusion into the administrative process[30] was balanced against his hunch (proved correct by subsequent events) that the FCC had acted prematurely in a field where further technical developments were bound to occur. Consequently, after delivering some obiter dicta about how television might be "a new barbarism parading as scientific progress," he withdrew from the ordeal of decision and listed himself as "dubitante."[31]

This review indicates how seriously and systematically Frankfurter has been guided in his decisions by a conscious standard of judicial self-restraint. But how can we tell whether this is a reflection of genuine libertarian reluctance to expand the powers of the Court or merely convenient rationalization for a fundamentally antilibertarian set of personal preferences? One method of answering this question is to review his active and courageous career in the civil liberties field before his appointment to the Supreme Court. Another method, more relevant to the materials of this study, is to examine more carefully the data of Table 9 (p. 190).

If Frankfurter's restraint philosophy is genuine, it should manifest itself in a general reluctance to invalidate state action, whether constitutionality of statutes or criminal prosecutions is at issue. But at the federal level his principles of restraint should operate only to protect legislation from declarations of unconstitutionality. So far as mere interpretation of statutes and checking on the operations of federal prosecuting machinery are concerned, a libertarian bias should have a chance to demonstrate its existence, unencumbered by restraint notions.

An inspection of Table 9 reveals precisely this situation. It is in dealing with state criminal convictions and in passing on the constitutionality of various types of state restrictions on freedom that Frankfurter fails to arrive at libertarian results. But in federal proceedings involving aliens (where the typical problem is statutory interpretation rather than constitutionality), in enforcing procedural protections in federal criminal prosecutions (where the Supreme Court admittedly has supervisory responsibility for the federal judicial system), and even in the variegated federal free speech cases (arising mostly out of the prosecutions of Communists), Frankfurter consistently favored the libertarian result. So far as treatment of aliens was concerned, he was more favor-

TABLE 10

VOTING RECORD OF SUPREME COURT JUSTICES IN FEDERAL AND STATE CIVIL LIBERTIES CASES, 1946–52 TERMS

(In Percentages)

	Support for Libertarian Claims	
	State Cases	Federal Cases
Murphy	100	100
Rutledge	100	89
Douglas	98	78
Black	89	85
Frankfurter	40	83
Court	36	35
Jackson	11	54
Clark	26	20
Burton	22	22
Minton	20	9
Vinson	19	9
Reed	19	7

able to their claims than Douglas was. In enforcing procedural protections in federal criminal cases, he was second only to Murphy on the Court.

This whole point can be made more clearly by combining the 113 cases covered in Table 9 into two categories according to their origin in federal or state proceedings, as is done in Table 10. This analysis shows that for the Court as a whole the level of support for the libertarian result in the two types of cases was almost identical. Moreover, for all the justices except three, there was no significant difference in reaction between the two categories of cases. Douglas' tendency to take a less libertarian position in federal than in state cases was due almost entirely to his vote in alien matters. With Frankfurter and Jackson the situation was decidedly the reverse. Frankfurter's record of 83 per cent favorable votes in federal cases, contrasted with his 40 per cent figure in state cases, seems a definite indication that he finds a barrier of restraint in dealing with state proceedings which is not operative in the federal area.

XII. *The Vinson Majority*

In the two preceding chapters an attempt has been made to explore the motivations of five liberal justices who served on the Vinson Court. The obvious difficulties in applying such a vague concept as "liberalism" to the Court have been avoided by adopting an objective standard—whether a justice voted for the libertarian result in civil liberties cases more often than did the majority of the Court. Of the five libertarians identified by this test, only three were on the Vinson Court during its latter period.

The remaining six members of the Vinson Court favored the libertarian result less often than the Court as a whole in the cases covered by Table 9, ranging from Jackson's 31 per cent support to a low of 13 per cent for Reed. It is not easy to label this group. "Conservative" would be a misleading and largely meaningless term to apply, and "illiberal" or "antilibertarian" would be even more objectionable. After all, these justices were the dominant part of a Court which persistently rejected rationalizations for unequal treatment of individuals on racial grounds; which conscientiously sought to keep the loyalty-oath practice within some kind of bounds; which exhibited marked concern about the standards of federal and state criminal procedure; and which refused to abandon the clear-and-present-danger test as a basis for judicial check upon possible legislative excesses. Perhaps the most accurate and least invidious way of characterizing their position is to call them the "less libertarians."

THE LESS LIBERTARIANS

Table 9 (p. 190) shows that Jackson gave considerably more support to libertarian claims than did his colleagues in this group, but he was significantly below Frankfurter in every category. He was, however, more favorable than the Court as a whole in all three areas involving federal action (aliens, federal criminal defendants, and Communist cases).

Jackson's favorable ratio in federal criminal cases was largely due to his hyperactive concern about the search and seizure clause. In *Brinegar* v. *United States*, where the libertarians Black, Douglas, and Rutledge had refused to hold that the stopping and searching of a suspected bootlegger's car was unreasonable search and seizure, Jackson seized the opportunity for some sarcasm about their preferred-position philosophy. He himself, he said, had objected to that concept, because giving some constitutional rights a preferred position means "relegating others to a deferred position; we can establish no firsts without thereby establishing seconds. Indications are not wanting that Fourth Amendment freedoms are tacitly marked as secondary rights, to be relegated to a deferred position." But Jackson's votes seem to indicate that he also has a system of preferences, which ranks the Fourth Amendment above the First.

Some of the decisions in which Jackson arrived at antilibertarian results can be explained on judicial restraint grounds, as in Frankfurter's case. In the first sound-truck case he expressed his unwillingness to deny municipal power of control over these noisy abominations; and in *Kunz* v. *New York* he would not have had the Court interfere when a city undertook to handle hatemongering in the streets by a licensing system. In the former litigation he vigorously protested a description of the judicial function as that of balancing values and interests, contending that balancing was a matter for the legislatures, not the courts. He said: "I disagree entirely with the idea that 'courts must balance. . . .' It is for the local communities to balance their own interests—that is politics—and what courts should keep out of. Our only function is to apply constitutional limitations."[1] Yet it is obvious that he has been as much of a balancer as anyone on the Court. Consider his frank weighing of the proper public policy for dealing with suspected criminals in *Watts* v. *Indiana*, where he concluded that solving crimes was a higher social good than protecting suspects from arrest on suspicion and questioning without the presence of counsel.

The unpredictability of Jackson's performance leads one to

question whether he has developed any systematic theories about civil liberties or the judicial function. In the second flag-salute case in 1943 he wrote one of the ablest defenses of the preferred-position theory ever to come from the Court, a theory which he has subsequently rejected with scorn. In the Douds case his partial dissent was a blunt warning to Congress that it must let men's minds alone; but in the Dennis case he thought Congress should be able to provide for the punishment of speech as conspiracy.

The remaining five members of the Court divide into two groups on the basis of their degree of support for, or rather opposition to, libertarian claims, Clark and Burton being somewhat more favorable than Minton, Vinson, and Reed. However, there is not much basis in the statistics of Table 9 for attempting distinctions among them. Some of their votes in individual cases are worthy of note—Minton's and Reed's dissents in the Hanke picketing case, Burton's vote in the Joint Anti-Fascist Refugee case, and Vinson's dissent in the magazine solicitation case of *Breard* v. *Alexandria*. But the pattern of behavior is characteristically similar. For most purposes these five justices *were* the Vinson Court, and the general trend of their thinking should have been made fairly clear from the review of the Court's decisions in the preceding chapters.

The late Chief Justice Vinson, however, deserves some special consideration. It seems unfortunate that he should have been very nearly the most negative member of the Court on libertarian claims; for this inevitably handicapped his performance in the kind of task for which he otherwise seemed rather well suited. There are two possible roles which a Chief Justice can play that will appropriately exploit the potentialities of his position. He can be the intellectual leader of the Court, dominating it by the strength of his personality and the coherence of his idea system. Marshall was such a Chief Justice; but, of course, successful performance of this role requires a strikingly unusual combination of qualities. Where these qualities are present, it is almost irrelevant to be concerned about whether the Chief Justice is at the left, the center, or the right of the other justices, for wherever he is *will* be the center of the Court.

The other role which becomes a Chief Justice is that of compromiser or co-ordinator. He may lack the intellectual superiority or the creative imagination of the first type of Chief Justice, or he may have a Court which simply refuses to be dominated by its chief. Under these conditions he may make an equally significant contribution by fertility in devising formulas on which disparate elements of the Court can agree and by an ability to infuse his colleagues with a spirit of corporate responsibility which is conducive to co-operative effort. For this role the Chief Justice needs not only the appropriate personal qualities of patience, good will, tact, and administrative sense, but it is almost essential that he himself stand somewhere near the center of the Court's idea system.

Clearly, Vinson could not have been expected to fill the first role. There were at least four members of the Court who outranked him in intellectual power and mobility. He lacked the ability to handle large ideas easily or to write with force and compelling appeal. Nor was the Court he headed one which would take kindly to domination. The only role which he could have essayed with hope of success was that of integration and compromise. One has merely to look at the statistics of dissent for proof that he did not succeed in that task. But the business of judgment is not quite that simple; for we cannot be sure that under another Chief Justice the disintegration might not have been even worse. We cannot know how effectively he handled the Saturday conferences at which decisions were hammered out. We cannot know what pacifying or integrating influence he wielded. We are limited to the evidence of the decisions themselves.

On this score the record is not wholly unfavorable. Probably the two most important decisions for civil liberties theory which his Court handed down were Dennis and Douds. In both instances he accepted the responsibility of writing the opinion for the Court, and his product, whatever one may think of the result reached, was a capable and serious attempt to reconcile the diverse formulations of preceding opinions with "the felt necessities of the time" as he felt them. There was naturally nothing novel in his thinking. The only new element was the revised statement of the clear-and-present-danger test developed by Judge Learned Hand in the Dennis court of appeals review, which, as Vinson artlessly remarked, was "as succinct and inclusive as any other we might devise at this time." But he did preserve the continuity of thought in this field, and, while the immediate result was antilibertarian, he at least maintained a basis for judicial control over subsequent legislative action.

There was another case in which we can detect the hand of Vinson the compromiser, and that was the first restrictive-covenant case, *Shelley* v. *Kraemer*. In fact, as the preceding discussion of the case has suggested, the art of compromise succeeded too well there. On the surface everything was perfect—a desirable social result, a unanimous Court, and not a single precedent overruled by Vinson's opinion. But there was a fatal defect—the restrictive covenant remained legal. And so the problem came back to haunt the Court, which had to break out of the equivocal position in which Vinson's compromise had left it as best it could.

When the benefit of every doubt has been given to Vinson, however, it seems clear that his success as an integrating force on the Court was quite limited. He had, from 1949 on, an automatic majority for the point of view congenial to him in most of these controversies, and so it was unnecessary to maneuver toward a more common ground. Yet the two preceding chapters certainly show a divergence of attitudes outside the Vinson majority group which should have made such maneuvering fruitful. What happened, however, in an increasing number of cases was that the Vinson majority drove all the libertarians into opposition.

It is a serious indictment of the Vinson majority that many of its decisions were unacceptable to the practitioners both of libertarian activism and of libertarian restraint. When Black, with his impetuous drive for freedom, agreed with Frankfurter, with his meticulous concern for jurisdictional niceties, that the Court had come to a wrong decision, the case against the Vinson majority is strong indeed.

BLACK AND FRANKFURTER, DISSENTING

Applying this standard to the Vinson Court from 1949 to 1953, we find that 50 of the 281 nonunanimous decisions of those four terms saw both Black and Frankfurter in dissent. Of these 50 decisions, 34 raised civil liberties issues,[2] and in all but one of these the Court majority had given an answer which achieved an antilibertarian result.[3] Most of these decisions have been covered in preceding chapters, but here we are interested in seeing what characteristics of the Vinson majority are highlighted by the Black-Frankfurter criticisms.

The first thing that emerges from a review of these disputed decisions is a difference in approach toward the interpretation of federal legislation touching on civil liberties. On several occasions the Black-Frankfurter dissents were occasioned by their insistence on interpreting legislation so as to secure the least possible conflict with libertarian and humanitarian goals, a consideration which has not seemed so important to the Vinson majority. This difference is particularly obvious in the nine alien cases. We have already noted, for example, Burton's comment in the Eichenlaub case, where he said in effect that Congress had passed a deportation statute because it wanted aliens deported, and the Court ought to help it achieve that goal. Frankfurter proceeded on a quite different line in his dissent, saying: "Where, as here, a statute permits either of two constructions without violence to language, the construction which leads to hardship should be rejected in favor of the permissible construction consonant with humane considerations."

Again, consider the varying reactions in the 1953 case of *Orloff* v. *Willoughby*. Orloff, a doctor, had applied for and received a commission as captain in the Air Force Medical Corps, but the commission was revoked on his refusal to execute the required loyalty certificate. Subsequently he was drafted into the army, though beyond draft age, under the provision authorizing conscription of over-age men in certain "medical and allied specialist categories." This time he executed the loyalty certificate but refused to give other information or to say whether he had ever been a member of the Communist party. The army refused him a commission, and at first assigned him to nonmedical duties, but later made him a laboratory technician. He sought habeas corpus on the ground that he was being illegally detained in the army, not having been given the specialized duties or the commission to which he was entitled under the statute. The majority did not interpret the statute as justifying his claim, but Frankfurter, Black, and Douglas did. Frankfurter believed Congress had rather clearly indicated that doctors over draft age were to be inducted only for service as doctors; and if they were unfit for commissions, then they should be discharged.

Perhaps even more important than their attitude toward statutory interpretation is the Black-Frankfurter concern with enforcement of the constitutional and traditional guaranties of a fair trial in the federal courts. Again we may pass lightly over cases demonstrating this concern which have already been discussed,[4] and turn to the 1950 decision in *Dennis* v. *United States*.[5] Dennis, a high Communist party official, was convicted of wilful refusal to obey a subpoena served on him by the Un-American Activities Committee, before a District of Columbia jury on which sat seven government employees.[6] Dennis contended that a Communist could not get a fair trial from government employees, because the "aura of surveillance and intimidation" resulting from the federal loyalty check would make them fearful of rendering anything but a guilty verdict. The Court ruled against him, saying that jurors could be challenged for actual bias but that no presumption of bias on the part of all government employees could be accepted. Frankfurter and Black, on the other hand, thought it was merely recognizing "the facts of life" to see that government employees would be "peculiarly susceptible" to the pressures generated by antagonism toward a politically unpopular group.

But probably the most revealing instance of the Vinson majority's failure to bend over backward in rigorous insistence upon maintenance of protective procedures was *Sacher* v. *United States*. This case grew out of the contempt of court sentences which Judge Medina passed on the Communists' lawyers in the second Dennis case. The nine months' trial of this case was certainly among the most turbulent and hectic in American court annals. The five principal defense lawyers carried on a running battle with Judge Medina which appeared "wilfully obstructive"[7] of the conduct of the trial. The trial judge, as Justice Black summarized the situation, was convinced that the lawyers had deliberately and calculatedly badgered and insulted him throughout the long months of trial. Among these insults, so the Judge believed and declared, were insolent, sarcastic, impudent and disrespectful charges that he angled for newspaper headlines; connived with the United States Attorney; entertained racial prejudice; judicially acted with "bias, prejudice, corruption, and partiality." He found and repeatedly declared that these lawyers were acting in concerted agreement in an attempt to create confusion, provoke incidents and break down his health.

Judge Medina on many occasions warned counsel that their conduct was contemptuous; but, in order not to delay the trial or deprive defendants of counsel, he did not cite them for contempt until after the jury had brought in its verdict and was discharged. Immediately thereafter he asked the lawyers to stand up, read them a small portion of a lengthy "contempt certificate" he had prepared, listing numerous instances of alleged contemptuous conduct, found them all guilty of contempt without giving them an opportunity to say a word in reply, and sentenced them to prison. The court of appeals reviewed Judge Medina's action, both on facts and on law, reversed some of the specifications of contempt, but by a two to one vote affirmed the conviction and sentences.

The Supreme Court initially refused to review the case, though Black and Douglas noted that they believed certiorari should be granted.[8] After the summer recess of 1951, however, the Court reconsidered because of "the importance of clarifying the permissible practice in such cases" and granted certiorari, but limited to the single question as to whether the judge was himself authorized by law to determine and punish contempt or whether contempt could be adjudged and punished only by a judge other than the accusing one and after notice, hearing, and opportunity to defend.[9]

The Supreme Court majority, speaking through Justice Jackson, upheld Medina's procedure. The Federal Rules of Criminal Procedure contemplate that convictions for contempt will normally involve notice and hearing and be tried before a different judge, with the possibility of participation of a jury. However, Rule 42(*a*) permits "summary disposition" of a contempt charge by a judge if he certifies "that he saw or heard the conduct constituting the contempt and that it was committed in the actual presence of the court." The contention of the Communists' counsel was that under this rule Medina had power of summary punishment of contempts only immediately after they were committed in his presence and that, after the trial was over, when summary action was unnecessary to prevent obstruction of justice, the regular procedures must prevail. Jackson held that Rule 42(*a*) permitted use of summary contempt procedures either during a trial or at its termination and added that the latter "more deliberate course" might well be the fairer of the two.

Justices Black, Frankfurter, and Douglas dissented (Clark not participating). They all agreed that the contempt citation should have been tried regularly, not summarily, and before a different judge. Rule 42(*a*), Frankfurter observed, "merely permits summary punishment" of contempts committed in the actual presence of the court. It does not command it. The power of summary punishment is subject to "the inherent limitation that the power shall be fairly used" for the purpose for which it is conferred.

> Among the restrictions to be implied, as a matter of course, are two basic principles of our law—that no judge should sit in a case in which he is personally involved and that no criminal punishment should be meted out except upon notice and due hearing, unless overriding necessity precludes such indispensable safeguards for assuring fairness and affording the feeling that fairness has been done.

Here Judge Medina was personally involved in an extraordinary degree. To make clear just how recriminatory and generally low a level the repartee between judge and counsel reached, Frankfurter quoted in an appendix to his opinion page after page of the colloquies which had gone on,

> more suggestive of an undisciplined debating society than of the hush and solemnity of a court of justice. Too often counsel were encouraged to vie with the court in dialectic, in repartee and banter, in talk so copious as inevitably to arrest the momentum of the trial and to weaken the restraints of respect that a judge should engender in lawyers . . . he failed to exercise the moral authority of a court possessed of a great tradition. He indulged them, sometimes resignedly, sometimes playfully, in lengthy speeches. These incontinent wrangles between court and

counsel were punctuated by occasional minatory intimations from the Bench. As in the case of parental warnings to children, feckless repetition deprived them of authority.

Much should be forgiven a judge who operated under the physical strain of a nine months' trial and was subjected to the provocations which were heaped upon him in this case. But when all allowances are made, certainly the dissenters had ground for believing that Medina had failed to satisfy minimum standards of judicial deportment and that the contempt charge should have been tried before a different judge.[10]

What seems to join Frankfurter with Black and Douglas in such a case as that of Sacher is a deep reverence for the basic notion of due process, which in the Joint Anti-Fascist Refugee case Frankfurter called "perhaps the most majestic concept in our whole constitutional system," containing "the garnered wisdom of the past in assuring fundamental justice." The intensity of his feeling about due process, as well as his recognition of the creative problems in its interpretation, is conveyed by this quotation from that decision:

> The requirement of "due process" is not a fair-weather or timid assurance. It must be respected in periods of calm and in times of trouble; it protects aliens as well as citizens. But "due process," unlike some legal rules, is not a technical conception with a fixed content unrelated to time, place and circumstances. Expressing as it does in its ultimate analysis respect enforced by law for that feeling of just treatment which has been evolved through centuries of Anglo-American constitutional history and civilization, "due process" cannot be imprisoned within the treacherous limits of any formula. Representing a profound attitude of fairness between man and man, and more particularly between the individual and government, "due process" is compounded of history, reason, the past course of decisions, and stout confidence in the strength of the democratic faith which we profess. Due process is not a mechanical instrument. It is not a yardstick. It is a process. It is a delicate process of adjustment inescapably involving the exercise of judgment by those whom the Constitution entrusted with the unfolding of the process.

An unstable majority in the Joint Anti-Fascist Refugee case came to the same conclusion as Frankfurter about due process; but the difference between the Vinson majority and the Frankfurter-Black-Douglas conception manifested itself in the 1953 decision of *United States* v. *Nugent.* The issue arose out of procedures for exempting conscientious objectors from military service. Statutory arrangements for persons making such a claim include reference of their appeals to the Department of Justice for "inquiry and hearing." It was the practice to have the FBI make the inquiry. At the hearing, the person was entitled to be instructed as to the general nature and character of any unfavorable evidence developed by the inquiry, but he was not permitted to see the FBI report or to be told the names of the persons interviewed. The Court majority held that the "hearing" required by statute was not a full-fledged trial and was not invalidated by failure to reveal the FBI report. Frankfurter, dissenting along with Black and Douglas, agreed with the trial judge that the statute must be construed to require the investigative reports to be made part of the record if the hearing was to fit "within our Anglo-Saxon concepts of justice and due process." He added: "The enemy is not yet so near the gate that we should allow respect for traditions of fairness, which has hitherto prevailed in this country, to be overborne by military exigencies. . . . In a country with our moral and material strength the maintenance of fair procedures cannot handicap our security."

Of course, the Nugent case was a federal proceeding. It takes more of a showing at the state level before Frankfurter will join Black in charging lack of due process, but that can happen, as it did in *Daniels* v. *Allen.*[11] Here the defendant had received the death penalty in a proceeding where admittedly Negroes had been unconstitutionally excluded from the jury. The trial judge gave the defense attorneys 60 days to make up their appeal document, though the state law prescribed no set period for taking an appeal. Daniels' attorney completed the document on the sixtieth day, but, because the prosecuting attorney was away on vacation, the papers were not delivered to his office and receipted for until the sixty-first day. On the ground that the notice was one day late, the judge dismissed the appeal, thus denying any opportunity to raise the objection as to racial discrimination in the trial.

The Supreme Court majority held that the failure to use the

available state remedies barred resort to a writ of habeas corpus in the federal courts; for, technically, habeas corpus cannot be made to do service for an appeal. It should lie, Jackson said, "only for defects not disclosed on the record, going to the power, legal competence or jurisdiction of the committing state court." Frankfurter, dissenting along with Black and Douglas, said this was a "jejune abstraction." The real question for him was not preservation of technical rules but whether the refusal of the judge to permit an appeal to be filed one day late, when there was no state law limiting time of filing, was "an act so arbitrary and so cruel in its operation, considering that life is at stake, that in the circumstances of this case it constituted a denial of due process in its rudimentary procedural aspect."

When a question of this gravity was asked, Frankfurter was clear that habeas corpus should be available to provide means of answering. Availability of the writ was essential "for the moral health of our kind of society"; and he added:

> It is not the boasting of empty rhetoric that has treated the writ of habeas corpus as the basic safeguard of freedom in the Anglo-American world. . . . Its history and function in our legal system and the unavailability of the writ in totalitarian societies are naturally enough regarded as one of the decisively differentiating factors between our democracy and totalitarian governments.[12]

These examples may give some insight into the judicial attitudes which led Black and Frankfurter, with the rather frequent concurrence of Douglas and occasional support from Jackson, to join in significant challenges to the decisional pattern of the Vinson majority. It is not easy to summarize their differences, which, again, are in degree rather than in kind, with the majority. But it does seem clear that what Black and Frankfurter share and what the Vinson majority frequently failed to exhibit is a warm humanitarian sympathy, a conviction that libertarian values are tremendously important, an insistence that the Court use the full measure of its legitimate power to compel adherence to procedural safeguards, and a tough-minded scrutiny of the plausible rationalizations which are always available to explain away infringements of human liberty.

XIII. *Democracy and Judicial Review*

Military men are often accused of planning to fight their next war on the basis of the lessons taught by the last one. Thus the French, having spent World War I in the trenches, readied themselves for World War II by building a bigger and better trench—the Maginot Line—only to find it useless in dealing with dive bombers and Panzer divisions. Now that we come to cast up the accounts of the Vinson Court, we may conclude that it has been guilty of a similar error in attempting to apply the lessons of 1937 to a new and far different judicial world. The "nine old men" had made the mistake of challenging a grass-roots political movement and its legislative expression. The task of the Roosevelt Court was to get back in step with the country and to provide appropriate constitutional rationalizations for popular economic policies. The attitude of legislative deference came easily to the members of the Roosevelt Court, who were all liberals in the Holmesian sense. Their acceptance of the strong legislature–weak judiciary formula was, after 1941, fortified by the necessities of a global war, which had to be won by vigorous executive and legislative action, with little time for concern with legal niceties.

By the time the Vinson Court came on the scene, the situation had changed. The shooting war was over, and the government's power of direction over the economy was established so firmly as to be beyond challenge. "The pressing issue for the New Court," wrote Eugene V. Rostow in 1947, was "to help articulate the public law of a free society, competent to fulfill its democratic dream in the turbulent second half of the twentieth century."[1] The shooting war was over, but the cold war was just beginning, and it proved harder to work out judicial relationships to a cold war than to a hot one. The emergencies of the latter are so pressing as to leave the judiciary no real choice of disapproving legislative and military solutions. The Court bows to *force majeur*, always consoling itself with the thought that the situation is merely temporary and that, come peace, things will return to normal. In fact, when the hot war is safely over, the Court may even recover sufficient courage to declare unconstitutional some of the measures by which the war was won.[2] But in a cold war the emergency with which legislatures must deal, though less urgent, is of indefinite duration, so that the Court cannot merely postpone decisions and wait for V-Day. It must face up to the question, Who makes the rules for a society in a state of siege?

The Vinson Court's solution was almost entirely within the tradition of the strong legislature–weak judiciary formula which Holmes developed for the quite different purpose of controlling judicial review over state economic legislation. In fact, the Vinson Court even refused to give full faith and credit to the one doctrine Holmes proposed which did have the potentiality of strengthening judicial review, the clear-and-present-danger test. The Dennis decision preserved that test in form but applied it in such a way as to make it quite unlikely that any legislative action could fail to meet its requirements.

Even more significant, however, is the encouragement which the Vinson Court gave to the view that judicial review is inherently undemocratic in character. Such a contention can, of course, call upon a long history of American liberal thought for support. Judges are appointed, not elected; and, since they serve for life, they may easily be out of tune with the times. The Court's role is essentially negative; it cannot accept any real responsibility for formulation of public policy, and so, the argument runs, it should not stand in the way of the political branches which do have that responsibility. If the Court undertakes to strike down legislation as unconstitutional, the process of self-government is necessarily weakened; for assurance that the Court is on guard may convince the people that vigilance in protection of their liberties is unnecessary, and the legislature and executive may conclude that constitutional scruples can be disregarded.

By relying on judicial review, sums up Henry Steele Commager, "we concede that the majority is not to be trusted."[3]

Such contentions, as noted, have been heard throughout our history, but seldom, if ever, have they been so persistently affirmed by members of the Supreme Court itself as in recent years. Justice Frankfurter has been merely the most articulate in sponsoring this view, as when he referred to the Court as "oligarchic"[4] or when he said on another occasion: "Courts are not representative bodies. They are not designed to be a good reflex of a democratic society."[5] What, then, should we accept as the best reflex of a democratic society? According to Frankfurter's opinion in the Dennis case, an unfettered legislature seems to be what is needed, for he said that a refusal to enforce the Smith Act in that proceeding would have "impaired or restricted . . . the democratic process." The Court's inaction had the effect that "power and responsibility remain with the people and immediately with their representatives."

But no one, Frankfurter included, would really contend that the most democratic system is that one in which the legislature is most unfettered. Certainly, it is the American theory that the legislature needs to be subjected to the competition of a system of checks and balances and that this competition must proceed within boundaries laid down in a written constitution. The American Constitution does not assume that the majority is always right; it does not equate majoritarianism with democracy; it is careful to safeguard certain conditions deemed essential to the maintenance of a free political community from what Madison called "the superior force of an interested and overbearing majority."[6] Democratic government is limited government, not unlimited government.

There are some who still doubt that the framers of the Constitution intended the Supreme Court to participate in this limiting process to the extent of passing on the constitutionality of congressional legislation,[7] but the overriding fact is that such authority has been exercised since 1803. There are, of course, many reasons of the soundest sort, reviewed in a previous chapter, for the Supreme Court to use its power of invalidating legislative action with the greatest circumspection and restraint.

But is there any reason for the Court to cast doubt on its own credentials as an able and valued participant in the process of interpreting the Constitution?

The Vinson Court did just this, not only by questioning the democratic character of judicial review, but also by a rather alarming fragmentation of opinion, in the course of which, as Carl Swisher has recently said, "even the ideal of unanimity tends to fade away . . . and we move back in the direction of the seriatim opinions, opinions by many or all the justices in each case, which characterized the Court during the first decade of its history."[8] Freedom of individual opinion, even on the Supreme Court, is certainly an indispensable part of the American heritage. But the effect of these multiple opinions, Swisher believes, is to deny to the country "the benefit of the best that a Court of nine carefully selected justices—well paid, deferentially treated, and fully protected in their positions—can do in the way of stating the fundamentals of our constitutional system."

Open disagreement among the justices on these fundamentals and their application has inevitably weakened the moral authority of the Court, a development to which the justices themselves have not hesitated to call attention. Justice Jackson remarked in a 1953 decision with characteristic brashness: "Rightly or wrongly, the belief is widely held by the practicing profession that this Court no longer respects impersonal rules of law but is guided in these matters by personal impressions which from time to time may be shared by a majority of Justices." Then, drawing the judicial robe back still further to expose the Court's feet of clay, he added: "We are not final because we are infallible, but we are infallible only because we are final."[9]

Devotion of the Court's talents to the sharpening of diversity rather than to the creation of synthesis has fatally hampered the building of the strong case that can be made for effective judicial protection of civil rights. How did it come about that the preferred-position concept, which around 1940 was apparently well under way toward general adoption as a tenet of constitutional interpretation, later lost the active support of all the Court except Black and Douglas? Why did preferred position become almost a fighting issue for Frankfurter and Jackson, who on occasions have subscribed to an almost identical conception of the primacy of libertarian values? Thus in the same opinion in which he completely rejected the preferred-position argument, Frankfurter agreed that "those liberties of the individual which history has attested as the indispensable conditions of an open as against a closed society come to this Court with a momentum for respect lacking when appeal is made to liberties which derive merely from shifting economic arrangements."[10]

But perhaps it is more fruitful to turn from an analysis of past mistakes to the charting of a course for the future of judicial review in the civil liberties field. What could a Court which truly believes in the principles of an open society legitimately do to further those principles?

The basic requisite is to establish some workable consensus justifying the Court's exercise of independent judgment on alleged invasions of civil liberties, based on its own interpretation of the Bill of Rights. The legal fiction of the reasonable man, long used as a guide in judicial review, is too fictitious for any useful purpose here. On the other hand, the promising line which Justice Stone opened up in his 1938 Carolene footnote has never been adequately exploited. As noted in chapter ii, Stone suggested, first, that "legislation which restricts those political processes which can ordinarily be expected to bring about repeal of undesirable legislation [might] be subjected to more exacting judicial scrutiny . . . than are most other types of legislation."[11] His point was that the Court should police the *process* by which political decisions are reached; for, unless there is freedom to circulate ideas and unless the representative system is in good order, there can be no confidence in its end-product. Acceptance of this standard would have given a considerably different result, for example, in the voting cases from *Colegrove* v. *Green* to *South* v. *Peters*, for it would have convinced the Court that it is not undemocratic to insist that legislatures be elected in the fullest possible conformity with the principles of representative democracy.

Stone's second query in the Carolene footnote was "whether prejudice against discrete and insular minorities may be a special condition, which tends seriously to curtail the operation of those political processes ordinarily to be relied upon to protect minorities, and which may call for a correspondingly more searching judicial inquiry." Would a Court which accepted this view have written the kind of opinions handed down by the majority justices in the Dennis case? In dealing with these "miserable merchants of unwanted ideas" who are completely outside the pale of political support, should not the Court have tightened up its canons of review instead of loosening them?

What the Court actually did in Dennis was itself to supply, by the process of judicial notice, the missing links necessary to make the government's use of the Smith Act successful. The indictment was for teaching, and organizing a party to teach, Communist doctrine. The Court held that the defendants could be constitutionally convicted on such speech charges because actually they were guilty of much graver crimes, though the graver crimes were not charged nor was evidence presented to prove them. This is a matter of more than technical significance, for, by ratifying the government's victory in a Smith Act prosecution for teaching and organizing, instead of insisting that the Communist party be indicted for what it is, a conspiracy to overthrow the government, the Court inevitably raised serious questions about the future scope of protection for freedom of speech and freedom of assembly.

If the Vinson Court had devoted itself to appropriate articulation of the two suggestions made by Stone, its civil liberties record could have been much different. It might have produced standards of judicial review with limits binding enough to satisfy justices genuinely concerned about judicial nullification of the popular will, while at the same time providing a positive guide to replace the negativism and undue deference of the self-restraint philosophy. For self-restraint, as Rostow says, "is a working rule of limited utility. On those aspects of American life which fall within the jurisdiction of the Court, the question becomes: What positive goal is served by the Supreme Court's decision—or refusal to decide?"[12]

The self-restraint for which Stone pleaded in the Butler decision was certainly not intended as a route to judicial abdication.

Walton Hamilton usefully reminds us that "respect for the province of the legislature does not carry an immunity to judicial responsibility."[13] Deciding Supreme Court cases is a positive job. There are responsibilities of judging which cannot be put off on a legislature or a lower court. Frankfurter, by his conscientious efforts to apply the restraint idea, has carried it to a logical extreme and thereby demonstrated its hollowness as a guide for action. Thus in the Feiner case he deferred to the New York court of appeals because it was an able and sensitive court. Application of this rule would give the preposterous situation of the Court's responsibility varying in different cases, depending upon the reputation of the supreme court of the state from which the appeal came.[14]

The restraint doctrine also has potentialities of degenerating into a self-consciousness which compels the judge to demonstrate anew with every case that arises the fitness of judicial review in general and his own participation in particular. Justice Frankfurter has carried his preoccupation with restraint to almost pathological extremes in an effort to insure and demonstrate that his own decisions are the product of legal principles operating under antiseptic conditions and untouched by personal preferences. In case after case he has prefaced his decision by a disquisition on the duality of Frankfurter the man and Frankfurter the judge. Mostly he has been concerned with showing why as a judge he has felt compelled to come to conclusions which as a citizen he would never support. Thus in the second flag-salute case he explained his refusal to hold unconstitutional the compulsory flag salute in public schools as follows:

> One who belongs to the most vilified and persecuted minority in history is not likely to be insensible to the freedoms guaranteed by our Constitution. Were my purely personal attitude relevant I should wholeheartedly associate myself with the general libertarian views in the Court's opinion, representing as they do the thought and action of a lifetime.

In *Haley* v. *Ohio* he referred to the fact that as a judge he could not give effect to his personal disbelief in capital punishment. In the curious case of *Louisiana* v. *Resweber*, where a condemned man had failed to die in the electric chair because of its faulty mechanism, Frankfurter supplied the fifth vote for the Court's ruling that a second trip to the chair would not be double jeopardy or cruel and unusual punishment. He said:

> I cannot rid myself of the conviction that were I to hold that Louisiana would transgress the Due Process Clause if the State were allowed, in the precise circumstances before us, to carry out the death sentence, I would be enforcing my private view rather than that consensus of society's opinion which, for purposes of due process, is the standard enjoined by the Constitution.

But how does Frankfurter propose to find standards which are external to his own value system? In the electric-chair case, he professed to rely on "the consensus of society's opinion." But how did he know what the consensus of opinion was on a subject that had never arisen before? Instead of the result at which he arrived, could he not have assumed with equal validity that his own personal aversion to sending this man on a second trip to the electric chair was what any normally sensitive human being would have felt?

In the Haley case he went further, indicating that judicial humility, plus self-administered psychoanalysis, was the answer:

> Humility in this context means an alert self-scrutiny so as to avoid infusing into the vagueness of a Constitutional command one's merely private notions. Like other mortals, judges, though unaware, may be in the grip of prepossessions. The only way to relax such a grip, the only way to avoid finding in the Constitution the personal bias one has placed in it, is to explore the influences that have shaped one's unanalyzed views in order to lay bare prepossessions.

These statements afford fascinating glimpses into a sophisticated judicial mind at work; but as public bulletins of successful inner purgation they carry a "holier than thou" inference with respect to disagreeing justices which seems quite unjustified; for Frankfurter's accounts certainly misstate or oversimplify the problem of judicial motivation. No matter how conscious or even heroic the efforts, the man and the judge can never be separated, and the gratifications of deprivation are as personally rooted as the gratifications of indulgence.

In opposition to the restraint conception, the belief that the Court must concern itself with the promotion of positive libertarian goals was most actively espoused on the Vinson Court by Justices Black and Douglas, earlier supported also by Murphy and Rutledge. Their defense of the cause of freedom in various guises has been vigorous and hard-hitting. No one should underestimate or undervalue the courage manifested by the Black and Douglas dissents in the Dennis case or fail to appreciate the strength of their conviction that "right" will ultimately triumph. Black concluded his dissent in that case with these words:

> Public opinion being what it now is, few will protest the conviction of these Communist petitioners. There is hope, however, that in calmer times, when present pressures, passions and fears subside, this or some later Court will restore the First Amendment liberties to the high preferred place where they belong in our free society.

It is very useful and provocative to have the pure free speech doctrine defended in such an influential forum. In spite of the looseness of their arguments about preferred position, such talk unquestionably has an educational value for an unsophisticated public. Both Frankfurter and Douglas wrote dissenting opinions in *United States* v. *Nugent*, but there can be little doubt that Douglas' biting and scornful single paragraph was more effective than Frankfurter's admirable disquisition on due process. Here is Douglas at his best:

> The use of statements by informers who need not confront the person under investigation or accusation has such an infamous history that it should be rooted out from our procedure. A hearing at which these faceless people are allowed to present their whispered rumors and yet escape the test and torture of cross-examination is not a hearing in the Anglo-American sense. We should be done with the practice—whether the life of a man is at stake, or his reputation, or any matter touching upon his status or his rights.

Nor has there been a better defense of academic freedom or a more vivid picture of the results of a "1984" type of thought control than in Douglas' dissent in the New York teachers' loyalty case:

> What happens under this law is typical of what happens in a police state. Teachers are under constant surveillance; their pasts are combed for signs of disloyalty; their utterances are watched for clues to dangerous thoughts. A pall is cast over the classrooms. There can be no real academic freedom in that environment. Where suspicion fills

the air and holds scholars in line for fear of their jobs, there can be no exercise of the free intellect. Supineness and dogmatism take the place of inquiry. A "party line"—as dangerous as the "party line" of the Communists—lays hold. It is the "party line" of the orthodox view, of the conventional thought, of the accepted approach. A problem can no longer be pursued with impunity to its edges. Fear stalks the classroom. The teacher is no longer a stimulant to adventurous thinking; she becomes instead a pipe line for safe and sound information. A deadening dogma takes the place of free inquiry. Instruction tends to become sterile; pursuit of knowledge is discouraged; discussion often leaves off where it should begin.

This, I think, is what happens when a censor looks over a teacher's shoulder. This system of spying and surveillance with its accompanying reports and trials cannot go hand in hand with academic freedom. It produces standardized thought, not the pursuit of truth. Yet it was the pursuit of truth which the First Amendment was designed to protect. A system which directly or inevitably has that effect is alien to our system and should be struck down. Its survival is a real threat to our way of life. We need be bold and adventuresome in our thinking to survive. A school system producing students trained as robots threatens to rob a generation of the versatility that has been perhaps our greatest distinction. The Framers knew the danger of dogmatism; they also knew the strength that comes when the mind is free, when ideas may be pursued wherever they lead. We forget these teachings of the First Amendment when we sustain this law.[15]

Why, then, were not the Black-Douglas arguments more successful on the Vinson Court? More particularly, did these two justices contribute in any way to the defeat of their own goals? It is quite possible that they did, by inadequate recognition of the fact that a Supreme Court justice has a task which is broader than that of safeguarding or enforcing one set of values. He must balance the competing claims of liberty and authority. As Jackson has well said:

The Court's day-to-day task is to reject as false, claims in the name of civil liberty which, if granted, would paralyze or impair authority to defend existence of our society, and to reject as false, claims in the name of security which would undermine our freedom and open the way to oppression.[16]

If a justice automatically takes the libertarian side on every issue, he is scarcely functioning in a balancing capacity, no matter how persuasive his opinion may seem. Swisher points out that "the eloquent defenses of civil liberties, formerly written by Justices Murphy and Rutledge and now by Justices Black and Douglas, take much of their drive from the fact that the dynamics of opposing positions are largely ignored."

The preferred-position philosophy of Black and Douglas is not necessarily incompatible with the balancing process. Its result is simply to throw an extra weight on one side of the scales, like the butcher who consistently weighs his thumb along with the meat. What does seem incompatible with the balancing process is what Justice Cardozo called "the tyranny of labels."[17] "Label thinking" starts off with the assumption that certain kinds of restrictions are unconstitutional and limits the judicial task to determining whether the restriction in the instant case fits into one of the proscribed categories. If so, it is automatically void. Perhaps the best example of this practice is found in the "prior-restraint" label. For Black, prior restraint is prior restraint, and therefore unconstitutional, whether the restraint is aimed at Jehovah's Witnesses ringing doorbells or the gigantic conspiracy of the Communist party. It would seem preferable that the determining factor in a judgment of unconstitutionality should be, not the label by which the restraint is called, but rather the seriousness of the threat to freedom and the justification offered for the limitation.

Label thinking unfits a justice to make distinctions based on matters of degree, and it results in the kind of absolutistic standards seen at work in Black's steel seizure decision. Label thinking leads a judge into a world of abstractions in which the facts of a particular case are unimportant, as Douglas demonstrated by his unrealistic approach to the Terminiello case. Label thinking encourages a justice to apply to a statute legal rather than empirical tests, as Murphy did when he declared the Thornhill antipicketing act unconstitutional "on its face." It would have been a better guide for future decisions if he had set the holding in a framework of circumstances rather than of concepts. Paul A. Freund makes this point well in comparing the Court's treatment of commerce and civil liberties questions:

> A free market in ideas and a free national market in goods are basic processes in our constitutional system. Each must nevertheless submit

to qualifications in collision with other public interests. If the Court has on the whole been more successful in finding serviceable accommodations under the Commerce Clause between a national free market and the claims of local welfare than under the First Amendment between liberty of the mind and the claims of public order, one reason may be the more empiric, particularistic approach that has generally characterized the performance of the former role.[18]

So it came about that no completely satisfactory case for a democratic judicial review was ever presented to the Vinson Court. The effort to escape from the old liberal stereotype of a strong legislature and a weak judiciary was too much even for Black and Douglas. Believing as they do that courts must challenge legislative threats to civil liberties, they should appreciate that this can be done only by a strong and protected judiciary. But they could not rid themselves of the effects of the old liberal suspicion that judges are not to be trusted with democratic ideals, and they fell back on their earlier beliefs in restricting judicial power. Thus in the Dennis case they insisted that the question of whether the Communist party was a clear and present danger should have been left to the jury, not decided by the judge. Why they would expect a sounder determination or one more favorable to the libertarian viewpoint on this issue from a jury of twelve untrained newspaper-reading laymen than from a federal judge is difficult to understand. Again, in a series of cases dealing with the power of judges to protect pending litigation from newspaper or other outside pressure, Black and Douglas have been unconvinced of the need to shelter the judge from expressions of public opinion. Such expressions, they say, are part of the democratic process, to which the judge must reconcile himself. In *Craig* v. *Harney* Douglas quoted a 1918 comment by Justice Holmes that "a judge of the United States is expected to be a man of ordinary firmness of character."[19]

Frankfurter's problem in adjusting the strong legislature–weak judiciary formula has been just the opposite. He sees clearly the need of giving judges the status they must have successfully to challenge legislative or popular assaults on libertarian values. He does not believe it is somehow undemocratic to shield the judge and the courtroom from popular clamor. He believes judges are humanly sensitive to such clamor, and, in rebuttal to Douglas' quotation from Holmes, he remarked: "That was said by an Olympian who was so remote from the common currents of life that he did not read newspapers."[20] But while Frankfurter wants the judicial process strong enough to defend itself, he is reluctant to admit that judges can use their powers against legislatures.

There are those who believe that the argument for democratic judicial review is naïve in its expectation that any court, even one with the prestige and power of the Supreme Court, can protect democratic values in a society if it is bent on destroying them. This view that judicial power over the tide of events is no greater than Canute's has been well stated by Judge Learned Hand:

> I often wonder whether we do not rest our hopes too much upon constitutions, upon laws and upon courts. These are false hopes; believe me, these are false hopes. Liberty lies in the hearts of men and women; when it dies there, no constitution, no law, no court can save it; no constitution, no law, no court can even do much to help it. While it lies there it needs no constitution, no law, no court to save it.[21]

Admittedly, there is some truth in what he says, but it would be fatal to the Supreme Court's sense of responsibility for any justice to act on such a gospel of despair. In an absolute sense the responsibility in a democratic society of every citizen and every public instrumentality to maintain the conditions which make democracy possible may well be equal. Certainly, Congress and the executive share this obligation equally with the Court. But as a practical matter our expectations of the Court are higher. The justices enjoy a perspective and an opportunity for reflection which is not available to more direct participants in the political process. Supreme Court discussion should not be on a par with legislative debates. It should be representative, not of our current thought, but of our best thought. We want assurance that the Court is judging us by our highest ideals, not on the basis of our average performance.

American democracy is a complex affair, but if there is any one key to its past successes and its future maintenance, that key must be found in the all-pervasive pluralism of American society.

At the level of governmental institutions that pluralism is reflected in a separation of powers, the purpose of which has never been better expressed than by Justice Brandeis when he said:

> The doctrine of the separation of powers was adopted by the Convention of 1787, not to promote efficiency but to preclude the exercise of arbitrary power. The purpose was, not to avoid friction, but, by means of the inevitable friction incident to the distribution of the governmental powers among three departments, to save the people from autocracy.[22]

"Autocracy" is an old-fashioned word, but perils to democracy are real and present, and a deliberate refusal of the Supreme Court to participate in the pluralistic system set up to protect democratic values is a poor kind of contribution to make to its success. If the Court gets delusions of grandeur or forgets what democracy means, there are ways of bringing it back to reality, as the events of 1937 demonstrated. But if the executive or the legislature should lose contact with basic democratic principles, it would be difficult to restore the balance without the vigorous weight of the Court.

During the period of the Vinson Court, the peril to libertarian principles came primarily from the legislature. The sobering facts about legislative irresponsibility have not been better put than by Walter Lippmann:

> If the free world is in . . . great peril, it is not because the adversaries of freedom are so strong or so attractive but because so many, indeed most, of the large democratic states are at the moment so badly governed. In many of them, the U.S. included, good government is undermined by the usurpation of the sovereign power by the popular assembly. In the crisis of Western society this usurpation has brought about a paralysis and panic fear which threaten to wreck the position of the whole free world, and to destroy the freedom and the kindly community of men with one another at home.
>
> That usurpation of the sovereign power is a popular assault, incited by demagogs, against the prerogatives, the guarantees, and the very structure of free constitutions. That has become possible in what should be law-abiding and freedom-loving communities because of the wide and general acceptance of the heresy that has corrupted and would destroy democracy. The heresy is that majorities can do no wrong, that there is no higher truth than the transient opinions of contem-

porary majorities, and that there is no higher law than the ambitions and the maneuvers of the persons they are persuaded to elect.

Against that heresy, which must subvert a free society and desecrate its most sacred principles, free men will prevail when they have learned once again to carry the shield of faith, to wear the helmet of salvation and to wield the sword of the spirit.[23]

In such a noble, yet difficult, crusade as Lippmann envisions, the United States Supreme Court has an important role to play. In carrying out that task, neither emotional zeal, which prejudges the issues, nor judicial neutralism, which seeks ways of avoiding the substantive questions, will do. A Supreme Court justice must be able, and willing, to balance some of the most delicate, intangible, yet superlatively important, issues that can arise in a democratic society. He must be a creature of the times and sensitive to the same currents of opinion as move legislators, to the end that the standards of reasonableness by which he judges legislative action will not be detached from reality. But he must at the same time be sensitive to the system of expectations which has made the Supreme Court the American conscience, with the responsibility not merely of preaching to legislatures but of passing judgment on their actions in the light of the great libertarian principles of the Bill of Rights.

Notes

CHAPTER I

1. Except when he dissents from the Court's conclusions, in which event the senior justice in the majority determines who will write the Court's opinion.

2. Merlo J. Pusey, *Charles Evans Hughes* (New York: Macmillan Co., 1951), p. 802. There is disagreement on this point, President Truman contending that Hughes had finally wound up their conversation by recommending Vinson.

3. Throughout this book, Supreme Court terms are identified by the year in which they began. They run from October to June.

4. For an account of this episode see C. H. Pritchett, *The Roosevelt Court: A Study in Judicial Politics and Values* (New York: Macmillan Co., 1948), pp. 26–29.

5. "The United States Supreme Court, 1948–49," *University of Chicago Law Review,* XVII (1949), 1.

6. "Court and Constitution: The Passive Period," *Vanderbilt Law Review,* IV (1951), 400.

7. See Pritchett, *op. cit.,* pp. 72–77. In 1950 Justice Frankfurter, in upholding the system of market quotas on sugar set up under the Sugar Act of 1948, against claims that the quotas were contrary to due process, said: "If ever claims of this sort carried plausibility, they seem to us singularly belated in view of the unfolding of the Commerce Clause" (*Secretary of Agriculture* v. *Central Roig Refining Co.* [1950]).

8. See Pritchett, *op. cit.,* pp. 78–81; Virginia Wood, *Due Process of Law, 1932–1949* (Baton Rouge: Louisiana State University Press, 1951).

9. See Hollis W. Barber, "Religious Liberty v. the Police Power: Jehovah's Witnesses," *American Political Science Review,* XLI (1947), 226–47.

10. *Dennis* v. *United States.*

11. *American Communications Assn.* v. *Douds.*

12. *Carlson* v. *Landon* (1952).

13. *New York Times,* March 7, 1952.

14. 340 U.S. 948. Naturally, Justices Reed and Frankfurter took no part in consideration of the petition for review. In 1953 the Court

rejected Hiss's appeal for a new trial and disbarred him from practice (73 S. Ct. 830, 834).

15. 195 F. 2d 583, 73 S. Ct. 20.

16. The fact that Justice Black was the only justice to make public his favorable vote does not necessarily mean that he was alone in wanting to review the case, for in the past the customary practice has been that the Court simply announces the granting or denial of the petition, with no indication of how individual justices voted. Justices Black and Douglas, however, on a substantial number of occasions have announced their position when they wished to review but did not get the other necessary votes. The fact that Douglas made no such statement as Black's on this occasion might thus support the conclusion that he did not favor review, but this cannot be certain.

17. 73 S. Ct. 134.

18. 73 S. Ct. 949.

19. 73 S. Ct. 1151. On the petition for rehearing, Black and Douglas noted that it should be granted. Frankfurter again said that he never announced his dissent from the Court's action on certiorari petitions and added: "Partial disclosure of votes on successive stages of a certiorari proceeding does not present an accurate picture of what took place."

20. 73 S. Ct. 1152.

21. Justice Black filed objection to the convening of a special term.

22. 73 S. Ct. 1152.

23. 73 S. Ct. 1166.

24. *Cochran* v. *Louisiana Board of Education.*

25. *Zorach* v. *Clauson,* 343 U.S. at 317 (1952).

26. "The Supreme Court as National School Board," *Thought,* XXIII (1948), 665–83.

27. An attempt had been made in the trial court to prove that the system was, in fact, administered in a coercive manner; but trial on this issue was refused.

28. One of the plaintiffs, who sued as a father, did not assert that his child was injured or even offended by the Bible reading. The other plaintiff, a taxpayer, did not allege that the Bible reading added anything to the cost of conducting the school. Thus they did not meet the requirement that the constitutionality of a statute may be challenged only by someone who sustains a direct injury through its enforcement (see *Massachusetts* v. *Mellon* [1923]).

29. Another recent case raising issues in this field is *Kedroff* v. *St. Nicholas Cathedral* (1952). Among the many discussions of the establishment issue see Wilber G. Katz, "Freedom of Religion and State Neutrality," *University of Chicago Law Review,* XX (1953), 426–40; and Lyn-

ford A. Lardner, "How Far Does the Constitution Separate Church and State?" *American Political Science Review*, XLV (1951), 110–32.

30. For a fuller exposition of this view see Pritchett, *op. cit.*, chap. i.

31. See *Leland* v. *Oregon* (1952).

32. This count includes the appointment of Harlan F. Stone, originally appointed to an associate justiceship by Coolidge, to the chief justiceship. One associate justiceship was filled twice by Roosevelt, as James F. Byrnes, named in 1942, resigned in 1943. Personal accounts of all the Roosevelt appointees are found in Wesley McCune, *The Nine Young Men* (New York: Harper & Bros., 1947).

33. For a biographical account of Black and some selected decisions see John P. Frank, *Mr. Justice Black: The Man and His Opinions* (New York: A. A. Knopf, 1949).

34. Some representative opinions are collected in *The Constitutional World of Mr. Justice Frankfurter*, ed. S. J. Konefsky (New York: Macmillan Co., 1949).

35. See William O. Douglas, *Beyond the High Himalayas* (New York: Doubleday, 1952).

36. This does not count Republican Stone's elevation to the chief justiceship by Roosevelt in 1941.

37. The availability of these four votes on certiorari petitions helps to explain the unprecedented number of civil liberties cases accepted by the Court during the 1940's.

38. In June, 1953, Clark declined an invitation to testify before a House judiciary subcommittee concerning some of his activities at Attorney General, on the ground that such an appearance would be a violation of the independent position of the judiciary. The House group voted 22 to 5 against issuing a subpoena for Clark (*New York Times*, June 24, 1953).

39. For comparable data on the 1930–39 terms see Pritchett, *op. cit.*, p. 25. The count of cases includes all those decided by full opinion, plus per curiam opinions reported in the same manner as full opinions. Differences of policy in counting per curiam opinions may result in lack of uniformity in the statistics assembled by different commentators on the Court.

40. Incidentally, Table 1 also calls attention to the Vinson Court's rather drastic reduction in workload. For the six terms 1940–45, the average number of cases disposed of by full opinion per term was 157. For the 1946–52 terms, the figure was 112. Since the Court largely determines its workload by granting or refusing certiorari, this drop must be attributed to a definite policy on the part of the Court. In so far as the decline has been principally manifested since 1949, it is probably traceable to the deaths of Murphy and Rutledge. As already noted, the four-judge group of Black, Douglas, Murphy, and Rutledge must have

been responsible for the acceptance of many certiorari petitions. John Frank has collected examples of denial of certiorari in recent terms where the importance of the public question involved seemed to be considerable. (See "The United States Supreme Court, 1949–50," *University of Chicago Law Review*, XVIII [1950], 52–54; and "The United States Supreme Court, 1950–51," *ibid.*, XIX [1952], 231–36.)

41. *The Supreme Court of the United States* (New York: Columbia University Press, 1928), p. 68.

42. *The Commerce Clause* (Chapel Hill: University of North Carolina Press, 1937), p. 9. For Chief Justice Vinson's defense of dissenting opinions, see 69 S. Ct. ix–xi.

43. "Behind the Split in the Supreme Court," *New York Times Magazine*, October 9, 1949.

CHAPTER II

1. One section of the act provided criminal punishment for anyone who published false and malicious statements with intent to defame Congress or the President or to bring them into contempt or disrepute.

2. *Debs* v. *United States* (1919).

3. *Free Speech in the United States* (Cambridge: Harvard University Press, 1946), p. 82.

4. *Schaefer* v. *United States* (1920); *Pierce* v. *United States* (1920). Justice Clarke also dissented in *Schaefer*.

5. See discussion in chap. viii.

6. *Prudential Insurance Co.* v. *Cheek* (1922).

7. *Meyer* v. *Nebraska* (1923).

8. *Pierce* v. *Society of Sisters* (1925).

9. Charles P. Curtis, Jr., comments: "I do not believe we can find anything that happened either inside or outside the Court which had caused this complete, sudden, and really revolutionary change. The water had been rising for a hundred and thirty odd years, until in 1925 it lapped quietly over the sill" (*Lions under the Throne* [Houghton Mifflin Co., 1947], pp. 266–67).

10. Alexander Meiklejohn, *Free Speech and Its Relation to Self Government* (New York: Harper & Bros., 1948), pp. 54–55: "Never when the ordinary civil processes of discussion and education are available, says Mr. Brandeis, will the Constitution tolerate the resort to suppression. The only allowable justification of it is to be found, not in the dangerous character of a specific set of ideas, but in the social situation which, for the time, renders the community incapable of the reasonable consideration of the issues of policy which confront it. In an emergency, as so defined, there can be no assurance that partisan ideas will be given by the citizens a fair and intelligent hearing. There can be

no assurance that all ideas will be fairly and adequately presented. In a word, when such a civil or military emergency comes upon us, the processes of public discussion have broken down. In that situation as so defined, no advocate of the freedom of speech, however ardent, could deny the right and the duty of the government to declare that public discussion must be, not by one party alone, but by all parties alike, stopped until the order necessary for fruitful discussion has been restored. When the roof falls in, a moderator may, without violating the First Amendment, declare the meeting adjourned."

11. *Minersville School District* v. *Gobitis* (1940); *West Virginia State Board of Education* v. *Barnette* (1943); see C. H. Pritchett, *The Roosevelt Court* (New York: Macmillan Co., 1948), pp. 91–99.

12. It may be appropriate to mention at this point still another newspaper contempt case, *Craig* v. *Harney*, decided in 1947 after Vinson had come onto the Court. Here the Court again followed the Bridges doctrine, over the protests of Frankfurter, Jackson, and Vinson. This time Frankfurter charged that clear and present danger had become "merely a phrase for covering up a novel, iron constitutional doctrine" that misbehavior could not be punished as contempt unless it took place in a courtroom or its immediate proximity. Contemptuous behavior in the courtroom itself was at issue in *Fisher* v. *Pace* (1949).

13. *Cantwell* v. *Connecticut* (1940). In this case the Court invalidated a state statute prohibiting persons from carrying on house-to-house solicitation for religious or philanthropic purposes without the prior approval of a public official.

14. *Kovacs* v. *Cooper*, 336 U.S. at 90 (1949).

15. *Palko* v. *Connecticut.*

16. *United States* v. *Carolene Products Co.*

17. *Kovacs* v. *Cooper*, 336 U.S. at 90–91. But Frankfurter's contention that the footnote did not even "have the concurrence of a majority of the Court" is less sound. He relies on the fact that Cardozo and Reed did not participate in the decision, McReynolds dissented, Butler concurred only in the result, and Black did not concur in that part of the opinion where the footnote occurred. This leaves only four votes for the footnote, but Black's subsequent adoption of the preferred-position argument supplies at least a retrospective fifth vote.

18. *Schneider* v. *New Jersey.*

19. *Prince* v. *Massachusetts* (1944); *Follett* v. *Town of McCormick* (1944); *Marsh* v. *Alabama* (1946); *Saia* v. *New York* (1948).

20. *West Virginia State Board of Education* v. *Barnette.*

CHAPTER III

1. *Commentaries*, IV, 151; quoted in Zechariah Chafee, Jr., *Free Speech in the United States* (Cambridge: Harvard University Press, 1946), p. 9.

2. Chafee, *op. cit.*, p. 18.

3. *Mutual Film Corp.* v. *Industrial Cmsn. of Ohio.*

4. This argument was uncomplicated by situations that might arise in time of war.

5. *Lovell* v. *Griffin* (1938); *Schneider* v. *New Jersey* (1939). Justice McReynolds dissented in the latter case.

6. *Cantwell* v. *Connecticut.*

7. *Martin* v. *City of Struthers.*

8. *Tucker* v. *Texas; Marsh* v. *Alabama.*

9. *Jones* v. *Opelika.*

10. *Murdock* v. *Pennsylvania* (1943). The majority in *Murdock* was composed of Stone, Rutledge, Murphy, Black, and Douglas; the minority was Frankfurter, Jackson, Reed, and Roberts.

11. *Mutual Film Corp.* v. *Industrial Cmsn. of Ohio.*

12. *Gelling* v. *Texas* (1952).

13. *Fowler* v. *Rhode Island* (1953) was a case which Douglas considered "on all fours" with Niemotko. A Pawtucket ordinance forbade addresses at "any political or religious meeting in any public park," and a Jehovah's Witnesses minister was convicted for making such an address. However, the ordinance admittedly did not prohibit the holding of church services in public parks, and the Court decided that this address was a form of church service, which could not be banned without unconstitutionally preferring other church groups over Jehovah's Witnesses, contrary to the First Amendment. Frankfurter would have based the holding on the equal protection clause, as in Niemotko.

14. Frankfurter subsequently commented to the following effect on the Kovacs ruling: "The limits of the decision of the Court upholding the ordinance are therefore not clear, but the result in any event does not leave the Saia decision intact" (*Niemotko* v. *Maryland*, 340 U.S. at 280 [1951]).

15. *Public Utilities Commission* v. *Pollak* (1952). In 1953 the laws of economics stopped what the Bill of Rights had failed to halt. The streetcar programs were abandoned because profits had not come up to expectations (*New York Times*, June 1, 1953).

16. This count excludes the Kovacs case on the ground that the holding there is somewhat qualified by its confusion. Also excluded is *Lorain Journal Co.* v. *United States* (1951). This controversy, which the paper involved tried to blow up into a free-press case, arose from a Sherman Act prosecution growing out of an Ohio paper's alleged attempt to enforce a news monopoly in its area by forcing its advertisers to boycott a competing radio station. The publisher contended that the injunction issued by the federal district court against such practices amounted to a "prior restraint upon what it may publish." Justice Burton disposed of this claim in a single paragraph. His decision was in accord with the

Roosevelt Court's rulings on similar transparent efforts to use the First Amendment as a shield against federal regulation of the business practices of the publishing industry, e.g., application of the Wagner Act to the Associated Press, *Associated Press* v. *NLRB* (1937); application of the Sherman Act against the monopoly provisions in Associated Press franchises, *Associated Press* v. *United States* (1945); and application of the Fair Labor Standards Act to a newspaper, *Oklahoma Press Pub. Co.* v. *Walling* (1946). *Times-Picayune Pub. Co.* v. *United States* (1953) was an antitrust suit against a newspaper company which published both a morning and an evening newspaper. There was no other morning newspaper, but there were two other competing afternoon papers. The *Times-Picayune* required advertisers in its morning paper also to place the same advertising in the evening paper. The Court majority, speaking through Clark, held that this unit advertising practice was not undertaken with an intent to monopolize. Justices Burton, Black, Douglas, and Minton dissented.

17. *Bunger* v. *Green River*. It was a brief per curiam opinion. Other factors encouraging a new constitutional test were the 1943 decision invalidating a ban on doorbell-ringing, *Martin* v. *City of Struthers*, and the two 1946 holdings that a company town and a federal housing project could not forbid distributors of literature on their premises, *Tucker* v. *Texas* and *Marsh* v. *Alabama*.

18. This statement is reminiscent of Justice Holmes's attack on the absolutist aphorism that "the power to tax is the power to destroy." "The power to tax," he said in *Panhandle Oil Co.* v. *Mississippi*, "is not the power to destroy while this Court sits."

19. *Milk Wagon Drivers Union* v. *Meadowmoor Dairies*.

20. *Bakery and Pastry Drivers Local* v. *Wohl*.

21. *Cafeteria Employees Union* v. *Angelos*.

22. "Strikes, Picketing, and the Constitution," *Vanderbilt Law Review*, IV (1951), 595.

23. *Giboney* v. *Empire Storage & Ice Co.* (1949); *Building Service Employees Union* v. *Gazzam* (1950); *Hughes* v. *Superior Court of California* (1950); *International Brotherhood of Teamsters* v. *Hanke* (1950); *Local Union No. 10* v. *Graham* (1953).

24. The constitutionality of such legislation, widely adopted in the states as a means of outlawing the closed shop, had been upheld by the Court unanimously in *Lincoln Federal Labor Union* v. *Northwestern Iron & Metal Co.* (1949).

25. The Virginia courts had accepted the former theory, though the trial judge made no findings as a basis for this conclusion. Douglas, dissenting, would have remanded the case for specific findings on this point, but he did not appear to deny that if the trial court's view of the facts was correct, the picketing was properly enjoined. Black dissented but gave no reasons.

26. Clark concurred in the result.

27. In addition to the 1953 case of *Local Union No. 10* v. *Graham*, already discussed, there was a 1952 decision, *Montgomery Trades Council* v. *Ledbetter Erection Co.* The Court, having once accepted this case, then dismissed the petition for certiorari on the ground that the injunction in question was a temporary one, thus lacking the finality of judgment necessary for Supreme Court review. Douglas and Black dissented, saying that it was usually the temporary injunctions which did the irreparable damage in picketing cases and that the state court's assertion of power to issue an interlocutory injunction was a final action which could be adjudicated without reference to any future proceedings that might be taken.

CHAPTER IV

1. *Chaplinsky* v. *New Hampshire.*

2. Douglas had defended the action as analogous to what the Court had done in the 1931 case of *Stromberg* v. *California;* but Frankfurter's dissent left little of this contention standing.

3. Jackson pointed out that in an earlier dissent he had also had to supply the facts which the majority opinion had neglected to relate (*Douglas* v. *Jeanette*, 319 U.S. at 166 [1943]).

4. Doubt as to whether Feiner actually used this latter language is expressed in Black's dissent, with support from the record.

5. The quotation is from the dissent of Justice Douglas, well known as an out-of-doors man. Justice Black's opinion reports the term used as "S—O—B—."

6. In his excitement Black forgot that radio and television programs are not subject to state control but to that of the federal government.

7. Black's prediction that this decision would open the way to practically unlimited state censorship was dramatically verified less than three months later, when the Chicago motion-picture censor board banned *The Miracle* from showing in Chicago. The police commissioner held that the movie exposed adherents of a religion to contempt and was therefore a violation of the ordinance which the Supreme Court had upheld in the Beauharnais case (*New York Times*, July 22, 1952).

8. Here the Court cited, among others, *In re Summers* (1945), holding that a state may exclude a conscientious objector from admission to the bar, and *Hirabayashi* v. *United States* (1943), approving the wartime evacuation of Japanese from the West Coast.

9. Francis D. Wormuth, "Legislative Disqualifications as Bills of Attainder," *Vanderbilt Law Review*, IV (1951), 603–19, supports Black's contention that the oath requirement was a bill of attainder.

10. Since Frankfurter, Jackson, and Black all held the "belief" pro-

visions of the act unconstitutional, the vote for this portion of the decision was a tie, three to three, a fact to which Vinson's opinion did not call attention but which should have precluded him from discussing the issue. These circumstances generated a great interest in a case raising the same issues and decided one month later by the Court with eight justices participating, *Osman* v. *Douds* (1950). However, the two new participants, Minton and Douglas, took opposite sides on the "belief" issue, so that another tie vote, four to four, resulted. Black again announced his view that the entire section was unconstitutional. Douglas, who might have been expected to agree with Black's contention, failed to indicate whether he did or not. He found that the provisions of the oath were not separable, and consequently his holding that the "belief" provisions were unconstitutional made it unnecessary for him to consider the constitutionality of the other part of the oath.

11. 18 USC 2384.

12. 183 F. 2d 201 (1950).

13. Justice Black protested that the limited grant of certiorari prevented the Court from considering at least two other reasons for reversing the convictions—the alleged discriminatory selection of the jury panel and the alleged violent hostility of one juror to the defendants before and during the trial.

14. In spite of Douglas' statement, the issue was discussed in *Whitney* v. *California* (1927) by Justice Sanford in his majority opinion. However, Justice Brandeis' critique of the state statute there at issue would seem to be the more authoritative statement, and it directly denies the Jackson thesis: "The felony which the statute created is a crime very unlike the old felony of conspiracy or the old misdemeanor of unlawful assembly. The mere act of assisting in forming a society for teaching syndicalism, or becoming a member of it, or assembling with others for that purpose is given the dynamic quality of crime. There is guilt although the society may not contemplate immediate promulgation of the doctrine. . . . The novelty in the prohibition introduced is that the statute aims, not at the practice of criminal syndicalism, nor even directly at the preaching of it, but at association with those who propose to preach it."

15. John Frank comments: "What it all comes to is that intellectual non-restraint has the Frankfurter intellectual sympathy but not his vote," and adds: "This opinion is the very epitome of intellectual liberalism at its most ineffective" ("The United States Supreme Court, 1950–51," *University of Chicago Law Review*, XIX [1952], 187).

16. *Albertson* v. *Millard* (1953). Black and Douglas dissented, on the ground that the issues were clear enough for Supreme Court action.

CHAPTER V

1. "The principle of disclosure is, we believe, the appropriate way to deal with those who would subvert our democracy by revolution or by encouraging disunity and destroying the civil rights of some groups" (*To Secure These Rights* [Washington: Government Printing Office, 1947], p. 52).

2. The definitive study of the committee is Robert K. Carr, *The House Committee on Un-American Activities, 1945–1950* (Ithaca, N.Y.: Cornell University Press, 1952), from which the material following is largely drawn.

3. *Cummings* v. *Missouri* (1867), *Ex parte Garland* (1867).

4. *United States* v. *Josephson,* 165 F. 2d 82 (1947), cert. denied 333 U.S. 838, 858 (1948), 335 U.S. 899 (1948); *Barsky* v. *United States,* 167 F. 2d 241 (1948), cert. denied 334 U.S. 843 (1948); *Eisler* v. *United States,* 170 F. 2d 273 (1948), cert. granted 335 U.S. 857 (1948); *Lawson* v. *United States,* 176 F. 2d 49 (1949), cert. denied 339 U.S. 934, 972 (1950); *Marshall* v. *United States,* 176 F. 2d 473 (1949), cert. denied 339 U.S. 933, 959 (1950).

5. Certiorari was granted in the Eisler case, argument was heard, briefs were submitted and read, and the Court had "all but made the announcement" of its decision when Eisler fled the country on the Polish steamship "Batory." The Court then ordered the case removed from the docket, "pending the return of the fugitive." Justices Murphy and Jackson dissented, Murphy arguing that it was the legal issues that were important in the case, not the individual petitioner, and "those issues did not leave when Eisler did" (*Eisler* v. *United States* [1949]).

6. The court of appeals ruling in the Eisler case was also by a two to one vote.

7. Congress, the Court held, possesses no "general power of making inquiry into the private affairs of the citizen." If an inquiry relates to "a matter wherein relief or redress could be had only by a judicial proceeding," it is not within the range of the legislature but must be left to the judicial power. In 1953 Justice Frankfurter criticized the "loose language" of *Kilbourn* v. *Thompson,* and pointed out "the inroads that have been made upon that case by later cases" (*United States* v. *Rumely,* 73 S. Ct. at 546). However, Justice Douglas cited the decision favorably in a concurring opinion in the same case.

8. As just noted, one of the few pieces of legislation resulting from the work of the committee was declared unconstitutional in *United States* v. *Lovett.*

9. Justices Douglas and Black adopted essentially the same position in their concurring opinion in *United States* v. *Rumely,* 73 S. Ct. at 547: "Inquiry into personal and private affairs is precluded . . . and so is any matter in respect to which no valid legislation could be had. . . .

Since Congress could not by law require of respondent what the House demanded, it may not take the first step in an inquiry ending in fine or imprisonment."

10. Judge Edgerton in the Barsky case said that the committee had intentionally inflicted punishment on certain witnesses by bringing about their dismissal from employment and subjecting them to "publicity and opprobrium," and held that this met the bill of attainder test stated in *U.S.* v. *Lovett.*

11. However, the possibility of applying the Rumely precedent against the Un-American Activities Committee "seems dubious indeed" (*University of Chicago Law Review,* XX [1953], 594).

12. The widespread adoption of the tactic of claiming the privilege of the Fifth Amendment has engendered many interesting discussions of the conditions under which the privilege may be validly claimed and whether inferences as to guilt may be validly drawn from such a claim. Courts enforce a strict "no-inference" rule, but it is difficult to explain this position to the general public. In fact, by 1953 the various congressional investigating committees appeared to regard their inquiries as successful whenever they produced a claim of immunity from a witness, because of the widespread assumption that such claims are made to hide Communist party membership (see L. B. Frantz and Norman Redlich, "Does Silence Mean Guilt?" *Nation,* June 6, 1953; also Bernard Meltzer and Harry Kalven, "Invoking the Fifth Amendment," *Bulletin of the Atomic Scientists,* IX [1953], 176–86).

13. *Blau* v. *United States* (1951); see also *Hoffman* v. *United States* (1951).

14. *New York Times,* February 27, 1951.

15. *Ibid.,* March 22, 1951.

16. *Tenney* v. *Brandhove* (1951). For an account of the operations of this group and comparable committees in other states see Walter Gellhorn (ed.), *The States and Subversion* (Ithaca, N.Y.: Cornell University Press, 1952).

17. The resolution setting up the committee directed it, among other things, "to ascertain . . . all facts relating to the activities of persons and groups known or suspected to be dominated or controlled by a foreign power, and who owe allegiance thereto because of religious, racial, political, ideological, philosophical, or other ties, including but not limited to the influence upon all such persons and groups of education, economic circumstances, social positions, fraternal and casual associations, living standards, race, religion, politics, ancestry and the activities of paid provocation."

18. See generally the symposium, "Congressional Investigations," *University of Chicago Law Review,* XVIII (1951), 421–685.

19. The following discussion relies largely on Leonard D. White, "The

Loyalty Program of the United States Government," *Bulletin of the Atomic Scientists*, VII (1951), 363–66; see also Eleanor Bontecue, *The Federal Loyalty-Security Program* (Ithaca, N.Y.: Cornell University Press, 1953).

20. 53 Stat. 1148.

21. The constitutionality of commission action in enforcing these regulations was upheld in *Friedman* v. *Schwellenbach* by the lower courts, and the Supreme Court denied certiorari (65 F. Supp. 254, 159 F. 2d 22 [1946]; 330 U.S. 838 [1947]); see also C. H. Pritchett, *The Roosevelt Court* (New York: Macmillan Co., 1948), p. 127.

22. Subsequently amended by Executive Order 10241, April 28, 1951.

23. The standard originally fixed in 1947 was that "reasonable grounds exist for belief that the person involved is disloyal to the Government of the United States."

24. 182 F. 2d 46 (1950).

25. 182 F. 2d 368 (1950).

26. "The Supreme Court and the Loyalty Program," *American Bar Association Journal*, XXXVII (1951), 434.

27. "The Federal Employee Loyalty Program," *Columbia Law Review*, LVII (1951), 546.

28. In addition to the loyalty program, federal employees were subjected to a security check. Under Public Law 733, passed August 26, 1950, the heads of twelve named agencies engaged, in part at least, in sensitive activities were authorized summarily to suspend any employee in the interest of national security; but, after suspension, charges and hearings were provided. The President was authorized by the act to extend its provisions to other departments.

Acting on this authority, President Eisenhower on April 27, 1953, issued Executive Order 10450. Effective May 27, it abolished the Truman loyalty program and provided combined loyalty-security criteria for dismissal from the federal service. The Loyalty Review Board and its regional boards were abolished. The authority of department heads for decisions as to their own personnel was affirmed, but suspended employees could request hearings before a three-man board chosen by the department head from a roster of federal officials maintained for the purpose by the Attorney General. The department head would be free to accept or reject the board's recommendations (as was also the case with the Loyalty Review Board's recommendations).

Executive Order 10450 makes no reference to a list of subversive organizations to be maintained by the Attorney General, but Sec. 13 does authorize that official to "render . . . advice" to department heads. Actually, the list has been continued and expanded. On April 29, 1953, Attorney General Brownell redesignated the 192 organizations on the list and added 62 more. He said that these 62 organizations would have

Administra-
], chap. 3).
hat no per-
o which he
ns (*Federal*

rter helped
nited States
d Rutledge
turalization
thizer, was
izenship in
of violating
ther in per-
entered by
charges.
ailable or
he Supr
eviewe
Admir
l.
rk o
ve

ation and ask for a hearing (*New York*
st will thus continue to be a principal
federal employees are members of, or
with, subversive groups.

eals for the District of Columbia ruled
rship in an organization listed by the
was not sufficient ground for the dis-
der loyalty regulations (*Kutcher* v. *Gray*,

k Times, March 5, 1952.
dissented, but on the quite different ground
eclined jurisdiction in this case.

CHAPTER VI

nting in *Shaughnessy* v. *U.S.* ex rel. *Mezei*,
ee also *New York Times*, April 23, 1953.
, 342 U.S. at 536 (1952).
tates.
States.
Bridges v. *United States*, an effort to revoke the
idges, West Coast labor leader, for perjury in
gs was blocked by a four to three vote of the
hat the statute of limitations barred the prosecu-
t

United States (1943); *Baumgartner* v. *United*
St

d States (1946).
8.
kins (1886); *Truax* v. *Raich* (1915).
1 *teer Fleet* v. *United States* (1931).
1 *hiu* v. *United States* (1892).
12 v. *United States* (1896).
13 *lifornia* (1941).
14. Security (McCarran) Act of 1950 does not accept
this p *Martinez* v. *Neelly*, 197 F. 2d 462 (1952), a native of
Mexic n the United States since 1924 was ordered deported
becaus en a Communist for a few months in 1932. On review,
the Su rt divided four to four, thus leaving the deportation
order i 73 S. Ct. 345).
15. C *ederal Regulations*, VIII, sec 150.6 (6).
16. T 's stand in this case was promptly nullified by Congress,
which a a provision exempting proceedings relating to the ex-

clusion or expulsion of aliens from the requirements of the
tive Procedure Act (Public Law 843 [81st Cong., 2d sess., 195
However, the Immigration Service did provide in its rules t
son should serve as a hearing officer in a case with respect t
had performed investigative or other enforcement functio
Register, XV [November 10, 1950], 7637).

17. 41 Stat. 593.

18. But it is relevant to note that Jackson and Frankfu
make up the Court majority in the case of *Klapprott* v. *U*
(1949), where the attempt of Black, Douglas, Murphy, an
to throw some procedural protections around the den
process was defeated. Klapprott, an alleged Nazi sympa
subjected to proceedings for the cancellation of his cit
New Jersey while he was in jail in New York on a charge
the Selective Service Act. When he made no appearance, ei
son or by counsel, judgment canceling his citizenship was
default, the government offering no evidence to support its

19. The principal difficulty is that habeas corpus is av
after the alien is in custody. In *Heikkila* v. *Barber* (1953) t
Court rejected a claim that a deportation order could be
declaratory judgment under the provisions of sec. 10 of the
tive Procedure Act. Justices Black and Frankfurter dissente

20. In this connection Frankfurter quoted Jackson's rema
months earlier in *Woods* v. *Miller* (1948) that "we . . . ha
peace terms with our allies not to mention our enemies."

21. 55 Stat. 252.

22. But cf. Jackson in the Mezei case: "Because the respon
right of entry, does it follow that he has no rights at all?" (
636).

23. Ellen R. Knauff, *The Ellen Knauff Story* (New Y
Norton & Co., 1952). Jackson subsequently called this case '
saved by further administrative and congressional hearing
petuating an injustice" (*Shaughnessy* v. *United States* ex
73 S. Ct. at 635 [1953]). In a 1953 decision, *Kwong Hai Chew*
the Court, with only Minton dissenting, refused to extend t
of the Knauff decision to an alien resident of the United
mitted to permanent residence in 1945 after war service in
States merchant marine, Kwong was excluded from the cou
when the vessel in which he was chief steward returned d
Eastern voyage. He was given no notice of any charge aga on
no opportunity to be heard. Bail was denied, and he was was
Ellis Island. The Supreme Court rescued him by ruling e ex-
within the protection of the Fifth Amendment and so coul
cluded without notice and hearing.

24. *Stack* v. *Boyle* (1951).

25. The disappearance of these four Communists led to legal difficulties for the Civil Rights Congress, which had provided bail for them. Three trustees of the congress' bail fund, Frederick V. Field, Dashiell Hammett, and A. W. Hunton, refused to answer questions of a grand jury concerning the operations of the fund, on the ground that self-incrimination might result, and were convicted of contempt. The court of appeals upheld the convictions in October, 1951 (190 F. 2d 554), and the Supreme Court denied certiorari (342 U.S. 894).

26. After *conviction* on this charge, the Los Angeles Communists were admitted to bail in the amount of $20,000 each.

27. As Jackson said: "Since we proclaimed him a Hercules who might pull down the pillars of our temple, we should not be surprised if peoples less prosperous, less strongly established and less stable feared to take him off our timorous hands." Of coure, Jackson added, Mezei would be free to leave the country "if only he were an amphibian!" (73 S. Ct. at 633).

28. For a remarkable study of the factors which went into the making of this decision see Morton Grodzins, *Americans Betrayed* (Chicago: University of Chicago Press, 1949).

29. *Hirabayashi* v. *United States* (1943); *Korematsu* v. *United States* (1944).

30. *Terrace* v. *Thompson* (1923); *Cockrill* v. *California* (1925).

31. *Civil Liberties Quarterly*, XVII (1948), 1. On April 17, 1952, the California supreme court did what the U.S. Supreme Court had been too timid to do, and declared the Alien Land Law unconstitutional on the ground of the Fourteenth Amendment (*Fujii* v. *State*, 242 Pac. [2d] 617). A lower appellate court in California had invalidated the law on the ground of conflict with the provisions concerning human rights in the United Nations Charter (*Fujii* v. *State*, 217 Pac. 2d 481, 218 Pac. 2d 595 [1950]); see Quincy Wright, "National Courts and Human Rights—the Fujii Case," *American Journal of International Law*, XLV (1951), 62–82.

CHAPTER VII

1. *An American Dilemma* (New York: Harper & Bros., 1944), p. 24.

2. This chapter relies very considerably on a doctoral dissertation at the University of Chicago by Ralph Jans, "Negro Civil Rights and the Supreme Court, 1865–1949."

3. *Washington, Alexandria & Georgetown R. Co.* v. *Brown*. The woman involved was in charge of the ladies' restroom in the Senate building, which may have helped develop interest in her case.

4. 18 Stat. 335.

5. *Louisville, New Orleans & Texas R. Co.* v. *Mississippi* (1890).

6. *Chiles* v. *C. & O. Rwy. Co.* (1910).

7. *McCabe* v. *Atchison, Topeka & Santa Fe Rwy. Co.* (1914).

8. *South Covington & Cincinnati Street Railway Co.* v. *Kentucky* (1920).

9. *South Covington & Cincinnati Street Railway Co.* v. *Covington* (1915).

10. *Mitchell* v. *United States* (1941).

11. In 1951 the Supreme Court denied certiorari in a case where a railroad regulation requiring segregation had been declared invalid as a burden on commerce (*Atlantic Coast Line* v. *Chance*, 186 F. 2d 879; cert. denied, 341 U.S. 941).

12. *Missouri* ex rel. *Gaines* v. *Canada* (1938).

13. *Fisher* v. *Hurst* (1948).

14. *New York Times*, October 10, 1950.

15. *Ibid.*, August 2, 1952.

16. *Gray* v. *Board of Trustees of University of Tennessee* (1952).

17. *Briggs* v. *Elliott.* Justices Black and Douglas dissented on the ground that "the additional facts contained in the report to the District Court are wholly irrelevant to the constitutional questions presented by the appeal to this Court."

18. *Brown* v. *Board of Education of Topeka*, 98 F. Supp. 797, 343 U.S. 989; *Briggs* v. *Elliott*, 103 F. Supp. 920, 343 U.S. 979.

19. *New York Times*, January 9, 1952.

20. See 73 S. Ct. 1 (1952).

21. *Davis* v. *School Board of Prince Edward County, Va.*, 103 F. Supp. 337.

22. *Bolling* v. *Sharpe.*

23. *Gebhart* v. *Belton*, 87 A. 2d 862 (1952), 91 A. 2d 137 (1952), 73 S. Ct. 213 (1952).

24. 73 S. Ct. 1114–18. Argument was subsequently postponed to December 7, 1953, on the request of the Attorney General.

25. See *Harmon* v. *Tyler* (1927); *City of Richmond* v. *Deans* (1930); *City of Birmingham* v. *Monk*, 185 F. 2d 859, cert. denied, 341 U.S. 940 (1951).

26. *Mays* v. *Burgess* (1945). The Supreme Court had in the meantime passed on another restrictive-covenant case, *Hansberry* v. *Lee* (1940), but without examining either the validity of covenants in general or the right of state courts to enforce them.

27. *Weiss* v. *Leaon*, 225 S. W. 2d 127.

28. *Roberts* v. *Curtis*, 93 F. Supp. 604 (1950). The Michigan and Oklahoma supreme courts also stated conflicting views (*Phillips* v. *Naff*, 52 N.W. 2d 158 [1952], and *Correll* v. *Earley*, 237 P. 2d 1017 [1951]).

29. Reed and Jackson did not participate.

30. On the same day that *Barrows* v. *Jackson* was decided, the Court unanimously held that an 1873 statute adopted by the District of Colum-

bia prohibiting racial discrimination in restaurants was still valid and enforcible (*District of Columbia* v. *John R. Thompson Co.* [1953]).

31. The Court reiterated the holding of the Steele case, particularly as to the availability of judicial redress, in *Graham* v. *Brotherhood of Locomotive Firemen and Enginemen* (1949).

CHAPTER VIII

1. *Upshaw* v. *United States* (1948); *United States* v. *Carignan* (1951).
2. *Von Moltke* v. *Gillies* (1948).
3. *Frazier* v. *United States* (1948); *Dennis* v. *United States* (1950).
4. For an account of the Roosevelt Court's adventures with this problem, see C. H. Pritchett, *The Roosevelt Court* (New York: Macmillan Co., 1948), pp. 153–55.
5. *United States* v. *Rabinowitz*, 339 U.S. at 67.
6. *Trupiano* v. *United States,* 334 U.S. at 705 (1948).
7. *Trupiano* v. *United States,* 334 U.S. at 715.
8. In the McDonald case, police of the District of Columbia broke into a boarding-house and arrested men engaged in a numbers game payoff, seizing the evidence of their crime. All the justices except Burton, Vinson, and Reed thought this was unconstitutional. In the Bringar case, the majority held that federal agents who stopped and searched an auto being used to bring liquor into "dry" Oklahoma had acted on probable cause. Jackson, Frankfurter, and Murphy dissented.
9. *Olmstead* v. *United States* (1928).
10. This discussion of the application of the search and seizure clause to federal criminal prosecutions has not included a consideration of the use of compulsory powers of discovery by federal administrative agencies. On this point see two important decisions of the Vinson Court: *Shapiro* v. *United States* (1948) and *United States* v. *Morton Salt Co.* (1950).
11. "Does the Fourteenth Amendment Incorporate the Bill of Rights: The Original Understanding and the Judicial Interpretation," *Stanford Law Review*, II (1949), 5–173.
12. On the other hand, Professor William W. Crosskey, in *Politics and the Constitution in the History of the United States* (Chicago: University of Chicago Press, 1953) supports Black's position. In chap. xxxi, "The True Meaning of the Fourteenth Amendment," he contends that these matters are "very simple and very obvious." His argument, however, is based entirely on a logical and textual analysis of the amendment. He takes the surprising position that the kind of historical evidence used by Fairman "is illegitimate in the case of a provision, like the first section of the Fourteenth Amendment, which is clear in itself, or clear when read in the light of the prior law. . . . Mr. Fairman apparently

forgets that the ultimate question is not what the legislatures meant, any more than it is what Congress or the more immediate framers of the amendment meant: it is what the amendment means" (p. 1381).

13. Justice Black, who was at this time (1949) still somewhat aloof from the liberal wing on the search and seizure issue, supported the majority view that "the federal exclusionary rule is not a command of the Fourth Amendment but is a judicially created rule of evidence."

14. Such as private action for damages against the searching officer, or "the internal discipline of the police under the eyes of an alert public opinion"!

15. Douglas was again the only dissenter in *Schwartz* v. *State* (1952), where intercepted telephone conversations were used in securing a Texas conviction. A federal statute forbids use in federal proceedings of evidence thus obtained, but the Court majority refused to make this statutory rule applicable to the states. Douglas stood on the position he had taken in his On Lee dissent, saying that the Court's current interpretations "give the police the right to intrude into the privacy of any life."

16. The six cases are *Townsend* v. *Burke* (1948), *Wade* v. *Mayo* (1948), *Uveges* v. *Pennsylvania* (1948), *Gibbs* v. *Burke* (1949), *Palmer* v. *Ashe* (1951), and *Keenan* v. *Burke* (1951). Absence of counsel was also one of the issues, though not the principal one, in *In re Oliver* (1948), *Gallegos* v. *Nebraska* (1951), and *Stroble* v. *California* (1952).

17. *Gibbs* v. *Burke.*

18. The 1951 case of *Keenan* v. *Burke* was decided per curiam on the authority of *Townsend* v. *Burke.* Here again the trial judge had been "facetious" in sentencing to prison. Justice Minton, dissenting, said: "It is utterly incomprehensible to me how a judge can commit a denial of federal due process by being facetious in the sentencing of defendants when the sentences he imposes are within the limits prescribed by statute."

19. The six cases were: *Carter* v. *Illinois* (1946), *Foster* v. *Illinois* (1947), *Gayes* v. *New York* (1947), *Bute* v. *Illinois* (1948), *Gryger* v. *Burke* (1948), and *Quicksall* v. *Michigan* (1950).

20. This tabulation excludes *Lee* v. *Mississippi* (1948), which found the Court unanimously deciding that a defendant did not lose the right to contend that his confession had been coerced by reason of the fact that he had testified—untruthfully—at the trial that he had never made a confession.

21. *Watts* v. *Indiana* (1949), *Turner* v. *Pennsylvania* (1949), *Harris* v. *South Carolina* (1949).

22. Except that Jackson, for reasons not apparent, did not dissent in the Watts case, making the vote there six to three.

23. *Congressional Record,* XCIII, 1392; House Rept. No. 29 (80th Cong., 1st sess.).

24. Frankfurter also dissented in Stroble, but on other grounds.

25. For developments on the Roosevelt Court, see Pritchett, *op. cit.,* pp. 141–43.

26. *Patton* v. *Mississippi* (1947), *Brunson* v. *North Carolina* (1948), *Shepherd* v. *Florida* (1951), and *Avery* v. *Georgia* (1953).

27. New York's system of "blue-ribbon juries," specially selected panels made up of the more intelligent, educated, able, and experienced members of the community, was upheld by identical five to four alignments in two cases, *Fay* v. *New York* (1947) and *Moore* v. *New York* (1948). Jackson wrote the opinions in both cases, pointing out that the Court had challenged state juries only on grounds of racial discrimination. Murphy, Rutledge, Black, and Douglas contended that "the systematic and intentional exclusion of all but the 'best' or the most learned or intelligent of the general jurors" was "completely at war with the democratic theory of our jury system" (333 U.S. at 570).

28. *Woods* v. *Nierstheimer* (1946).

29. *Ex parte Hawk* (1944).

30. *Marino* v. *Ragen* (1947). Of the 322 petitions from Illinois filed during the 1946 term, only 2 were granted.

31. *Young* v. *Ragen* (1949).

32. Ill. Rev. Stat. (1951), chap. 38, secs. 826–32.

33. *Jennings* v. *Illinois* (1951). In this case Minton and Frankfurter dissented, the latter because he felt that no proper federal question had been presented.

34. 28 U.S.C. 2241 (c) (3).

35. See *Frank* v. *Mangum* (1915); *Moore* v. *Dempsey* (1923); *Mooney* v. *Holohan* (1935).

36. *Brown* v. *Allen* (1953). In 1952 only 1.8 per cent of the petitioners were successful.

37. Jackson made three points: (1) Habeas corpus should not raise any question which was, or could have been, decided by appeal or other procedure for review of conviction. (2) Unless a petition stated facts which, if proved, would warrant relief, the applicant would not be entitled as of right to a hearing. (3) Petitions should be required to set forth every previous application to any court for relief on any grounds.

38. Interestingly enough, the argument against presidential authority which Black used in this case without success was much the same as that he stated five weeks later in the opinion for the Court in the steel seizure case (p. 206). He wrote here: "No part of the Constitution contains a provision specifically authorizing the President to create courts to try American citizens." The notion that the President has no powers except those specifically stated in the Constitution is, of course, absurd and was ignored by the Court in *Madsen* v. *Kinsella.*

39. *Wade* v. *Hunter* and *Humphrey* v. *Smith*. In the former case, however, the Court did agree that the double-jeopardy provision must be observed in military trials, but said it had not been infringed in this instance.

40. *Burns* v. *Wilson;* see also *Whelchel* v. *McDonald* (1950) and *Gusik* v. *Schilder* (1950).

41. See Pritchett, *op. cit.*, pp. 155–56. Murphy and Rutledge dissented in the Yamashita case.

42. Murphy dissented, but gave no reasons. Rutledge appended this statement to the opinion: "Mr. Justice Rutledge reserves decision and the announcement of his vote until a later time." He died half a year later without ever having announced his vote or, apparently, having made up his mind.

43. This point was rather a sore one with him, for he had written the opinion in *Ahrens* v. *Clark* (1948) holding that habeas corpus proceedings had to be brought in the judicial district where the petitioner was physically located. His three colleagues of the liberal wing had attacked him for thus contracting "the writ's classic scope" and had specifically raised the question as to what happened under the Douglas doctrine when "the place of detention lies wholly outside the territorial limits of any federal jurisdiction."

44. This is the clause limiting the original jurisdiction of the Supreme Court.

45. 334 U.S. 824 (1948).

46. On the authority of *Ahrens* v. *Clark*.

47. *Stein* v. *New York*, 73 S. Ct. at 1101, 1104 (1953).

CHAPTER IX

1. The limitations of this type of treatment should also be noted. One objection is that the statistical approach treats all cases as of equal importance, and agreement or disagreement between a pair of justices in an insignificant case contributes just as much to a tabular total as the vote in a case of first importance.

The so-called "companion cases" create further problems. The Court often consolidates cases which raise the same or similar problems and disposes of them in a single opinion. But on other occasions it fails to follow this practice and, instead, writes separate opinions covering two or more similar controversies. Usually the main problems are discussed in the first of the cases, and the companion cases are disposed of by a skeleton of the argument in the main case or by a mere reference to it. As separate decisions these companion cases are entitled to a place in the statistics, but the counting of them does result in giving multiple weight to alignments on a single issue arising out of almost identical factual situations.

Finally, the justices may agree as to the way a case should be decided but for different reasons. Two justices may disagree with the opinion of the Court; but one may think it goes too far, while the other sees it as not going far enough; or one justice may have in mind the substantive problem in the case, while for another it turns on a procedural question. In such cases the dissenting justices may need to be shown as disagreeing with the majority but also as disagreeing with the other dissenters. All these difficulties can be minimized by careful and understanding handling of the data, but they are none the less real.

2. For the detailed story, see C. H. Pritchett, *The Roosevelt Court* (New York: Macmillan Co., 1948), pp. 32–44, 240–52.

CHAPTER X

1. Quoted in Jerome Frank, *Law and the Modern Mind* (New York: Brentano's, 1930), p. 104.

2. C. H. Pritchett, "Divisions of Opinion among Justices of the U.S. Supreme Court, 1939–41," *American Political Science Review*, XXXV (1941), 890–98. John Frank has written: "Since Pritchett began his work some years ago he has had a host of imitators and followers, of whom this reviewer will readily admit to being one. The result is that almost everyone working in the field of Supreme Court study has become a sort of one-scholar census taker after his own fashion" (*Iowa Law Review*, XXXIV [1948], 144). For Frank's methods see his series of annual articles on the work of the Court in the *University of Chicago Law Review*, beginning in 1947.

3. "Truman Reshapes the Supreme Court" and "Justice in a Democracy," *Atlantic Monthly*, CLXXXIV (1949), 30–36.

4. January 30, 1950.

5. Frank, *op cit.*, p. 145. Moreover, it must never be forgotten that the hard certainty, the calm objectivity, which make a statistical table so convincing are to a considerable extent illusory. Actually, subjective judgments of the analyst—as to what the "real" issue was in a case, as to how judicial decisions should be translated into Yes and No votes—play a great part in producing the "objective" evidence for the box score. Frank's warning on this point is fully justified: "A major vice of the statistical method is that the reader is dangerously likely to accept the capsulated knowledge in the omniscient columns of figures without realizing how dubious was the compiler's judgment on which the figures were based. The statistics are no better than the scholarly comprehension of their compiler, and he must be cautious indeed. His questions should be reserved in footnotes, and the most dubious cases should be set aside altogether" (*ibid.*, p. 146).

6. Commenting on Dilliard's article, Howe says that if Dilliard would admit the complex of issues present in a typical civil liberties case and then "go on to argue that his tables at least show that his heroes gave to civil liberties, in relation to other interests with which the Supreme Court is necessarily concerned, a relatively high valuation I should agree with him" (*op. cit.*, p. 36).

7. *Falbo* v. *United States* (1944).

8. *Milk Wagon Drivers Union* v. *Meadowmoor Dairies* (1941).

9. "The United States Supreme Court, 1948–49," *University of Chicago Law Review*, XVII (1949), 51.

10. John Frank, "Justice Murphy: The Goals Attempted," *Yale Law Journal*, LIX (1949), 9.

11. *Seminole Nation* v. *United States* (1942), two cases; *Creek Nation* v. *United States* (1943); *Northwestern Shoshone Indians* v. *United States* (1945); and *Ute Indians* v. *United States* (1947).

12. *Creek Nation* v. *United States.*

13. 53 Stat. 1404.

14. *Wilkerson* v. *McCarthy*, 336 U.S. at 67, 71. In 23 nonunanimous decisions in federal workmen's compensation cases from 1946 to 1952, none of the four libertarian activists ever cast a vote against an employee claim.

15. See C. H. Pritchett, *The Roosevelt Court* (New York: Macmillan Co., 1948), pp. 93–101.

16. *Minersville School District* v. *Gobitis.*

17. *Jones* v. *Opelika* (1942).

18. One exception was *Prince* v. *Massachusetts* (1944).

19. A useful word, apparently invented by Christopher Morley, who defines it as "the helper of the underdog" (see Preface to *The Complete Sherlock Holmes* [New York: Doubleday & Co., Inc., 1953], p. xv).

20. *Application of Yamashita* (1946).

21. Italics supplied.

22. *Eakin* v. *Raub* (1825); quoted from R. E. Cushman, *Leading Constitutional Decisions* (8th ed.; New York: F. S. Crofts Co., 1946), p. 218.

23. *Urie* v. *Thompson* (1949).

CHAPTER XI

1. *United States* v. *Butler* (1936). For a conservative attack on such "judicial deference" toward legislatures see Arthur T. Vanderbilt, *The Doctrine of the Separation of Powers and Its Present-Day Significance* (Lincoln: University of Nebraska Press, 1953), chap. iii.

2. *United States* v. *California* (1947); *United States* v. *Louisiana* (1950); *United States* v. *Texas* (1950).

3. *American Federation of Labor* v. *American Sash & Door Co.*, 335 U.S. at 555 (1949).

4. *Ibid.*, at 557.

5. For more complete analyses of the decision see Glendon A. Schubert, Jr., "The Steel Case: Presidential Responsibility and Judicial Irresponsibility," *Western Political Quarterly*, VI (1953), 61–77; and Paul G. Kauper, "The Steel Seizure Case: Congress, the President, and the Supreme Court," *Michigan Law Review*, LI (1952), 141–82.

6. See Paul A. Freund, "The Supreme Court, 1951 Term: Foreword," *Harvard Law Review*, LXVI (1952), 89–95.

7. Judge Pine's decision stated: "The fundamental issue is whether the seizure is or is not authorized by law. In my opinion, this issue should be decided first, and that I shall now do." Judge Pine was so anxious to get to the constitutional issue that he decided it before determining whether he had jurisdiction in the case.

8. By Executve Order 10233, April 21, 1951. The President relied on the general language of Title IV of the act for this step.

9. Justice Clark thought that the Selective Service Act of 1948 would have justified the seizure, but the President did not invoke it.

10. *Our Chief Magistrate and His Powers* (New York: Columbia University Press, 1916), pp. 139–40.

11. *Autobiography* (New York: Macmillan Co., 1913), pp. 388–89. In accordance with this belief he was prepared, if it had proved necessary, to take over the anthracite coal mines during the strike of 1902 (*ibid.*, pp 504–18).

12. His opinion cites, in all, only three precedents, and they all bear on the jurisdictional issue.

13. The conceptualism of Douglas' approach is shown by the fact that for him the basic question was whether the President's action was of a "legislative nature." Since he decided it was, it followed that the President's action was illegal.

14. At the beginning of his opinion he said: "We must . . . put to one side consideration of what powers the President would have had . . . if the seizure had been only for a short, explicitly temporary period, to be determined automatically unless Congressional approval were given."

15. A kadi is an inferior Mohammedan judge or magistrate.

16. The best treatment of the federal civil rights laws and their enforcement is Robert K. Carr, *Federal Protection of Civil Rights: Quest for a Sword* (Ithaca, N.Y.: Cornell University Press, 1947).

17. See C. H. Pritchett, *The Roosevelt Court* (New York: Macmillan Co., 1948), pp. 149–52.

18. Frankfurter, Jackson, and Minton dissented for the same reasons

as in Screws, but they were joined by Black, who had been in the Screws majority. He gave no reasons for his reversal of attitude.

19. Actually, Black's concurring vote was based on separate grounds, so that Frankfurter's opinion for the Court in the second Williams case spoke for only four justices.

20. While Frankfurter's position in these cases is consistent with his principle of limiting federal incursion into local law enforcement, his attacks on Congress for having passed the civil rights laws after "inadequate deliberation" seem hard to reconcile with his general deference to legislative action.

21. The case of *Tenney* v. *Brandhove*, already discussed, also arose under a federal civil rights law.

22. See Pritchett, *op. cit.*, pp. 123–24. In the 1953 case of *Terry* v. Adams, the Court, with only Minton dissenting, applied the principle of *Smith* v. *Allwright* to invalidate the unofficial primaries conducted in a Texas county by the Jaybird party, a Democratic political organization which excluded Negroes. The winners in the Jaybird primaries were then entered in the regular Democratic party primaries, where over a sixty-year period they were never defeated for county office. In fact, other candidates seldom filed. The Court ruled that the "Jaybird primary has become an integral part, indeed the only effective part, of the elective process that determines who shall rule and govern in the county" and consequently that the Fifteenth Amendment was applicable and must be observed.

23. In October, 1946, the Court had denied certiorari in the case of *Cook* v. *Fortson*, which had also sought to test the Georgia county unit system. Black, Murphy, and Rutledge would have granted the writ, but Douglas apparently did not supply the fourth vote that would have resulted in acceptance of the case.

24. The government attorney, Mr. Jesse Climenko, smarting under this judicial innuendo, rose to defend the government's action, though the time allotted to him for argument had expired. His demeanor was probably as near insubordination as any counsel has ever exhibited before the bar of the Supreme Court, particularly since he ignored the first reminder from Chief Justice Vinson that his time had expired. Climenko was only inches away from a contempt citation, as the Chief Justice repeated the warning with fire in his eyes, and Climenko then subsided. The author was present in the courtroom during this episode.

25. See discussion, p. 196.

26. *Carter* v. *Atlanta & St. Andrews Bay R. Co.*, 338 U.S. at 439 (1949).

27. See also *Affolder* v. *New York, C. & St. L. R. Co.* (1950) and *Moore* v. *Chesapeake & O. Ry. Co.* (1951).

28. In *Layne & Bowler* v. *Western Well Works* (1923), Chief Justice

Taft for a unanimous Court held that a writ of certiorari could be dismissed even after it was granted "where argument exposed a want of conflict or revealed that the case involved no more than its particular facts," Frankfurter asserted in *Wilkerson* v. *McCarthy*, 336 U.S. at 67.

29. Since the departure of Rutledge and Murphy, fewer workmen's compensation cases have secured the necessary four votes for granting certiorari, but Frankfurter has continued to urge his method of disposing of cases which he feels are not worth the Court's attention. In 1952 he proposed that the writs granted in two land damage claims against the United States be dismissed, because the cases had proved to be "legal sports," presenting a unique set of circumstances unlikely to recur (*United States* v. *Shannon*, 342 U.S. at 294). He added his opinion that attorneys were abusing the certiorari privilege by pressing unworthy cases on the Court, citing the 987 petitions which the Court had had to wade through in the preceding term.

Further indication of the special responsibility which Frankfurter feels for successful operation of the certiorari review mechanism was given in 1950, when he took the unusual course of writing a 25-page opinion explaining why the Court's failure to grant certiorari in *Maryland* v. *Baltimore Radio Show* did not mean that the Court necessarily approved of the result arrived at in the lower court.

30. See Pritchett, *op. cit.*, pp. 192–95.

31. Again, in *United States* v. *Public Utilities Cmsn. of California* (1953) he reported that "preoccupation with other matters pending before the Court" prevented him from doing the research on legislative history he believed necessary to decide a case properly, and he was "therefore constrained to leave the decision of this case to those who have no doubts about the matter."

CHAPTER XII

1. *Saia* v. *New York*, 334 U.S. at 571.

2. Nine cases involved aliens or naturalized citizens: *Savorgnan* v. *United States*, *United States* ex rel. *Knauff* v. *Shaughnessy*, *United States* ex rel. *Eichenlaub* v. *Shaughnessy*, *Ackermann* v. *United States*, *Jordan* v. *De George*, *Carlson* v. *Landon*, *United States* v. *Spector*, *Heikkila* v. *Barber*, and *Shaughnessy* v. *United States* ex rel. *Mezei*. Nine involved federal criminal convictions: *United States* v. *Alpers*, *United States* v. *Rabinowitz*, *Dennis* v. *United States* (1950), *Williams* v. *United States*, *United States* v. *Williams*, *On Lee* v. *United States*, *Lutwak* v. *United States*, *United States* v. *Grainger*, and *United States* v. *Nugent*. There was one habeas corpus proceeding seeking release from the army, *Orloff* v. *Willoughby*. Eight cases were related in one way or another to the drive on communism: *American Communications Assn.* v. *Douds*, *United*

States v. *Bryan*, *United States* v. *Fleischman*, *Rogers* v. *United States*, *Garner* v. *Board of Public Works*, *Sacher* v. *United States*, *In re Isserman*, and *Rosenberg* v. *United States*. Finally, there were seven state criminal prosecutions questioned on constitutional grounds: *Darr* v. *Burford*, *Stroble* v. *California*, *Stembridge* v. *Georgia*, *Leland* v. *Oregon*, *Brown* v. *Allen*, *United States* ex rel. *Smith* v. *Baldi*, and *Stein* v. *New York*.

3. The exception was *Williams* v. *United States*, where the Court majority applied the federal civil rights law to state police officers who obtained confessions by force. Frankfurter's hostility to these statutes is well known (see *Screws* v. *United States*), but Black gave no reason for his dissent.

4. For example, the two most recent decisions weakening the protection of the search and seizure clause, Rabinowitz and On Lee. It was, of course, only with the Rabinowitz case that Black got over to the libertarian side on this issue, where Frankfurter had been all along.

5. This decision is not to be confused with one of the same name in 1951, involving prosecution of the same Dennis for violation of the Smith Act.

6. In 1948 the Court had, by a five to four vote, upheld a conviction for violation of the federal Narcotics Act in the District of Columbia, where the jury was composed entirely of federal employees (*Frazier* v. *United States*). In connection with the Dennis decision see also *Morford* v. *United States* (1950).

7. So characterized by Judge Augustus Hand, *U.S.* v. *Sacher*, 182 F. 2d at 423.

8. 341 U.S. 952 (1951).

9. 342 U.S. 858 (1951).

10. In addition to the holding that another judge should have tried the contempt charge, Black and Douglas believed that the lawyers were entitled by the Constitution to a trial by jury. Frankfurter did not join them in this conclusion.

A second aftermath of the Dennis case was the disbarment of Abraham J. Isserman, another of the defense counsel, by the state of New Jersey. Under its rules, the Supreme Court then required Isserman to show cause why he should not be barred from practice before the Supreme Court. By a four to four vote in *In re Isserman* (1953) the Court held that he had failed to meet this test and ordered his disbarment. Jackson, dissenting along with Black, Frankfurter, and Douglas, argued that Isserman had already been sufficiently punished for his contempt of court by a jail sentence. He knew of no other instance where a lawyer had been disbarred because of a contempt conviction. He added: "To permanently and wholly deprive one of his profession at Isserman's time of life, and after he has paid so dearly for his fault, impresses us as a severity which will serve no useful purpose for the bar, the court, or the delinquent."

11. This was one of the three cases decided by the Court in the *Brown* v. *Allen* opinion (1953).

12. 73 S. Ct. at 449.

CHAPTER XIII

1. *Yale Law Journal*, LVI (1947), 1472.

2. For example, *Ex parte Milligan* (1866) and *Duncan* v. *Kahanomoku* (1946).

3. *Majority Rule and Minority Rights* (New York: Oxford University Press, 1943), p. 67.

4. *American Federation of Labor* v. *American Sash & Door Co.*, 335 U.S. at 555 (1949).

5. *Dennis* v. *United States*, 341 U.S. at 525.

6. *The Federalist*, No. X ("Everyman's Library" ed.; 1911), p. 41.

7. William W. Crosskey concludes after his extensive research on the subject that "judicial review was not meant to be provided generally in the Constitution, as to acts of Congress" (*Politics and the Constitution in the History of the United States* [Chicago: University of Chicago Press, 1953], p. 1007).

8. "Needed: A Rededicated Supreme Court," *Johns Hopkins Magazine*, April, 1953; subsequent quotations from Swisher in this chapter are from the same source.

9. *Brown* v. *Allen*, 73 S. Ct. at 424, 427.

10. *Kovacs* v. *Cooper*, 336 U.S. at 95.

11. *United States* v. *Carolene Products Co.*, 304 U.S. at 152, n. 4.

12. *Yale Law Journal*, LVI (1947), 1472; see also the very useful article by the same author, "The Democratic Character of Judicial Review," *Harvard Law Review*, LXVI (1952), 193–224.

13. *Yale Law Journal*, LVI (1947), 1460.

14. Recent decisions suggest that Frankfurter himself has become increasingly aware of the dangers of too much restraint. In the 1953 case of *Stein* v. *New York*, he remarked significantly that "the duty of deference cannot be allowed imperceptibly to slide into an abdication by this Court."

15. *Adler* v. *Board of Education*, 342 U.S. at 510–11.

16. *American Communications Assn.* v. *Douds*, 339 U.S. at 707.

17. "The tyranny of labels . . . must not lead us to leap to a conclusion that a word which in one set of facts may stand for oppression or enormity is of like effect in every other" (*Palko* v. *Connecticut* [1937]).

18. "The Supreme Court, 1951 Term: Foreword–the Year of the Steel Case," *Harvard Law Review*, LXVI (1952), 97.

19. *Toledo Newspaper Co.* v. *United States* (1918).

20. His own view, characteristically expressed in *Craig* v. *Harney*, is that "judges are not merely the habitations of bloodless categories of the law which pursue their predestined ends." It is also relevant to note *Shepherd* v. *Florida* (1951), where the Court majority invalidated a state conviction because of discrimination against Negroes in selection of the jury. But Frankfurter and Jackson, concurring, voted for reversal because "prejudicial influences outside the courtroom, becoming all too typical of a highly publicized trial, were brought to bear on this jury with such force that the conclusion is inescapable that these defendants were prejudged as guilty and the trial was but a legal gesture to register a verdict already dictated by the press and the public opinion which it generated." See also *Stroble* v. *California* (1952).

21. *The Spirit of Liberty*, ed. Irving Dilliard (New York: A. A. Knopf, 1952), pp. 189–90.

22. Dissenting in *Myers* v. *United States*, 272 U.S. at 293.

23. *Chicago Sun-Times*, June 4, 1953.

Table of Cases

Index